❖ ❖ ❖

CURRICULUM PRACTICE IN THE ELEMENTARY AND MIDDLE SCHOOL

J. Allen Queen

University of North Carolina at Charlotte

Merrill,
an imprint of Prentice Hall
Upper Saddle River, New Jersey   *Columbus, Ohio*

Library of Congress Cataloging-in-Publication Data

Queen, J. Allen.

    Curriculum practice in the elementary and middle school/J. Allen Queen.

        p. cm.

    Includes bibliographical references and index.

    ISBN 0-02-397051-0

    1. Education, Elementary—United States—Curricula. 2. Middle school educa-
tion—United States—Curricula. 3. Curriculum planning—United States. 4. Instructional
systems—Design. 5. Curriculum change—United States. I. Title.

    LB1570.Q45   1999

    375'.001—dc21

                                      98-29176

                                          CIP

Editor: Debra A. Stollenwerk
Production Editor: Mary Harlan
Photo Coordinator: Patty Carro
Design Coordinator: Diane C. Lorenzo
Text Designer: Mia Saunders
Cover Designer: Rod Harris
Cover photo: © PhotoEdit
Production Manager: Pamela D. Bennett
Copy Editor: Kathy Tracy
Electronic Text Management: Marilyn Wilson Phelps, Karen L. Bretz, Tracey B. Ward
Illustrations: Tracey B. Ward
Director of Marketing: Kevin Flanagan
Marketing Manager: Suzanne Stanton
Marketing Coordinator: Krista Groshong

This book was set in Zapf Elliptical by Prentice Hall and was printed and bound by
R. R. Donnelley & Sons Company. The cover was printed by Phoenix Color Corp.

 © 1999 by Prentice-Hall, Inc.
Simon & Schuster/A Viacom Company
Upper Saddle River, New Jersey 07458

Photos copyrighted by the companies or individuals listed. Photo credits: Scott Cun-
ningham/Merrill: pp. 72, 91, 182, 216; KS Studios/Merrill: p.164; Library of Congress:
p. 60; Anthony Magnacca/Merrill: pp. 28, 154; NASA: p. 84; Barbara Schwartz/Merrill:
p. 128; Silver Burdette Ginn/Merrill: p. 280; Anne Vega/Merrill: pp. 2, 100, 133, 197.

Printed in the United States of America

10 9 8 7 6 5 4 3 2 1

ISBN: 0-02-397051-0

Prentice-Hall International (UK) Limited, *London*
Prentice-Hall of Australia Pty. Limited, *Sydney*
Prentice-Hall of Canada, Inc., *Toronto*
Prentice-Hall Hispanoamericana, S. A., *Mexico*
Prentice-Hall of India Private Limited, *New Delhi*
Prentice-Hall of Japan, Inc., *Tokyo*
Simon & Schuster Asia Pte. Ltd., *Singapore*
Editora Prentice-Hall do Brasil, Ltda., *Rio de Janeiro*

In memory of Professor John F. Leahy,
University of Virginia,
my mentor, colleague, and friend.

PREFACE

Curriculum and instructional design texts on the market today focus on preparing graduate students for central office and leadership positions in curriculum development and instructional design in the schools. Unfortunately, many of these texts are inadequate in preparing teachers for their increasingly complex role in curriculum development and instructional design. Furthermore, most textbooks are written from historical, sociological, and theoretical perspectives that are limited in addressing issues for modern development in the elementary and middle schools.

Teacher educators must change the approach used in preparing future teachers. Prospective teachers today are overtrained in the area of methodology and undertrained in the areas of curriculum and instructional development. Most courses in elementary curriculum focus more on the historical and sociological influences on curriculum development than on the critical and practical elements of modern and future curriculum processes leading to the delivery of quality classroom instruction.

Elements of the major historical, philosophical, and social influences on past curriculum development are integrated into this text. An in-depth study of these issues, however, is better left to texts in the areas of educational foundations and curriculum theory. While a balanced coverage of viewpoints has been attempted, this book clearly is intended to open "new avenues" to undergraduate and graduate students by including educational Futurism in a curricular model.

Features

An outstanding feature of this text is that it was specifically designed for undergraduate and graduate students majoring in elementary and middle grades education without a background in curriculum development. Another, perhaps more significant, feature is the practical approach of the text, which guides students into the expanded role that practicing teachers will use in curriculum and instruction in the decades to come.

The book was designed for interactive instruction. Models with related class, group, and activities are included for analysis and study. A unique characteristic of this text is the detailed description of the developmental aspects of children and their changing needs and interests within a framework of instructional expectations at specific grade levels. Nongraded designs are included for expanded instructional development and flexibility.

Organization

The book consists of four parts. In Part I, Pathways for Change, Chapter 1 focuses on the recent challenges to and criticisms of the nation's schools and the reform efforts during the last two decades of the twentieth century. It offers various perspectives and challenging viewpoints at the national and state levels. In Chapter 2, concepts of growth and development and recently discovered risk factors in a rapidly changing society are presented for critical analysis for educators preparing to work with the ever-changing elementary and middle school-age child. Global concerns, changing technology, and special populations require significant changes in curriculum and instructional design. The many parties involved in educational improvement must unite for world class schools. The influences of philosophy on curriculum, from traditional influences to contemporary restructuring efforts, are presented for analysis. Futurism as an educational philosophy is presented along with a discussion of how it impacts curriculum.

In Part II, Pathways from the Past to the Future, Chapters 3 and 4 introduce prospective teachers to historical and social curricula patterns and designs for the twenty-first century. Chapter 5 discusses factors of curriculum design, organizational patterns, and ways in which teachers must become leaders in major curricular change. Movement to site-based management for curriculum decision making has changed the role some teachers play in curriculum interpretations, design, and implementation. This role is expanded within a futurist scope. Prospective teachers are introduced to an array of curriculum paradigms. Barriers to success in the modern curriculum efforts are examined. Issues for future curriculum development are continued with respect to curriculum goals, curriculum translations, and curriculum pacing of content and process. Attention is given to the delicate task of balancing subject content and processes. A comparison of the elements of a subject-centered curriculum and a process-oriented curriculum is presented as related to the producers and consumers of these two designs. Educators are introduced to the field-tested procedures that will guide them in easily and effectively integrating curriculum and instruction in a more structured, graded environment and in a less structured, nongraded setting. Attention is also given to the role changes teachers must make to facilitate the changing education process.

Part III, Pathways to Programs, examines an application focus on how children's developmental needs and interests can be interrelated to curricular and instructional decisions in the lower elementary program (Chapter 6), the upper elementary program (Chapter 7), and the middle school program (Chapter 8). For each of the three levels, proposed national curriculum standards from several sources are included for critical examination. Examples of state standards and local guidelines are included and compared with specific curriculum requirements for the elementary and middle school grades in a variety of settings. Subject content and process skills and instructional considerations are included for each level from kindergarten through Grade 8. After the presentation of subject and process models for each grade level, each chapter concludes with a nongraded program and positive and negative reactions to the model.

Part IV, Pathways to Instruction, guides the prospective teacher through a step-by-step procedure to integrate several types of units. Chapter 9 presents elements of an integrated unit with use of a model in process of development. Exemplary, field-tested integrated units are included for further practice and study. Master lesson design is also presented in a similar fashion. Field-tested models are provided. Weekly and daily lesson planning procedures are clearly outlined in a timesaving, organized chart format. In Chapter 10, curriculum and instructional evaluation procedures are presented in a variety of formats. The uses of portfolios, authentic assessment, and standardized testing are presented for analysis of the practicality of each in a rapidly changing society.

ACKNOWLEDGMENTS

I would like to acknowledge the following reviewers for their valuable contributions: Nancy Benz, South Plains College; Kenneth E. Cypert, Tarleton State University; Bernard J. Fleury, Westfield State College; Maureen Gillette, College of St. Rose; Susan Hahn, Dominican College; Lowell Horton, Northern Illinois University; Honor Keirans, Chestnut Hill College; Margaret A. Laughlin, University of Wisconsin–Green Bay; M. Lee Manning, Old Dominion College; Richard O. Peters, Nova Southeastern University (GTEP); Betty Jo Simmons,

Longwood College; Patti Trietsch, Sul Ross State University; and Leslie O. Wilson, University of Wisconsin–Stevens Point.

I would like to thank all my undergraduate and graduate students for their assistance in making this book possible. Their ideas, comments, and contributions are appreciated.

My sincere appreciation goes also to Debbie Stollenwerk, Penny Burleson, Mary Harlan, and the Merrill staff for their assistance and guidance in making this textbook possible.

And finally a special thanks to Beth Blackwelder for her content and editorial suggestions, which helped me stay practical in my approach in writing the manuscript.

❖ ❖ ❖

Brief Contents

CONTENTS

5 The Process of Curriculum Development

101

PART III

10   Curriculum and Instructional Evaluation   281

1

PATHWAYS FOR CHANGE

❖ ❖ ❖

❖ ❖ ❖

1

CHALLENGES FOR SCHOOL REFORM

Chapter Objective and Focus:

An examination of national and state reform
efforts as a result of *A Nation at Risk*

A Note to Alice and Dorothy

*"If you don't know where you are going, then any road will get you
there; and if you know and then get lost, just follow the yellow brick
road. In either case, hold on to the shoes, Dorothy!"*

These words, adapted from two childhood classics, may best parallel the
latest reform efforts of the past twenty years and the sense of hopeless
frustration that has grown toward America's system of public education.
Following the release of the infamous report *A Nation at Risk: The Imperatives for Education Reform* in April of 1983 by the National Committee on
Excellence in Education, numerous governmental and educational agencies at the national, state, and local levels produced goals, standards, programs, and incentives to solve the problems of America's ailing system of
public instruction. The general public blamed the schools and teachers.
Teachers blamed parents. Apathy rose. Attempts to fix the schools were

evident as presidents and governors pledged to emphasize educational reform in their administrations. School superintendents, principals, and parents focused on producing higher test scores. Every concerned citizen became aware that American children lagged behind academically when compared to children from other industrialized countries. Yet the needed route had no clear map. In fact, there was little agreement about where Americans wanted or needed the educational system to go.

In the recent past teachers were prepared to teach subject matter or specific skills such as reading and writing. They were expected to teach basic processing skills such as observing and classifying. Attempts at values clarification and citizenship development were included within the curriculum. For prospective teachers preparing to enter the teaching profession in the twenty-first century, these teaching skills will remain important, but additional skills also will be needed. One teaching skill that will be required by teachers is the skill to challenge a growing number of apathetic children and youth. Facing a multitude of reasons for such apathy, teachers of tomorrow will have to promote or create within these children and youth the desire to learn. This will be a most challenging task, but it must be achieved if the American system of public education is to survive. Designing curricula and instructional environments that revive the desire to learn and achieve must be an integral part of any road map to better education for which Americans keep striving.

What is educational reform? Reform can be viewed as a panacea to assure a concerned populace that change is being made to improve the condition of the nation's system of public education. It can be compared to applying a bandage to a festering wound to conceal the injury rather than treating the wound to promote a cure. The latest buzz words and educationese deflect attention from the malaise. Assessment and research data are often interpreted to provide the results people *want* to hear. The American educational system is ill. However, the Third Annual International Mathematics and Science Study of 1997 found improvement in math and science test scores for U.S. fourth grade students at international levels among 26 nations included in the study. While these results are positive, they must still be considered small first steps. True reform is much more than covering the wound and allowing nature to take its course. It is the process of bringing about sustained change that goes beyond treating an ailing system of education.

NATIONAL CONCERNS: *A NATION AT RISK*

Two events in recent American history produced alarm in terms of American education. The first was the Soviet launching of the satellite *Sputnik* in 1957, raising fears that America was losing out in the space race and in science technology. The second was the publishing of *A Nation at Risk*. In 1981, as President of the United States, Ronald Reagan appointed Terrel Bell as Secretary of Education. Secretary Bell formed the National Commission on Excellence in Education in August of 1981, for the most part to examine the U.S. educational system, report on the quality of education, and make any suggestions for improvement. The results of this examination were revealed in *A Nation at Risk* (1983).

The authors of *A Nation at Risk* reported the existence of an educational gap between America and other industrialized nations. They found that the American educational system was being bombarded by social, political, and personal problems that were flowing into the classroom and interfering with the quality of education. Foreign students were gaining on American children academically, and in some areas foreign students were surpassing children in the United States. Children in American schools had lost most of the gains made in the wake of Sputnik. Political leaders demanded action to lessen the widening gap.

Several indicators that showed American schools to be at risk were found by the authors of *A Nation at Risk* (1983):

- In an international comparison of school children, the U.S. was never first or second and was last seven times.
- Many American adults were functionally illiterate, including almost 40% of the teenage population.
- Achievement was lower than 26 years earlier when *Sputnik* was launched.
- Declining test scores were reported on high school and college measures.
- A decline in science achievement was observed.
- Costly remedial education was on the increase.

These declines occurred at a time when achievement needed to be higher than ever. Technology was booming and the need for highly skilled workers was increasing. Computers were becoming as common as televisions, and many lower-skilled jobs were being eliminated. Practically every profession across the country was being invaded by technology.

The authors of *A Nation at Risk* addressed many of the tools Americans already possessed to remodel the educational system, including voluntary efforts, traditions, natural abilities, dreams, and beliefs. The problem was that these were qualities that had been buried deep inside most Americans for the past thirty years and could work only if a way were found to rekindle a burning passion in society to revamp education (*A Nation at Risk*, 1983).

Ten years after the report was issued, Secretary Bell described his appointment of the Commission after President Reagan declined a presidentially appointed commission. Reagan had campaigned on the issue of a lesser role for the federal government in education and had vowed to dismantle the Department of Education and the cabinet post Secretary of Education. Included in the eighteen-member Commission group were scholars, corporate executives, and prominent educators. In a 1993 *Phi Delta Kappan* article, Secretary Bell stated that his purpose in establishing the National Commission on Excellence in Education was to conduct a study of the nation's schools and evaluate the quality of American education. He wrote:

> *A Nation at Risk* was front-page news in virtually every daily newspaper across the country and was a feature story on all the network television news shows. . . . The commission's findings were much more negative than I had anticipated. (p. 593)

The study concluded that the fabric of the American public school system had deteriorated tc the degree that the United States had lost much of its international status in the education of its youth. In conclusion, the National Commission on Excellence in Education (1983) found that the nation was at risk due to a "rising tide of mediocrity" which had permeated America's schools and society at large. The authors of the report warned that the status of American schools threatened the nation's future. Government and business leaders, educators, and the general public reacted with alarm to the Commission's report and were unpleasantly surprised by the extensive negative findings.

American educators and the general public were in for a major shock. The Commission's (1983) findings about indicators that put Americans at risk educationally will be quoted, debated, and analyzed for decades to come.

When the curriculum of the sixties was compared to the curriculum of the late seventies a decline in quality was noticed. Students were taking more general courses and were allowed to choose up to 50% of their high school courses required to graduate. The authors of *A Nation at Risk* suggested establishing five new basics as prerequisites for graduation: 4 years of English, 3 years of math, 3 years of social studies, and one-half year of computer science in high school. These new basics would increase standards and give American high schools a starting place in redesigning education.

The Commission also recommended strengthening standards and expectations in the schools. It suggested that colleges and universities create more challenging standards. Grades, in addition to standardized test results, should be used to assess student achievement. Textbooks should be reevaluated to determine whether more challenging books were necessary. New materials should include the latest in technology or the latest research in a content area (*A Nation at Risk*, 1983).

The Commission also focused on the time students spent in school and how effectively that time was used for instruction. The findings indicated that, compared to students in other industrialized countries, American students spent less time per day and fewer days per year in school. An average of 22 hours was used for instruction per week, significantly less than the norm in many other industrialized nations.

> In many elementary schools where time was used inappropriately, students received less than one-fifth of the instruction in reading comprehension that was received by students in classrooms where time was used more effectively.

In examining the role of teaching, the Commission found that more teachers were coming from the bottom quartile of college graduating classes. Teacher preparation programs were composed largely of courses in educational methods. Also, low teacher salaries required many teachers to supplement their income with additional jobs after school and during summer break. Teacher shortages existed in the fields of science, mathematics, foreign languages, and special education.

Although the majority of the Commission's findings and recommendations focused on secondary schools, implications were strong that elementary schools had failed to prepare children for successful study in secondary education. The impact was felt at all academic levels and generated strong reactions and much debate.

Reactions to *A Nation at Risk*

Reaction to *A Nation at Risk* was immediate. States established their own commissions to examine the problems of education. Professional organizations in almost every academic discipline began to rethink standards and required content. Emeral Crosby (1993), a member of the National Commission on Excellence in Education, termed the decade of the 1980s the "At-Risk Decade." Crosby stated that, although advancements in technology and commerce had improved at a steady pace, American education was still at great risk. He concluded that the concept of universal education found only in the United States and critical to its continuing national prominence was in such a state of disrepair that, in spite of tremendous technological advances, the nation's social ills in the areas of family, health care, guidance, housing, child care, and compassion were overwhelming the education system's ability to cope.

A lack of civility appeared to govern the discussions about improving education in general. Without a clear national direction, effective schools, and an engaged system of parental support for schools, academic gains by these students were limited.

Theodore Sizer (1989) presented an almost comical reaction to what had been accomplished in the reform efforts after *A Nation at Risk* was published. He compared the reform effort to entering a war without weaponry, suggesting that the nation's current course which required teachers to decrease the risk to the nation's future without the appropriate tools and the training to effectively use these tools was absurd.

The literature was divided as to the impact of *A Nation at Risk*. According to Crosby (1993) and Goldberg and Renton (1993), gains had been made in several of the recommended areas in the preceding decades. High school graduation requirements and college admission requirements were strengthened. The previously required one year of math was increased to three years in ten states, four states increased science requirements to three years, 37 states increased English to four or more years, and 28 states required three or more years of social studies (Goldberg and Renton, 1993). The content area of computer science boomed after *A Nation at Risk* was released. The number of schools owning computers increased from 18% in 1981 to 98% in 1991 (Crosby, 1993). Curriculum standards for athletes were raised, and the graduation rate of these athletes increased from 48.1% in 1984–1985 to 56.5% in 1986–1987 (Crosby, 1993). The school calendar was lengthened by 3 to 5 days in many systems. Although the cap of the school year remained at 180 days, many schools that previously had fewer days in the school year increased the length of the year. The recommendations on teaching received a lot of attention. Many school districts began administering competency tests to practicing teachers. In 1990, thirty-nine states required prospective teachers to pass such competencies (Goldberg and Renton, 1993). College admission standards for education programs increased and the courses themselves were changed. Teacher salaries increased as well (Crosby, 1993).

The opposite end of the spectrum included those who thought *A Nation at Risk* was only a spark to the system which, without direction and support, would not go very far. Asayesh (1993) stated, "It made a scapegoat out of education when the problems reflected in our schools are a symptom of profound shifts in American life that need to be addressed in a broader societal context" (p. 9). Some agreed that the focus of *A Nation at Risk* was wrongly placed. While it alerted the nation to a problem, its prime focus was on schools rather than the ever-changing community. Many acknowledged that, in order to be effective, a redesigning of communities as well as the school systems needed to occur. The focus could not be a national one in the beginning because not all communities and schools were starting at the same level for redesign. The focus needed to be school to school and community to community. An evaluation of what needed to be done regarding textbooks, attendance, teachers, administrators, quality of the buildings, and safe schools would be different for each school. Some would need slight changes and others would need extensive repair. Only when all schools were on the same playing field would it be possible to set standards across the board.

Edwards and Allred (1993) had three ideas as to why *A Nation at Risk* did not have a big impact on education. First, there was no financial support for changes that were too large. The report met with a natural resistance to change which was increased by the fact that the changes were not created at the local level and, therefore, were not owned by the communities responsible for assuring their accomplishment. Second, given that educators and government officials did not agree on school improvement needs, they also did not agree on the recommendations of *A Nation at Risk*. Finally, there was no strong leadership, and time constraints limited the amount that could be accomplished.

Goodlad (1990) stated that two basic reform movements followed *A Nation at Risk*. The first movement was "politically driven." In this movement national, state, and business organizations tried to cement an ill-defined reform effort. The second movement was "diffuse, sporadic, and local." This effort restructured or modified prior practices such as nongrading, teacher empowerment, and cooperative learning to improve test scores.

A decade after the publication of the report, Terrel Bell (1993) gave his personal reaction to *A Nation at Risk* and subsequent reform efforts. In his evaluation of the Commission's report and the present reform efforts, Dr. Bell stated that the nation had struggled for ten years with the problem of education and challenged American leadership to provide the support for learning that is needed to educate students from all backgrounds.

Confirming these findings, the Department of Education in 1993 released the results of a five-year study, Adult Literacy in America, which measured the literacy of 26,000 randomly selected individuals. Irwin Kirsch, project director, found that while many of the respondents had basic skills to decode words for reading, many lacked skills in using the information for practical application or problem solving. Estimates from the study projected that half of American adults were illiterate in translating information to solve daily problems. Individuals with more formal education and those with higher salaries usually scored higher on the survey, although a small percentage of college graduates scored at the lowest levels.

In an alarming interview in *Newsweek* magazine (Kaplan, 1993), Kirsch stated that employers were concerned that new workers would lack the basic skills required to complete tasks in the changing workplace in the move away from a manufacturing society to an information society.

Kirsch went on to say that many businesses had invested large sums of money to train employees in the basic skills they had not learned in school. In the same article, former Secretary of Education William Bennett reacted to the findings of the study and remarked, "Yeah, we're dumber than we thought we were."

On a more positive side, Crosby (1993) reported that many of the Commission's recommendations had been implemented. Most apparent were the increased high school graduation requirements as colleges and universities raised their admission standards. Techniques and technologies in teaching science and mathematics had improved significantly. The number of computers in schools and classrooms had increased dramatically.

At the beginning of the 1990s, a major reform effort in response to *A Nation at Risk* was initiated at the national level. President Bush presented his ideas to the nation's governors.

America 2000

In April 1991, eight years after the release of *A Nation at Risk*, President George Bush and the nation's governors held an educational summit in Charlottesville, Virginia, and produced a document entitled *America 2000: An Education Strat-*

egy. Following are the six major goals detailed within the document, designed to direct national efforts in regaining status as a leader of nations.

By the year 2000:

1. All children in America will start school ready to learn.

2. The high school graduation rate will increase to at least 90%.

3. American students will leave grades four, eight, and twelve having demonstrated competency in challenging subject matter including English, mathematics, science, history, and geography; and every school in America will ensure that all students learn to use their minds well, so they may be prepared for responsible citizenship, further learning, and productive employment in our modern economy.

4. Students will be first in the world in science and mathematics achievement.

5. Every adult American will be literate and will possess the knowledge and skills necessary to compete in a global economy and exercise the rights and responsibilities of citizenship.

6. Every school in America will be free of drugs and violence and will offer a disciplined environment conducive to learning.

The intentions of the authors of *America 2000* exceeded a listing of national goals and establishment of a time line for reaching these goals. *America 2000* was intended to be a strategy for restructuring the public schools.

Reactions to *America 2000*

In the 1992 Gallup/Phi Delta Kappa Education Poll (Elam, Lowell, and Gallup, 1992), the public was asked to indicate their level of awareness of the six national goals. Of the population sampled, 28% or less of the respondents were aware of the six national goals. The percentages were slightly less when the data were analyzed with respect to respondents with no children in school.

Thirty-three percent of those with children in public schools were aware of Goal 1, "By the year 2000, all children in America will start school ready to learn." Parents of children in public schools also exceeded the general population and the population with no children in school in awareness of all goals, scoring near or slightly above the 30% level with the following exception. Awareness of Goal 4, "By the year 2000, American students will be first in the world in mathematics and science achievement," was lowest for parents of public school children, with only 22% of those respondents aware of this goal. Surprisingly, the final group in the study, parents of children in nonpublic schools, indicated greatest awareness of Goal 4 with a total score of 32%. This group also scored the highest on the awareness scale of all groups with Goal 3, "By the year 2000, American students will leave grades 4, 8, and 12 having demonstrated competency in challenging subject matter, including English, mathematics, science, history, and geography," with a total of 36% aware of this goal. In the remaining areas (Goals 1, 2, 5, and 6) parents of public school children scored higher than those with children in nonpublic schools.

In the same Gallup Poll, these groups were asked to rate the progress being made toward achieving each goal. An overwhelmingly negative perception of the progress of America 2000 was given by the respondents. In fact, more than half of the respondents felt that there had been little or no progress in achieving individual goals and almost one-fourth either held no opinion or did not answer. These findings were consistent among all groups regardless of ethnic group, sex, and age.

During the election campaign of 1992, President Bush focused on *America 2000* while his opponents criticized the education initiative. Opponents asserted that the schools and school districts which were showing great gains in the six areas had, in fact, been performing well prior to the development of America 2000.

At several low points in recent history, the federal government has responded with national goals. Goals were set in the late 1950s after *Sputnik* was launched and during the War on Poverty in the 1960s.

Sewall (1991) observed that one of the problems of America 2000 was that no educators or parents had participated in the design process; yet these were the people most intimately engaged in the process of fulfilling the goals. He compared it to establishing goals for medicine without involving doctors. Would Americans stand for that? Would educators?

Howe (1991) noted that several factors were left out of the design of America 2000, including school finance, an increase in the number of children living in poverty, and the growing cultural and racial diversity of American society. America 2000 was doomed to failure without any financial support at the national and state levels.

America 2000, released by President Bush and Secretary of State Lamar Alexander in April of 1991, recommended four main support elements for the educational system: national assessment of achievement, new schools to act as models for American schools, a challenge to increase the skills of adults, and America 2000 communities which would work in conjunction with the new American schools (Lewis, 1991).

America 2000 had several major omissions, three of which were finances, poverty, and diversity. A possible explanation for the neglect of these issues may have been the mistaken idea that all schools were starting with enough resources to adopt America 2000. These issues were at the heart of the problems with the American educational system and needed to be addressed. In essence, America 2000 did not offer any real assistance to American schools.

In the beginning, America 2000 was supported by many. Five hundred thirty-five new American schools, one in each congressional district, would receive funding to begin a program to redesign the school and break the mold. These new schools would reevaluate everything—teaching, time, space, staffing, technology, administration, tools for education, even assessment (Howe, 1991). Schools not only would be required to apply for acceptance into the program in order to receive grant money, but would be required to be within America 2000 communities. To become an America 2000 community, a community was required to accept the national education goals of America 2000 as its own, develop a plan to achieve the goals, develop a form of assessment, and demonstrate that it was ready and willing to support the new school (Doyle, 1991).

National assessment was also proposed in America 2000. The goal of the testing was to measure the achievement of all students, not just those who were college-bound. Local educators would have to raise their educational standards in order to ensure that all the students in their schools were achieving at a high enough level to pass national tests proposed to be administered in fourth, eighth, and twelfth grades. The fact that the tests would be voluntary threw a wrench into the whole situation. Because of the tests' voluntary status, potentially only the highest achieving students would take them. Therefore, accurate assessment of the level of achievement would be nearly impossible (Sewall, 1991).

America 2000 met with opposition when people began to question the federal government's role in education. Although the disclaimers of the document acknowledged state control over education, the specific ideas of America 2000 did not seem to support that focus. The national standards, national testing, and requirement of communities to adopt goals as their own in order to be funded foreshadowed significant involvement of the federal government (Howe, 1991).

GOALS 2000

In 1993, newly elected President Bill Clinton appointed former governor of South Carolina Richard W. Riley as the new Secretary of Education to lead the national reform efforts in education. Secretary Riley lost no time in organizing a legislative package for submission to Congress. Riley had been extremely successful as an education governor in South Carolina, leading his state in improving test scores, increasing teacher salaries, developing business and school partnerships, and achieving a "bottom-up approach" to restructuring schools (Riley, 1993). The legislation developed under the leadership of Riley in the Clinton Administration expanded the elements of America 2000. Characterized by President Clinton as "reinventing education," the new legislation became law in March of 1994 and became known as GOALS 2000: Educate America Act. This legislation included the original six goals of America 2000 and two additional goals.

By the year 2000:

1. All children in America will start school ready to learn. (School Readiness Goal)
2. The high school graduation rate will increase to at least 90 percent. (School Completion Goal)

3. All students will leave grades 4, 8, and 12 having demonstrated competency over challenging subject matter including English, mathematics, science, foreign languages, civics and government, economics, the arts, history, and geography, and every school in America will ensure that all students learn to use their minds well, so they may be prepared for responsible citizenship, further learning, and productive employment in our nation's modern economy. (Student Achievement and Citizenship Goal)

4. United States students will be first in the world in mathematics and science achievement. (Mathematics and Science Goal)

5. Every American adult will be literate and will possess the knowledge and skills necessary to compete in a global economy and exercise the rights and responsibilities of citizenship. (Adult Literacy Lifelong Learning Goals)

6. Every school in the United States will be free of drugs, violence, and the unauthorized presence of firearms and alcohol and will offer a disciplined environment conducive to learning. (Safe, Disciplined, and Alcohol-and-Drug-Free School Goal)

7. The nation's teaching force will have access to programs for the continued improvement of the professional skills and the opportunity to acquire the knowledge and skills needed to instruct and prepare all American students for the next century. (Teacher Education and Professional Development Goal)

8. Every school will promote partnerships that will increase parental involvement and participation in promoting the social, emotional, and academic growth of children. (Parental Participation Goal)

Under the leadership of Secretary Riley, the Department of Education sought to keep educators, state law makers, and the public in general informed and involved in restructuring education. As part of GOALS 2000 (1994), the Department of Education established a 19-member board, known as the National Education Standards and Improvement Council for Voluntary National Standards. NESIC was the independent agency responsible for certifying criteria, content, and standards for national and state agencies.

NESIC was designed to certify state standards and assessment procedures to be appropriately aligned with the Educate America Act. Council members were appointed by the President from nominations received by Congressional leaders and the Secretary of Education. Appointed members included professional educators, business and industry representatives, and private citizens.

Directly overseeing GOALS 2000, also known as the National Education Goals, was the National Goals Panel. Its function and major responsibility were to monitor the progress of GOALS 2000 and to build a "nationwide, bipartisan consensus for the reforms" for implementing a national direction to ensure the success of the national goals. The Goals Panel could disapprove any national standards or state standards certified by the National Education Standards and Improvement Council for Voluntary National Standards.

Additionally, the Department of Education published the monthly community-oriented newsletter *Community Update* which was circulated to school systems and interested citizens to keep them informed of national progress, funding opportunities, and town meetings—many of which were rebroadcast on the Discovery Network. By late 1994, 31 states had received funding under GOALS 2000 (Department of Education, 1994).

Title III of the GOALS 2000: Educate America Act (1994) allowed states funding opportunities through the Department of Education. Title III also supported the development and implementation of education improvement plans that aligned state standards with the national goals. Opportunities for partnerships with universities and other organizations for funding were available as well.

Reactions to GOALS 2000

There was considerable reaction to GOALS 2000. All but two states participated in the program. Fully supporting the Clinton plan was Senator Edward Kennedy from Massachusetts, who asserted that the bill would change the way the federal government supports local schools.

Now began the process of giving real support and encouragement to teachers, parents, and school administrators who were willing to roll up their sleeves and get down to the hard work of using these funds to improve their schools.

One of the first adverse reactions came from Senator Strom Thurmond of South Carolina. Senator Thurmond was quoted immediately after a failed Republican filibuster to defeat GOALS 2000, stating that "it precludes state reform and could lead to a national curriculum" (Kaplan, 1993).

Jennings (1995) reported that there was much discussion in the United States Senate concerning GOALS 2000. The House version of the bill passed in 1993 was different from the version the Senate had examined earlier in that year. Several measures were added to the GOALS 2000 legislation in the House. Proposals to use money for private schooling were included, but defeated. The House approved amendments outlawing guns and the use of tobacco on school property. Once the Senate completed the passage of their version of the legislation, a House-Senate conference committee began to work toward agreement on the measure. This was difficult because the Senate and House were divided on two major issues. One issue was whether the states must have standards for content and student assessment as proposed by the House or be allowed to do whatever they desired with the federal funds as proposed by the Senate. The most critical issue was whether the states should have opportunity-to-learn standards in order to receive federal funds.

Not surprisingly, the state governors agreed with the position of the Senate. They argued that the focus should remain on student outcomes and not move back to the opportunity-to-learn standards, fearing that this would move education back into more emphasis on instructional inputs. Opportunity-to-learn standards were standards to assist students in poor school districts. The House felt that without these standards there would be no assurance that every student in America would have a fair or equal opportunity to meet the outcome-oriented standards.

The compromise that led to the completion of the act and to President Clinton's signature, making the bill law, was a requirement that any state wishing to receive federal funds for school reform have content standards and standards for performance and assessment, as required by the House version, and opportunity-to-learn standards.

One additional element that was included late in the GOALS 2000: Educate America Act was the Clinton administration's *Safe School Act*, which awarded the Department of Education funding programs to make public schools safer.

Secretary Riley (1993) was pleased with the passage of GOALS 2000. He believed this to be an important step in President Clinton's educational reform efforts to establish standards that would be challenging to all students. In an article written for *Principal* on the reinvention of education, he warned of the great task before the nation. He explained the four titles under GOALS 2000. In *Title I: National Education Goals,* the six national goals and objectives were described. Under this title, Congress became a "full partner with the President and the nation's governors" to provide the basic framework for a new system of public education. *Title II: National Education Reform Leadership, Standards, and Assessment* included the National Goals Panel. This panel was designed to monitor and report on state and national cooperation and success. *Title III: State Improvement* allowed for federal funding to states to implement programs at the local school level. *Title IV: National Skills Standards Board* called for the creation of a board composed of leaders from state and federal government, industry, business, and education to identify areas of major occupations, and to assist in the development of standards and assessments of skills in each of these areas.

Riley (1993) asserted that GOALS 2000 required numerous partnerships to make the Act successful. He believed that following this direction for education was going to take major cooperation among people to "reinvent education." This cooperation began to face a decline on January 4, 1995 with the induction of the 104th Congress with a new, conservative power base. As the new Republican-controlled Congress became dominant for the first time in forty years and inducted the first Republican Speaker of the House since 1954, newspapers throughout America reported the GOP's latest triumph to power. The day after the induction of the new Congress, *The Washington Post* printed comments of several members who were now in major power positions. House Speaker Newt Gingrich stated, "We owe it to our children and grandchildren to get this government in order."

Senator Robert Dole sounded his desire to roll back government regulations, stating, "We will roll back federal programs, laws and regulation from A to Z—from Amtrak to zoological studies." This rollback included a de-emphasis of the federal government's role in recent Democratic educational reforms.

STATE REFORM EFFORTS

Educational reform from national efforts moved rapidly to the states almost overnight. Reformers in many of the states sent messages that were well received by state legislators and local school boards. The reform efforts implemented included charter schools, public school choice, same-gender classrooms, and second language requirements for graduation. Most states attempted to implement GOALS 2000 within the established state curriculum. However, as the decade of the 1990s began to close, many reform efforts moved toward a greater accountability effort with regard to individual schools and individual teachers.

The Center for Education Reform in Washington, D.C., has kept a close watch on the reform efforts on a state-by-state basis. This agency will serve as a good source to keep researchers and educators updated and informed of the numerous reform efforts sprouting daily.

In order to give a sense of the scope of the reform efforts that have occurred throughout the United States, several states are profiled below.

In the Southeast, the North Carolina Education Standards and Accountability Commission in July 1996 presented benchmark standards for students in grades 4, 8, 10, and 12, in addition to other recommendations. These benchmarks represented North Carolina's first formal statewide attempt to hold students and teachers accountable for their performance. The Standards and Accountability Commission was created by the North Carolina General Assembly in 1993 to ensure that all graduates of North Carolina public schools mastered the skills needed to become productive workers and successful in life. The purpose of the commission was to develop high and clearly defined education standards, specify the skills and knowledge that high school graduates should possess in order to be competitive in the modern economy, and develop fair and valid assessments to assure that high school graduates met these standards.

In North Carolina in 1993, the first statewide grade level tests, known as End of Grade (EOG) and End of Course (EOC), were administered. The EOG tests are taken by students in third through eighth grades and include assessment in reading and math (grades 3–8), social studies (grades 4–8), and writing (grades 4, 6, and 8). EOC tests are taken by high school students and include assessment of the core subjects of Algebra I, Biology, Economic/Legal/Political Systems, English I, Physical Science, and U.S. History, as well as some advanced classes such as Geometry, Algebra II, Chemistry, and Physics.

Each year the "Report Card, the State of School Systems in North Carolina" is published. Its major focus is the results of the annual EOG and EOC tests. Growth in each area is expected each year. In 1995, 40.8% of students in high school scored at or above the proficient level on the EOC tests combined. The elementary school fared a little better. On the writing test, 53.1% of fourth graders scored at or above the proficient level; 47.6% of sixth graders scored in or above the proficient range; and 62.5% of eighth grade students scored at or above the proficient level. On the reading EOG Test, a total of 66% of all tested grades scored at or above the proficient level; in math, 66.1% scored at or above grade level; and in social studies 61.1% of combined grades scored at or above grade level.

In the Southwest, Parr (1993) discussed the Texas response to *A Nation at Risk* in the report "A State in Motion in the Midst of a Nation at Risk." This report provided the impetus for legislation (House Bill 72, 1984) which was influenced by Governor White and businessman Ross Perot. House Bill 72 emphasized equal funding for schools, pay increases for teachers, competency testing of teachers, exit testing of high school students, teacher appraisals, merit pay, and a career ladder for teachers. Reduced class size, the elimination of social promotions, and creation of the no-pass/no-play rule for student athletes was also included.

The 1997 legislative session made significant improvement to the Texas charter bill. Originally, the 1995 revamped education code provided for the creation of two types of charter schools, "open-enrollment" charters sponsored by the State Board of Education and district-sponsored "campus" charters. The original bill capped open-enrollment charters at 20, and by fall 1996 all 20 had been granted. Seventeen campus charter schools opened in the 1996–97 school year. One of the charters has already celebrated its first graduates, a teen mother and former dropout. During the same time, only one campus charter was approved to open in the Dallas area. However, in response to the competition from a handful of nearby open-enrollment charters, the Houston school board recently approved over a dozen "contract charter schools" to open under the jurisdiction of the local school district. Prior to the first charters, Houston principal Thaddeus Lott took on management of a cluster of autonomous schools under the new education code, although his expanded authority is limited to personnel and curriculum.

Legislation passed in 1997 raised the cap on open-enrollment charters to a total of 120 and allowed for additional charters to serve at-risk students. At that time the Department of Education had already received over 500 requests for charter applications. A 1997 report to the State Board found that existing charter schools in Texas primarily served minority and low-income students: charter school enrollment was 26% African-American (state average is 14%), 52% Hispanic (state average is 36%), and 19% white (state average is 47%).

On May 6, 1997, the Texas House of Representatives heard nearly two hours of debate before voting on a voucher bill that would allow children from low-income households attending poorly performing public schools to attend private schools. Henry Cuellar, a Democrat, introduced H.B. 318 to expand and improve the current Public Education Grant Program (public school choice). The bill was considered on the House floor on May 6, 1997, when an amendment by Representative Ron Wilson to allow private school choice was offered and debated for two hours. A move to kill the bill by tabling the amendment failed in a 68–68 tie vote. Representative Wilson, a black Democrat from Houston, saw that there was not enough support for passage so he withdrew the amendment from debate. In defeat, the tie vote showed a shifting of opinion toward parents who favor choice. Texas support is overwhelmingly bipartisan, and the Governor has added his support.

The 1995 legislative rewrite of the education code focused in large part on strengthening local control, but such provisions have resulted in little substantive action. Development of district-sponsored "campus" charter schools has made a dim showing thus far compared to the progress of state-sponsored "open enrollment" charters. Home Rule, which would allow districts with referendum approval to operate more autonomously from the state, has not been pursued by any districts. "Public education grants" (PEG), designed to give a hand up to the state's most at-risk student populations, have served a mere handful of students. PEGs allow students in low-performing or low-testing schools to attend a school in their district or a neighboring district.

KERA, the Kentucky Education Reform Act, was passed by the Kentucky legislature in June 1990, in response to the Kentucky Supreme Court ruling that the schools were inequitable and inefficient. This legislature totally revamped Kentucky's education system in areas of finance, governance, and curriculum in an attempt to provide equal educational opportunity for all children regardless of the property wealth of the district in which they lived. This act was not limited to setting higher educational standards, creating new organization structures and new statewide assessment with rewards and sanctions. It also created additional support systems for teachers, families, and students by increased funding for staff development to help teachers learn to implement the new mandate, preschool programs for economically at-risk four-year-olds and children with disabilities. In addition, it extended school services programs for all students who need more time to learn before or after school or in the summer and created family resource centers to put students and their families in touch with health and social services. KERA established learning standards for all students which were significantly higher than those in the past.

Mississippi is another state that, in the past decade, has implemented multiple educational reform programs. One of the first, Assistant Reading Instructor Program (designed to improve reading scores and decrease the rate of high school dropouts), has been under criticism recently. Over $340 million has been spent, without significant improvement in any of the target areas. Modifications to the program have been proposed to: (1) successfully implement the program, (2) convert it to a teacher aid program, (3) divert money into other similar programs, or (4) abolish and redirect funds.

The Mississippi Assessment System, a standardized achievement test, has been updated to a broader, non-traditional test. While the changes in the test were fairly well received by teachers, many expressed a need to change classroom instruction to better prepare students for the test.

A more recent reform is the Mississippi Accountability and Adequate Education Program (MAEP) Act, passed in 1997. Funding to implement this program has been raised through bonds. A per-student sum of $160 has been distributed to all 170 school districts. Counties receiving the funding are assessed on their planning and implementation of the program. Two counties have already received favorable ratings for their use of the funds and implementation of the program.

Reform programs in Maryland are more numerous than those in Mississippi. One program, funded by a grant from the National Science Foundation (NSF), is the Maryland Collaborative for Teacher Preparation (MCTP). This is an undergraduate program to prepare incoming teachers to use an interdisciplinary approach in teaching mathematics and science. One goal is to produce teacher proficiency in the use of technology in the classroom.

This technology thrust was the theme of many recent Maryland educational plans. Maryland's Plan for Technology in Education implemented in 1997 involved the use of $150 million over a five-year period. The funds are intended to meet the financial needs of schools as they cope with rising costs of technology. Each school submits a plan for use and the funds will be used for technology in the classrooms.

According to the Center for Education Reform, both Connecticut and Pennsylvania have implemented such initiatives as choice programs, private contracting, charter schools, and school curriculum revisions. Choice programs allow for open-enrollment among schools to help alleviate the imbalances of ethnic backgrounds between inner-city and urban school students. Another reform bill for private contracting and charter schools supports businesses, private organizations, universities, and colleges to manage and influence school instruction. Finally, these states have also prepared a new school code to increase graduation requirements and arts and science curriculum.

The state of California has been a leader in educational reform, and in the past few years has been seeking to spread educational reform efforts. In order to do this, educators are creating school networks that incorporate both state and district-level strategies. This reform effort is referred to as simply "networking." Networking in California consists of three major phases—two of which came from previous reform efforts. Phase One involves creating a vision of teaching and learning, that is, creating a vision of a thinking curriculum in each of the disciplines and then growing from that vision. Phase Two entails systemic reform. This involves creating a supportive climate for Phase One. This phase is the basis for the state plans that deal with the national GOALS 2000 legislation. These two phases have resulted in a genuine change in many schools. Phase Three involves the actual networking. This was a grand-scale attempt to link schools with support networks centered around improvement. One example of networking was 140 schools that received restructuring grants which were sponsored by businesses. One of every five schools submitted a bid for this money. More than 50 schools are participating in various new teacher projects.

The third phase has shown great promise for connecting large numbers of schools. Currently, there is a fourth phase in the making. Perhaps one of the reasons California has been successful in its reforms is because they have been built upon previous reform efforts.

In December 1996, California's State Board of Education voted to approve new textbooks which have a heavy emphasis on phonics for the state's reading curriculum. The state has also started implementing the Improving America's Schools Act (IASA) which provides funds for a variety of services to special needs students. The IASA has a plan, themes, standards and assessments, instructional strategies, and resources.

In comparing Washington, Oregon, and Utah, two of these states (Oregon and Utah) are receiving money allocated from the federally sponsored GOALS 2000 program. Three similarities in how these states have brought about changes in their educational systems can be identified.

The first similarity is the concept of Performance-Based Education. This is based on the premise that student achievement can be increased by setting clear standards and by holding both students and schools responsible for reaching higher levels of performance. The second concept is Opportunities to Learn, through which the schools work with the communities to ensure that all students come to school ready to learn, and that they receive instruction appropriate to their stage and style of learning, so that they will be able to succeed in the new performance-based system. The last similarity is Career Preparation. This involves making education more meaningful by connecting academics with the community and by introducing students to a variety of career options.

THE PROBLEM OF EDUCATIONAL REFORM

From the author's perspective, developed over years of experience as an elementary school teacher and principal, principals have long been viewed as the lone school decisionmakers, yet most have had limited knowledge of and experience with addressing the curriculum and instructional needs of children and in providing guidance and leadership to teachers. Historically, many came from coaching positions. Their limited success was most apparent in office management and discipline control, not in instructional leadership.

Teacher empowerment was the morale-boosting term of the early 1990s. In theory, empowerment allowed teachers to have more input into school curricular and instructional decisions. It went hand-in-hand with site-based management, which allowed principals, teachers, and parents to have direct input into the major decisions of the school. However, these efforts had limited success, primarily because the central administrative bureaucracy of local school districts did not allow sufficient change in the top-down power structure. However, by the late 1990s in schools across the United States, this began to change.

Within individual schools where principals were given more control in curriculum and fiscal matters, success was mixed. Schools with principals who allowed teachers to work as teams toward a common goal were more successful than those schools where principals did not encourage or allow faculty input into school decisions.

One real problem with the practice of principal as instructional leader and teachers as empowered decisionmakers was that most principals and teachers received limited training in participatory management and processes of curriculum and instructional alignment during the reform periods of the 1980s and 1990s. While they acknowledged that something had to be done, they often did not have the skills to be successful.

Americans continue to dream of having the best school system in the world. However, as the twentieth century ends, the United States is far from being in a global first place position. In fact, America's school children have lagged far behind children from other industrialized nations for the past two decades. The Third Annual Mathematics and Science Study of 1997 indicated that fourth grade students were only then beginning to improve in the areas of math and science.

Many of the reform efforts have had limited success. One problem was that reform efforts were attempted without the direction of grass roots initiatives and unified public support. Barriers to successful reform abounded. Schools in which the principal served as the instructional leader and classroom teachers were truly empowered to have constructive input into curriculum development and school decisionmaking were rare. Funding and fiscal support for innovative programs to establish standards and guidelines at the state and local levels which met or exceeded national standards were often inadequate and met with opposition. National standards were voluntary, having no real power over the states and local schools. Many school leaders did not or would not go beyond the vision of the present or the past. Most central offices were top heavy with administrative personnel who did not work directly with children and who often sabotaged, intentionally or unintentionally, good instructional plans or programs. Goals were short term, unclearly defined, unrealistic, or only remotely achievable given present resources. So much emphasis had been placed on outcome-based education, test scores, and how poorly the schools were educating American children, that developmental and environmental issues, perhaps the greatest set of factors that promote academic success, became secondary.

CREATING THE AMERICAN DREAM

What is the American Dream? At one time in the not too recent past, the American Dream was to get a quality education, establish a career, buy a home, and live in a community where the family felt secure and safe. Some Americans have believed that the American Dream, with the values of the 1950s, can be reclaimed through the existing system of education. However, American society has gone through such great change and reconfiguration that **any educational model based upon past principles and values will have only limited success.**

The American Dream that was once achievable by a large percentage of the population does not exist today, nor will the same dream be present tomorrow. America must let go of the past and deal with the future, and the place to start must be with the wounded system of public instruction. Obvious change is inevitable, and a two-step plan of action must be taken to assure that any change is relevant. First, we must as a nation develop a reconceptualization or creation of the American Dream based upon the individual and societal needs of the future. Secondly, America must create a new model of education for its schools that provides every child with an equal opportunity to reach a new generation of dreams.

American education needs a new direction. Address of the social, political, and personal problems that crept into the schools during the early 1980s must become part of the new mission of education. America needs a new American dream with as much hope as the old. Closer analysis of societal needs and the present political system for funding schools is a good place to start. American children no longer come to school on the bus from Mayberry. Children bring their baggage to school, along with their own—and their parents' or caregivers'—attitudes about education and society. Changing social influences and attitudes is an enormous task which must be tackled for the sake of America's youth. In the future, Americans may consider education as a privilege rather than a right and demand that students pass a test and sign an oath before entering high school. Students should have the choice of conforming to the school's cultural expectation or leaving. If schools had the freedom to remove students who were causing major disturbances and hurting educational progress, education would improve quickly.

Another problem with reform efforts has been that federal, state, and local leaders have not worked together. All levels of government have had their own ideas. None have been able to come to consensus on one reform strategy or agree upon a way to incorporate the most effective elements of each into unified educational goals. This lack of coordination between federal, state, and local programs has proven harmful to the schools. The result has been educational initiatives with no direction and educational programs with limited success in preparing students for the future. Schools need unified government direction backed by public support and involvement.

In 1993, former Secretary of Education Bell identified eight areas he believed needed to be addressed before America could move ahead as a united nation towards attaining realistic educational goals. The first area is technology, the most rapidly growing area in education and the most expensive. Computers can provide opportunity for students to interact with content in a broad range of activities, from drill and practice to simulations of real world experiences—allowing students to react to, interact with, and be proactive toward the curriculum.

The second area Bell addressed was staff. He believed that schools should be allowed and required to weed out teachers who do not have the instructional and/or interpersonal skills necessary to maintain an environment conducive to learning. Too many teachers remain in the classroom for years, long after they have lost the desire or ability to provide an appropriate and effective learning opportunity for students. Other teachers do not feel that their efforts and hard work are appreciated. Increasing teacher salaries and providing appropriate in-service training are ways to make teachers feel appreciated and keep their skills sharp.

A larger national role and increased coordination of action by all levels of government were the third and fourth issues Bell discussed. National standards can be a great asset to education—providing equitable educational opportunity for all students across the United States. The America we live in today is a transient society. With national standards, a fifth-grade child can move from Alabama to Washington in the middle of the year and remain on track. National standards will bring uniformity to educational opportunity and expectations.

The fifth issue Bell addressed was parental involvement. This will always be one of the most critical issues in education. The first five years of a child's life play a monumental role in his or her future success. Much of a child's learning happens in the home. Since so many homes are not environments that are conducive to learning, parents need to be educated in ways to raise responsible, intelligent children.

The size of American schools was the sixth issue Bell discussed. Districts, schools, and classrooms are far too large to be effective. Administrative duties appear to take precedence over teaching students and running effective schools.

Bell addressed leadership as the seventh area. School administration is another area of education where people stagnate. Schools need administrators with vision and who want to improve the condition and status of education. The way to get such effective administrators is to recruit only the best and train these recruits in school leadership. Administrators are a vital part of the future success of educational redesign.

The eighth and final issue Bell felt needed to be addressed was the recent discoveries in brain research. Scientists have determined that it is during the first years of a child's life that the brain grows at the most rapid rate. This is the time in a child's life that the brain should be constantly stimulated with new information. Parental involvement and good child care are extremely important. Bell listed many other issues that will need to be addressed by future educators but the focus of education was the most important.

Hodgkinson (1993) suggested the focus should be on improving the performance of the bottom third of students. He stated, "the top 20% of American students are the best in the world and getting better, of the 40% behind the top most are capable of completing college with a little remediation, and the bottom 40% are in need of some real help. Most of these students are in the shape they're in because of problems they bring to school every day." Hodgkinson went on to argue, "If American schools could bring half of the students in the bottom 40% into the middle class by teaching them some intellectual job skills the whole nation would benefit" (Hodgkinson, 1993, p. 623). The effects of such a focus can alter future generations. This may be where education of the future needs to focus.

"It is the best of times; it is the worst of times." Crosby (1993) characterized education today by borrowing these words of Charles Dickens in *A Tale of Two Cities* when he noted that, although Americans today have more money than ever before, more of our country is living in poverty. Poverty and deprivation exist side by side with comfortable affluence. While more high school students graduate, more high school students also drop out; more security, more uncertainty; more education, more miseducation; more success, more failure.

SUMMARY

A Nation at Risk gave the United States the greatest educational shock since the launch of *Sputnik* made every American fear that the United States might not be the greatest scientific society. America 2000 and GOALS 2000 were the first significant attempts to redesign education after the release of the 1983 report. These controversial attempts began a movement to improve American education at all levels. The biggest obstacle remaining for America to overcome is the division of federal, state, and local counterparts. Arguments arose that real improvements in education will come at the local school level. Other arguments espoused that this will be apparent at the national and/or state levels.

There was little disagreement that with the publication of *A Nation at Risk* the American public viewed the schools as inadequate to address the present expectations of society. While business and technology had made striking advances during this period, the public schools were still operating much in a mid-century model. Numerous reform efforts were initiated and many continue. However, few, if any, have impacted successful and sustained restructuring of the schools on a grand scale.

The desire to improve education and return America to a position of global dominance has become a mission for America. Most citizens believe that the current system of education has to be improved. The problem remains to find a solution with mutual agreement and support.

✛ ✛ ✛ DISCUSSION QUESTIONS

1. Define the term reform.

2. Why did the reform movements initiated after the release of *A Nation at Risk* fail?

3. How did GOALS 2000 differ significantly from America 2000?

4. What should be the major focus of a national curriculum, a state curriculum or a local curriculum?

5. What were some of the other reasons President Reagan might not have wanted a presidentially appointed commission to study education at the national level?

6. Examine the six goals of America 2000. How do you rate these with respect to appropriateness and the ability of our education system to achieve them?

7. What common threads or themes are present in the programs of the various states that are presented?

❖ ❖ ❖   CLASS ACTIVITIES

1. In a group of three or four, prioritize the list of points included within the chapter with respect to reconceptualizing the American Dream. Try to reach consensus.

2. Pretend that the class is a group of parents who have gathered to formulate five or six goals for the local school system. Construct these goals without educational jargon.

3. As a research project, compare the reform movements that followed the launching of *Sputnik* (1957) with the reform movements that arose after *A Nation at Risk* was published in 1983.

4. Interview a candidate running for the local school board. Have the candidate state the three most important changes needed for the school district. Ask how these changes can be accomplished.

5. Add two or three recommendations for action that should be taken to improve schools. How do your recommendations compare with those given by the National Commission on Excellence in Education?

6. President Clinton stated in 1993 that education had to be "reinvented." Prominent educators, business leaders, and industry officials view today's schools as inadequate to meet the challenges of today or tomorrow. As a prospective elementary school teacher, rate each of the goals in GOALS 2000 on a scale of 1 to 5 with respect to "appropriateness" and "prediction of attainment." Next describe how GOALS 2000 can act as a catalyst for the reinvention of education. Once these tasks are complete, interview several teachers, community leaders, and business and industry officials. Ask them to rate the goals with the same criteria and answer the question about reinventing. Analyze the data, design graphs to show comparisons, and give the results of your report to the class in a Power Point presentation.

❖ ❖ ❖ REFERENCES

Asayesh, G. (1993). Ten years after *A Nation at Risk*. *The School Administrator, 50*(4), 8–14.

Bell, T. H. (1993). Reflections one decade after *A Nation at Risk*. *Phi Delta Kappan, 74*(8), 592–597.

Bennett, W. (1988). *American education: Making it work*. Washington, DC: U.S. Department of Education.

Carnegie Task Force on Teaching as a Profession. (1986). *A nation prepared: Teachers for the 21st Century*. New York: Author.

Crosby, E. A. (1993, April). The at-risk decade. *Phi Delta Kappan*, 8, 598–602.

Doyle, D. (1991, November). America 2000. *Phi Delta Kappan*, 3, 184–191.

Edwards, C. H. & Allred, W. E. (1993). More on *A Nation at Risk*: Have the recommendations been implemented? *The Clearing House, 67*(2), 42–48.

Elam, S. M., Lowell, C. R., and Gallup, A. M. (1992). The 24th annual Gallup/Phi Delta Kappa poll of the public's attitudes toward the public schools. *Phi Delta Kappan, 74*(1), 41–53.

Goldberg, M. & Renton, A. M. (1993). Heeding the call to arms in *A Nation at Risk*. *The School Administrator, 50*(4).

Goodlad, J. I. (1990). *Teachers for our nation's schools*. San Francisco: Jossey-Bass Inc.

Hodgkinson, H. (1993). American education: The good, the bad, and the task. *Phi Delta Kappan, 74*(8), 619–623.

The Holmes Group. (1990). *Tomorrow's schools: Principles for the design of professional development schools*. East Lansing, MI: Author.

Howe, H. (1991). America 2000: A bumpy ride on four trains. *Phi Delta Kappan, 73*(3). 192–193.

Jennings, J. F. (1995). School reform based on what is taught and learned. *Phi Delta Kappan, 76*(10), 765–769.

Kaplan, D. A. (1993, Sept. 20). Dumber than we thought. *Newsweek*, 44–45.

Lewis, A. C. (1991, June). America 2000: What kind of nation? *Phi Delta Kappan, 72*(10), 734–735.

National Committee on Excellence in Education. (1983). *A nation at risk: The imperatives for educational reform*. Washington, DC: U.S. Government Printing Office.

North Carolina Department of Public Instruction (1996). *North Carolina standard course of study*. Raleigh, NC: NCDPI.

Parr, G. (1993). Educational reforms in Texas and their implications for school counselors. *The School Counselor (41)*, 44–47.

Riley, R. W. (1993). A new direction for education. *Principal, 73*(1), 5–7.

Sewall, G. T. (1991). America 2000: An appraisal. *Phi Delta Kappan, 73*(3), 204–209.

Sizer, T. R. (1989). Taking school reform seriously. *Preparing schools for the 1990s: An essay collection*. New York: Metropolitan Life Insurance Co.

U.S. Department of Education. (1997). Third international mathematics and science study. Washington, DC: U.S. Government Printing Office.

U.S. Department of Education. (1994, November). *Community update.* Washington, DC: U.S. Government Printing Office.

U.S. Department of Education. (1993). *Adult literacy in America.* Washington, DC: U.S. Government Printing Office.

❖ ❖ ❖   SUGGESTED READINGS

Adler, M. J. (1990). *Reforming education*: *The opening of the American mind.* New York: Collier Books.

Barth, P., & Mitchell, R. (1990). *Smart start: Elementary education for the 21st century.* Golden, CO: North American Press.

Berliner, D. C., & Biddle, B. J. (1995). *The manufactured crisis: Myths, fraud and the attack on America's public schools.* New York: Addison-Wesley.

Best, J. W. (1981). *Research in education* (4th ed.). Upper Saddle River, NJ: Prentice Hall.

Boyer, E. (1991). *Ready to learn.* Princeton, NJ: Carnegie Foundations for the Advancement of Teaching.

Boyer, E. (1995). *The basic school: A community for learning.* New Jersey: The Carnegie Foundation for the Advancement of Teaching.

Combs, A. W. (1991). *The schools we need.* New York: University Press of America.

Fiske, E. B. (1995). *Smart schools, smart kids: Why do some schools work?* New York: Alfred A. Knopf.

Gross, B., & Gross, R. (1969). *Radical school reform* (4th ed.). New York: Simon & Schuster, Inc.

Johnson, M. L. (1992). *Education on the wild side: Learning for the twenty-first century.* Golden, CO: North American Press.

Myers, C. B., & Myers, L. K. (1995). *The professional educator: A new introduction to teaching.* Boston: Wadsworth.

Ohlrich, D. C. (1989, March). Education reforms: Mistakes, misconceptions, miscues. *Phi Delta Kappan, 170*(7), 512–517.

Ornstein, A. C., & Behar, L. S. (1995). *Contemporary issues in curriculum.* Boston, MA: Allyn & Bacon.

Otto, R. (1994). A new social studies: The Kentucky education reform act of 1990. *The Social Studies, (85)*3, 106–111.

Postman, N. (1994). *The end of education: Redefining the value of school.* New York: McGraw-Hill.

Reese, W. J. (1988). Public schools and the common good. *Educational Theory, 38*(4), 431–440.

Tanner, D., & Tanner, L. (1995). *Curriculum development. Theory into practice* (3rd ed.). Upper Saddle River, NJ: Merrill/Prentice Hall.

Tye, K. (1992). Restructuring our schools: Beyond the rhetoric. *Phi Delta Kappan, 1.*

U.S. Department of Education. (1997). *A call to action for American education in the twenty-first century.* Washington, DC: U.S. Government Printing Office.

❖ ❖ ❖

2

THE CHANGING SOCIETY

Chapter Objective and Focus:

An analysis and discussion of the effects that the changing society has had on the American public schools curriculum

---

For the past few decades, educators have treated the symptoms of the United States' ailing system of public instruction instead of focusing on the problem. Business and industry continue to grow and change with the evolution of society. The American system of public instruction has not maintained the same pace of growth and change to meet the needs of an ever-changing society.

American society has changed dramatically since the 1950s in several respects. The norm is no longer the traditional two-parent family with the mother staying at home. In most two-parent homes, both parents work. In the 1990s many children lived in single-parent homes in which the parent worked long hours to meet basic living expenses. Children were often required to stay in child care facilities or in before- and after-school programs at school. In other situations, children stayed at home unattended and entertained themselves with unsupervised television or noneducational games.

The ethnic composition of the American population changed rapidly in the last quarter of the twentieth century. In the twenty-first century the ethnic composition of the United States will be much more diverse. In every large city and in many smaller towns, diverse population will be found. No one culture or ethnic group will be able to claim position as the majority group. The United States will be a nation of minorities. Accompanying this greater diversity will be continued debates of cultural separatism, cultural pluralism, and special populations.

Cultural changes in America have had a direct impact on children in school. Perhaps the most critical changes impacting education have been the changing family structure, increased violence, and an ever-present challenge to meet the needs of all students in a diverse society moving towards a global environment. These challenges will be magnified to an even greater extent in the future.

CHILD AND FAMILY

In 1980 African-American children accounted for the majority of the minority children. The other ethnic minorities combined outnumbered the African-American child population, and the traditional white child population began a continuing decline.

In a report by the Center for the Study of Social Policy (1992), children in 1990 composed a smaller portion of the American population than in 1980, but the number of children under the age of six increased by 12.5 percent. In the late 1990s young children were as numerous as during the baby boom of the 1950s.

The number of school-age children from the ages of six to eleven increased by 3.4 percent, while the teenage group decreased by 14 percent. The 1990 census reported that the number of non-Hispanic white children declined by seven percent, but they remained the largest group, a total of 70 percent of the population. African-American children composed the largest group of what was often referred to as "minorities" in the 1990s. This group of children totaled nearly 15 percent of the population. Closely following were Hispanic children who accounted for 12 percent of the population. Asian-Americans and Native Americans accounted for three percent and one percent, respectively.

In 1980, only seventy-one percent of all children lived in a home with two parents. This figure represented a dramatic decrease of 75 percent in only a decade. Nearly 20 percent of children lived in a single-parent environment with by far the majority 10.4 million living with the mother and 2.0 million of these children residing with their fathers. Particularly alarming was the fact that 5.7 million children (9 percent of the child population) lived in a home not headed by either parent. However, by 1990 the number of single-mother families had increased by 19 percent and the number of single-father families had increased by 68 percent. Among African-American families, the single-parent home outnumbered the two-parent home structure.

By 1990, the U.S. Census Bureau reported a historical shift in the population. Married couples with no children formed a larger percentage of the population than married couples living with children.

Children with working mothers increased by 55 percent in the decade from 1980 to 1990. Sixty-eight percent of women with children under the age of 18 worked, according to the 1990 census. Sixty percent of women with children under age six worked. This reflected an increase of 60 percent from 1980. The number of mothers who worked increased at about the age that children began school. Seventy-five percent of women with children six years of age or older worked. This was an increase of 63 percent from 1980.

In 1980, the traditional two-parent home, where 71 percent of children lived with both parents, sixty-two percent had two working parents. Of the 24 percent who lived with one parent, 69 percent of the parents worked. Sixty-four percent of all children living with a parent did not have a parent at home full time. Nearly 10 percent of all children lived with a parent who was unemployed.

Substantial population increases occurred during the decades from 1950 to 1990. The *U.S. Bureau of The Census, Statistical Abstract of the United States* (1993, 1995) recorded that the resident population grew from approximately 151 million to 249 million. Projections for the year 2000 neared 275 million. Campbell (1994), along with the U.S. Bureau of the Census, estimates that from 1990 to 2000 the number of students from preschool through college will increase by seven million.

As previously stated, some of the major changes in the family in the late 20th century are greater poverty among children and their families, the decline of the traditional family, and the entry of a large number of women into the labor force. Additional concerns are the high rate of teenage pregnancy, high-school dropouts, juvenile crime, a growing rate of child abuse, and how society, especially schools, can function effectively in this changing environment.

In the future, poverty and related social issues must be addressed more productively than during the twentieth century. Appropriate social programs and educational incentives must be designed and implemented nationwide if the educational system is to positively impact poverty and related issues.

The structure and function of the American family will continue to experience significant changes. Educators must be prepared to deal with the implications of increasing divorce rates, teenage pregnancy, and violence, all of which in the past resulted in emotional turmoil that children carried into the classrooms.

In the 1950s the American family was portrayed widely as traditional. The American dream included a father who had a steady job, a mother who tended house, two or three children, and home ownership. This family was portrayed as financially comfortable and living in a world with limited poverty.

As illustrated, much of this has changed, and more changes appear obvious in the future. Elementary school teachers will continue to instruct children in a culture in which no single set of characteristics will accurately describe the American family.

POVERTY AND VIOLENCE

The number of American children below the age of six living in poverty in the United States reached an all-time high in the final decade of the twentieth century, as reported by the National Center for Children in Poverty (1995). The director of the center, Aber Lawrence, stated that a record high of six million children under age six lived in poverty. That accounted for over one-fourth of all children in that age group in the United States. In a period of five years, from 1987–1992, the number of children under the age of six living in poverty increased by one million. This continued a trend of poverty that President Johnson's War on Poverty program in the 1960s failed to reverse.

The 1990 census reflected that 18 percent of all children under age 18 were poor. By 1992, the Current Population Survey placed that figure at 22 percent.

The Population Reference Bureau (1992) demonstrated that in 1990 more than 11 million children under 18 years of age lived in households with income below the poverty level. This was an increase of 14 percent from the 1980 census. Of that 11 million, 4.3 million children were under the age of six and 6.8 million were between the ages of 6 and 17. The percentage increases in children living in poverty according to race or ethnic groups in the ten-year period were:

Non-Hispanic White	1.5%
African-American	2.0%
Asian American	2.2%
Hispanic	3.1%
Native American	6.3%

Within these increases, 50 percent were in single-mother homes and 24 percent were in single-father homes.

In order to address the social implications of future reform efforts in education, programs must confront issues of poverty and health. Following the United States Supreme Court's ruling in *Brown vs. the Board of Education of Topeka, Kansas* in 1954, America began modern reform to equalize educational opportunity for all children by outlawing segregated schools. Much of this effort was impeded by slow social acceptance and the greater impact of the launching of *Sputnik* by the Soviets in 1957. While increased focus was placed upon science through passage of the National Defense Education Act of 1958, many schools remained poor and segregated well into the late 1960s.

President Johnson's War on Poverty, complete with compensatory educational programs and the passage of the Civil Rights Act of 1964, was the first social reform that attempted to affect education on a national level. Perhaps the real influence of these programs was the attention given to poverty-stricken children. Obviously the effects were limited. Although American schools are now legally desegregated, poverty, racial tensions, and violence will continue to plague the schools well into the next century.

Educators create some of the conditions that place culturally diverse children at greater risk by not recognizing and addressing their special needs. Prospective teachers must learn to recognize the individuality of children and agree that all children must have an equal chance to be successful in school.

In recent years, guns and violence have become major problems in society and in the schools. Education is essential to counter the widespread problem of violence. The schools must be supported by parents and the community in efforts to change the behavior patterns of youth by providing children with a drug-free and violence-free school environment and training in alternatives to violence in problem resolution. According to a 1994 survey conducted in seven hundred American cities by the National League of Cities, school violence in the preceding year caused the death or serious injury of students in 41% of these large cities. Survey responders in 38% of the cities reported a noticeable increase in school violence over the past five years. Seventeen percent said violence had gone down or was really not a problem. The remaining responders said it was about the same. Counting communities of all sizes, one-fourth of the respondents reported student deaths or injuries requiring hospitalization within the previous year as a result of violence. The figures were generally highest in large cities: 41% for cities with populations of 100,000 or more; 32% for cities of 50,000 to 100,000; and 19% for cities with populations fewer than 50,000. The largest cities were also the most likely to report increased violence over the preceding five years: 55% compared with 46% for the middle-size cities and 31% for smaller communities.

CHILDREN AND EDUCATION

School enrollment grew by less than 20 percent from 1980 to 1990 as reported by the Population Reference Bureau for the Center for the Study of Social Policy (1992). Sixty percent of preschool students attended private schools and 10 percent of elementary students attended private schools.

In 1991, eleven percent of all Americans aged 16–19 were not enrolled in school and were not high school graduates. Following are percentages of teens from several ethnic groups who were not attending school:

Non-Hispanic White	10%
African-American	14%
Hispanic	22%
Asian American	5%
Native American	18%

When compared with the total population of all dropouts, whites accounted for 66 percent. African-Americans and Hispanics accounted for 18 percent and 22 percent, respectively.

Marilyn McMillen (1993) reported for the National Center for Education that between 1982 and 1992, a 10 percent reduction in the number of high school sophomores who dropped out of school occurred. She stated that school failure and dislike of school were the major reasons students gave for quitting school.

During the period from 1982 to 1992, twenty-five percent of female students were reported to have dropped out of school due to pregnancy. In 1992, marriage was cited as the cause for leaving school significantly less often than in 1982.

According to a study conducted for the General Accounting Office in 1993, there were about 44.4 million school-age children (ages 5–17) in 1990. This was a decrease from 1980. School-age children make up less than 19 percent of the total population. The increase or decrease in school-age children by race was as follows:

Caucasian	decrease of 12%
African-American	decrease of 4%
Hispanic	increase of 57%
Asians	increase of 87%

According to the report, by 1990, white children comprised less than 70 percent of the school-age population, down from 75% in 1980.

The number of immigrant children rose by 24% during the last decade, a fact so significant that the State of California passed Proposition 187 which banned illegal aliens from attending school and receiving medical attention or any other state services except under emergency circumstances.

David Hamburg (1993) found that while adult pregnancy had declined since 1970, adolescent pregnancy had soared to one of the highest rates among technologically advanced nations. His findings indicate that teens accounted for 66 percent of all illegitimate births. Nearly 1.3 million children lived with teen mothers, only 50 percent of whom were married. Six million children under the age of 5 were living with mothers who were adolescents when they gave birth. Hamburg's findings verified that twenty-five percent of young American children were being raised in poverty and the trend was moving upward at an alarming rate.

Rubin and Borgers (1991) found that American families had undergone profound demographic transformations yet survived in spite of changing social conditions. However, the educational institutions that prepared children to become capable and responsible adults had failed to keep pace. For example, the 180-day school year with two months off in the summer was most compatible with the American lifestyle of the 1950s. Yet late-century family structural changes have required school boards and administrators to seriously examine such issues as magnet schools, alternative schools, and year-round schooling. Changes in the family have weakened the family support system essential for children's healthy development. This weakness has placed a greater burden on the schools to provide students with a stimulating and supportive environment.

One of the greatest influences on family systems has been the large and increasing number of working mothers. A review of several studies by the National Academy of Sciences indicated that, in general, the school achievement of children of working mothers differed very little when compared with children of mothers who did not work outside the home. Basically, it depended upon the parents, the child, and the circumstances that surrounded whether or not the mother was working. While a mother's work did limit involvement in her child's education, working mothers made significant efforts to maintain close contacts with teachers and schools. The National Institute of Education also researched the intellectual functioning of children from single-parent homes. The findings suggested that children from single-parent households had intelligence levels similar to children from two-parent households, but that children from one-parent homes tended to receive lower grades, display more disruptive behaviors, and have poorer attendance.

Also, the findings suggested that the degree to which the family and school worked together was critical in determining children's academic success. Each was necessary to the other. Home and school must be complementary.

In the past, society's responsibility for providing educational opportunities for children began with their entry into school. Because of the structural changes in families that have occurred, schools now must be restructured or recreated to respond more effectively to the ever-changing educational needs of children. Mounting societal pressures, the startling growth in the number of single-parent homes, and an increase in childhood poverty have forced public schools to assume responsibilities for the welfare of children that far exceed the traditional educational obligation. As a result, many public schools have pursued a broad social agenda and have provided a wide range of social services, including breakfast and lunch programs, health clinics, before- and after-school programs, and child care centers (Martin, 1992).

Weston (1989) noted that American families must continue to play a significant role in education. Every aspect of the family from organizational structure and value systems to the relationships established with the rest of society affects what a child learns. Whatever the structure, families must prepare children for formal schooling by ensuring a healthy birth and giving the physical attention, emotional nurturing, and intellectual stimulation necessary for successful early childhood development. Parents are literally and should be figuratively their children's first and perhaps most important teachers (Martin, 1992).

Schools that were originally designed to educate the traditional student must now adapt the curriculum and the instructional program to the needs of an increasingly diverse population. Rich (1987) asserted that changes encourage recognition of differences in racial and cultural heritage, language, health, and family situations. She encouraged educators to be prepared to handle issues of family diversity with awareness, acceptance, and respect. Schools must support and assign educational roles to the family and provide them with the practical information they need to help educate their children.

Joseph (1986) suggested that teachers provide a warm atmosphere in their classrooms by allowing the children to express their feelings. She further encouraged teachers to become more aware of their own attitudes toward student diversity. She strongly recommended that teachers convey the attitude that there is more than one acceptable family structure.

Rubin (1989) believed that teachers must develop greater awareness and skill in handling issues of family diversity. This should include reassuring children that it is normal for changes in families to cause unfamiliar feelings and emotions.

One example of the lack of planning for the need of today's families is the schools' reaction to the unpredictability of the direction in which American society is headed for the twenty-first century.

NEW CONCEPTS OF DEVELOPMENT AND NEW RISK FACTORS

As Americans approach the next decade, new thought patterns and research tenets concerning child development are beginning to emerge. As society changes, its children change as well. Ideas revolving around innate developmental characteristics may still be useful in interpreting the behavior of children, yet the rapidly changing environment of these children fosters a need for parents and educators to recognize the significant impact that environment has upon children.

Not all children develop and learn in the same manner. Family, culture, geographical location, and socio-economic status can significantly influence a child's well-being and degree of healthy development. As a result of environmental, social, cultural, and economic differences, children are not permitted equal opportunities for survival and success, and this state of inequality will continue, with even greater differentiation, into the next century.

Parents, schools, and communities must begin to predict the needs of future generations of children while accounting for changes in the economy and environments in which these children will attempt to thrive. New concepts of development will emerge, resulting in the necessity of a more educated and empathetic society. New risk factors, special populations of children, and global impacts upon children must be taken into consideration. A society is only as prosperous as its members. It is the responsibility of the present generation to become knowledgeable about the changing developmental needs of our children in the future.

Many parents of the twentieth century are limited in their knowledge of basic principles of growth and development. Children come to school unprepared to begin formal education. Many teachers forget the principles of child development and alienate the students they are trying to teach. Increased poverty, violence, and a growing apathy toward the poor contribute greatly to the inability of many of the nation's children to develop normally and be successful in school.

Early Learning and Education

According to *Starting Points: Meeting the Needs of Our Youngest Children*, a 1994 report by the Carnegie Corporation of New York, brain development before age one is more rapid and extensive than previously realized. The second half of the 20th century has seen a major change in the way the human brain is viewed. The old cliché, "Education is a lifelong experience," has taken on a whole new meaning.

Babies are born with billions of brain cells, almost twice the number they have as adults. During the first months of life, connections are made between these cells, forming the "wiring" that allows learning to occur. As a young child grows, nature acts as a sculptor, chipping away excess cells so this wiring can function more efficiently. Cells that are not stimulated by certain sensory experiences—tasting, touching, smelling, hearing, and seeing—ultimately die.

The threat to this cell wiring comes from giving insufficient stimulation to young babies to ensure that the sculpting process is successful. It is now known that brain growth and maturation are lifelong processes that are genetically and environmentally affected. As a result of this new information on how early learning takes place, parents and educators are faced with the new challenge of recognizing and adapting to the varied abilities children possess. It is now believed that there is no time that is too early to begin teaching a child skills such as reading and writing.

In his 1991 report, *Ready to Learn*, Boyer revealed that 88% of kindergarten teachers nationwide felt that their students had major problems with the complexity and structure of their language and language patterns. Of these same teachers, Boyer said that 43% felt that their incoming students were less equipped or less ready to learn than their students were five years previously.

As we move into the next century, the dynamics of family structures will continue to change and to evolve, moving away from what we recognize as traditional families. More than 85 percent of today's parents are either dual-career or single. Interestingly, single-father families are the fastest growing segment of our nation's population. Over the last 30 years, children have lost approximately 12 hours of time per week spent with their parents. Younger children are increasingly left with babysitters or placed in day care centers. For older children, time after school that was once spent with parents is now often spent on extra-curricular activities, sports or, less productively, in front of a television or video game.

As society approaches the next century, one of the most horrifying crises to be faced is that of child abuse. Any child, regardless of sex, age, ethnicity, or socioeconomic background, can be a victim of child abuse or neglect. Child abuse can be characterized by various forms of maltreatment including physical abuse, sexual abuse, mental injury, and child neglect, which includes the physical, educational, and emotional facets of negligence. Cases of physical abuse and those involving physical neglect are the most frequently occurring forms of child abuse (NCCAN, 1992).

The long-term consequences of the detrimental effects of child abuse directly influence the degree to which a child follows healthy growth and development patterns. Research on the effects of maltreatment on children has cited neurological, intellectual and cognitive, behavioral, emotional, and personality repercussions. Children who have suffered physical abuse resulting in head injuries often display signs of neurological disorders that pose obvious threats to intellectual and cognitive development.

Abused children do not necessarily exhibit identical behavioral and emotional dispositions, yet the presence of socio-emotional problems in many abused children is well documented (NCCAN, 1992). Researchers have noted common patterns of extreme characteristics in abused children, exemplified by either passive and withdrawn behavior or intensely active and aggressive behavior. Abused children have been found to be significantly more self-destructive. Symptoms of low self-esteem, social withdrawal, oppositionally deviant behavior, hyperactivity, and learning difficulties have been identified in abused children.

Sexual abuse, in relation to child abuse, is defined as indecent sexual liberties taken with a child by his caregiver. This horrific reality has tripled in its reported cases since 1980 (NCCAN, 1992). Empirical literature confirms the particularly devastating effects of sexual abuse, including fear, anxiety, depression, self-destructive behavior, anger, aggression, guilt and shame, impaired ability to trust, revictimization, sexually inappropriate behavior, school problems, truancy, running away, and delinquency. Each of these effects has a profound impact upon the development of children and influences the physical, emotional, intellectual, and moral realms.

Substantial increases in the incidence of child abuse and neglect will probably continue into the 21st century. Society must target the families of potential victims and provide appropriate measures for prevention and coping strategies for the victims. Children whose lives are threatened and torn apart by deranged parents cannot be expected to function "normally," let alone perform above average academically.

Child abuse is only one of many risk factors affecting the development of children at the dawn of the 21st century. Fundamental rudiments of humanity and of society will continue both to thrive and to deteriorate. Values and morals will change within families and will continue to challenge functions of formal schooling. One does not have to go far to see or hear evidence that a major concern today in the United States is the decline of morality among our nation's youth.

Society is inundated with problematic issues of youth morality today. Rates of drug abuse, alcohol use, and pregnancy among youths are on the rise, in almost epidemic proportions. The media is full of stories addressing this national crisis. Public service announcements encouraging reading and mentoring and discouraging smoking, alcohol use, drug use, and unsafe sex bombard viewers nightly. Politicians running for office advocate the need for a return to family values and raising children with the assistance of the entire community.

So what is causing this decline in morals and values? The causes are remnants of the problems of earlier generations from which contributing factors remain. Television, racism, poverty, materialism, greed, and the deterioration of the family are the main culprits.

Who is to blame? All sides seem to place the blame somewhere other than upon themselves. Many families blame the schools for not teaching morals, while schools blame the families. The teaching of morals, values, and moral development should be a partnership between the families and schools.

A parallel issue to morals and values in schools is character education. Character education, or actively teaching moral behavior by integrating it into classroom instruction and management, is another topic of heated discussion. Students seldom practice what the school-based character education programs preach. Principles of character education taught in schools must be reinforced at home in order to render the necessary improvements in personal values (Tyree, 1997).

Researchers have varied opinions about the effectiveness of character education. Hartshorn and Nelson found that youth can react in specific, nonconsistent ways. Children who are taught morals may act dishonestly if a situation rewards dishonest behavior. Professor Alan Lockwood of the University of Wisconsin reviewed over 70 years of research on character education and concluded that in real-life situations students who have been in character education programs often act as if they have never been taught about honesty, sharing, cooperation, and other important traits of character (Lockwood, 1993).

Increased substance abuse by America's youth has demonstrated that the "Just Say No" slogan of the 1980s has fallen on deaf ears. Coinciding with this is the view held by many parents that drug abuse is something their children will never experience. Yet youth substance abuse is an American epidemic. The face of substance abuse has no defining color and no particular socioeconomic status or educational background. A 1991 survey on drug abuse conducted by the Public Health Service revealed that out of an estimated 9.3 million youth between the ages of 12 and 17, 46% had used alcohol. Of those surveyed, 20% had used an illegal drug (marijuana, cocaine, heroine, speed, etc.).

These illegal drugs include so-called designer drugs like ecstasy. Ecstasy and other drugs like it were created to achieve the ultimate high. Other youths abuse chemicals by sniffing or huffing inhalants. This version of getting high is one of the scariest and deadliest because it involves the abuse of common household items such as hair spray, spray paint, glue, liquid paper, magic markers, whipped cream cans, and even freon from air-conditioning units.

Drug and alcohol abuse is not a new phenomenon among the youth culture. For years youth have experimented with whatever type of drug was available. One problem, however, is that now the drug is not limited to one or two types; there are hundreds of drugs from which to choose. Unlike in prior generations, the abuse is not limited to a small experimenting segment of the population; rather, it involves a growing percentage of the youth population.

Whole Child Perspective

Theories of child development differ in their explanations of how an individual changes physically, mentally, and emotionally throughout the course of life. Theories tend to emphasize different components of the developmental process, giving more importance and greater attention to particulars, such as cognition, behavior, or morality. Generally, theorists express concern for how an individual develops across the life span, although there is a tendency to compartmentalize this development rather than focus upon the overall process itself.

The past several decades have evinced an increasing trend in developmental psychology, a field in which practitioners are beginning to recognize that the individual is multi-variant, working from a framework that includes psychological, biological, and environmental dimensions. The life-span perspective of human development emphasizes the historical context of development, which acknowledges that human development in any one period of history tends to depict events that are specific to that period. Views on life-span development have also pointed out that development can take multiple directions. "Throughout life some people enhance their developmental outcomes while other people decrease them" (Roberts, 1994, p. 34). Many factors contribute to the changes an individual may experience in development. Changes occurring in one period of development are interrelated to changes taking place in other periods of development.

Coupled with individual development over time is the developmental process of the family unit. The family drama is also unfolding in a larger social context, which includes the extended family as well as the community. Transitions or changes in the individual, family, and community can direct many of the dynamic processes associated with human behavior. Changes in a child's intellectual ability also provide a map of expected behavior. This cognitive development is further refined by moral attitudes and an individual's ability to cooperate and communicate in a diverse society.

A systems paradigm of human development states that each facet of development is a holistic construct in which the whole is greater than the sum of its parts. Environment plays a large role in an individual's development, helping to shape the "whole" child. Development, from a systems perspective, is viewed not as a linear sequence of events but rather as an interconnected mesh of affective experiences and coping strategies which vary among individuals.

Parents, educators, and community members must invest interest in a child's "whole" development. This includes directing attention towards each entity of development, considering physical, cognitive, moral, and behavioral facets, and how these function together to make up the complete child. It also includes an attempt to understand the external influences and conflicts with which an individual is presented.

Perhaps the most alarming findings about children and their development were released in April 1994 by the Carnegie Corporation. In this report the researchers described that as many as one-half of the 12 million American children from birth to age three are developmentally at risk. The report found that many of these children under the age of three and their families are in an extremely negative environment that worsens daily.

David A. Hamburg, Carnegie president, found a lack of understanding of the critical nature of the situation. The panel of researchers found that changes in demographics and in society had placed these children from birth to age three in poverty. Research showed that these children lived in single-parent homes and were often victimized physically by adults. Low-quality child care was also cited as a major factor in the plight of children in poverty.

The Carnegie Report (1994) provided several statistics that demonstrated the risk factors of children from birth to age three. These included:

1. One-fourth of them were born to unwed mothers.
2. One half of all these children will experience divorce of their parents during childhood.
3. One-quarter of them live in poverty.
4. Infants are the fastest growing age group in foster homes.
5. Over one-third of children under age two are not properly immunized.
6. One-third of child abuse victims are under one year old.

In addition to these problems, scientists in the study discovered new evidence showing that in the first year of life infants are susceptible to both positive and negative influences. This evidence that the formation of synapses in the brain develops more rapidly than expected led to the conclusion that improper social environments can activate hormones that negatively affect brain functions related to learning.

Without intervention and change, these six million children and those to follow will continue to come to school unprepared to learn. These new findings about growth and development in the early years will have a great impact upon teaching and learning in the twenty-first century. Therefore, if educators are to be effective in designing appropriate curriculum and instruction models for the future, child growth and development must be evaluated closely in the design process.

Students with Special Needs

Historically, one of the most significant problems in special education has been how students are classified and placed in these programs. Children with special needs are often treated differently. Teachers may have unwarranted lower expectations of children classified as handicapped or learning disabled.

Achieving success in special education reform requires progress in policy-making, administration, and programming. Regular education teachers should be more knowledgeable and competent in their ability to teach children with special needs. They should not replace special education teachers or other professionals, but rather work in harmony with these educators to plan, guide, instruct, and evaluate the progress of students. Inclusion must be understood in terms of the whole education enterprise. All students, especially students with special needs, require a part in the regular education system that includes special intervention programs for limited periods of time in the regular classroom. For example, the deaf should be considered a legitimate cultural and linguistic minority and entitled to the inclusion of educational programs. The author believes that by the year 2010, mainstream programs will have departed from the one teacher/one class operation. Special education teachers will provide high density instruction, such as in small groups or one-on-one as part of their regular classroom operation to students showing the least progress. Children will not be labeled. Rather than adding separate units about various cultural groups, educators will transform the curriculum as a whole. Social studies, history, and literature classes are the most fertile grounds for this transition. By recognizing the contributions of individuals from all cultures, schools can foster the development of competent, secure young people who will become major players in a global society.

A particular problem at this time may be to improve the coordination of programs in the schools and communities that serve students who are exceptional or marginal in their school progress. Community agencies must first understand the cultures from which they are programming, critique their learning styles and their point of view, and plan for inclusion of the culture of their constituencies. Schools must place special emphasis on helping all special students become productive contributors to the economy of America.

Since the early 1970s, a national trend in redirecting the way we must educate children with disabilities has emerged. Public Law 94-142 was passed in 1975 (now updated to the Individuals with Disabilities Act, Public Law 101-476). Before this time, students in special education programs socialized with regular students only during social times such as recess, assemblies and lunch. Placement rates in restrictive settings have increased significantly (McLeskey & Pacchiano, 1994).

The first program after Public Law 94-142 was enacted was mainstreaming. The purpose of mainstreaming is to require schools to have both regular classrooms and special classrooms for children with special needs. It also requires special needs children to move back and forth between the two classrooms. This strategy was viewed positively, therefore full inclusion was added to the school day.

Friend (1993) defined inclusion as "an educational philosophy based on the belief that all students are entitled to fully participate in their school community." The term includes students with different cultural backgrounds and languages. Although it includes a wide array of individuals, inclusion is most often associated with students who have mental, physical, and/or emotional disabilities. Inclusion is not without controversy and, as with most new reform ideas, there are those who see it as negative and destructive for regular children. There are also people who believe inclusion is the best thing for children and society.

Proponents believe that students help each other based on individual strengths and needs and that disabled students can form friendships and associate with "normal students" (Stoler, 1992). Inclusion of handicapped students into the regular classroom is thought by many to be a way to eliminate segregation in the schools.

Additionally, the push for full inclusion embraces the theory that, if all students are put together in one classroom, regular children will learn to tolerate differences in others. Many believe that children benefit from being in an inclusive environment by learning or interacting with members of society regardless of their differences (Friend, 1993).

Supporters argue that inclusion is not only a positive influence for all students, but that it is a matter of civil rights. They reason that the only way to make sure that handicapped children have the same education is to place them in regular classroom. They argue that, if nothing else, children with disabilities will experience the same situations as regular students. When disabled students were moved into the regular classroom, it was found that they often benefited from role models who were age appropriate. These special students learned social skills and responded to natural cues when they were permitted to be directly involved in school activities (Block, 1994).

Proponents of inclusion believe that the old approach of pulling special education students out of class weakens communication between the regular and special education teachers (Semmel, 1991). They believe that labeling disabled students and taking them out of the regular classroom results in "stigmatization".

Although by law, educators are required to provide a "least restrictive environment" for students with disabilities, some teachers argue that inclusion benefits socialization more than education. Semmel (1992) found that both regular and special education teachers believe that disabled children have a right to be educated in a classroom with normal children. Regular classroom teachers indicate that they lack the appropriate skills to meet the instructional needs of the special child.

In the last part of the twentieth century, special students were those classified with a type of physical, mental, emotional, or behavioral handicap. In the twenty-first century, cultural factors alone will be grounds for inclusion.

For decades, educators have known that children from poverty-stricken areas, children of migrant workers, and immigrant children have always been viewed as special students. In the past these students were usually tolerated if they were not disruptive. However, most were considered hopeless by many teachers and, at best, caring teachers tried to teach these children some basic skills of reading, writing, and mathematics. By the 1990s American educators greeted the "crack babies" in kindergarten and homeless children at all grade levels. The movement has just started.

Homeless children will be a great concern affecting schools in tomorrow's society. By the middle 1990s an estimated 100,000 children were homeless (Eddowes, 1994). Many of these children have severe emotional, social, developmental, educational, or health problems. Many will not become productive citizens. Both the family and the school will need to share responsibility in assisting the homeless child in the learning process.

In 1987, Congress passed the Stewart B. McKinney Homeless Assistance Act which ensured that homeless children will have access to education. Even after this act was passed, homeless parents still had problems advocating for their children. Educators can help address this problem by reaching out to homeless parents. Well-designed child care and school programs that provide family support can allow homeless children to develop properly in spite of the great difficulties in their lives. Homeless children have many barriers to education and educators must make a greater effort to meet their needs. The importance of understanding homeless children's lifestyles must be stressed in the preservice training of teachers (McChesney, 1993).

Learning disabled and impaired children are another population of special children whose developmental needs may differ. These children often need additional one-on-one instruction and attention to help them become active and productive citizens. Programs that emphasize developmentally appropriate instruction must be implemented to ensure that their needs are addressed. Individual education plans (IEPs) should accompany academic expectations of learning impaired students.

Both preservice and in-service professional development require partnerships among schools and institutions of higher education to promote inclusive learning communities of all individuals who impact the learning and lives of students with special needs.

Urban and Rural School Comparisons

Urban and rural communities, as opposed to suburban areas, have higher concentrations of poor and/or limited English proficient students. Additionally, these groups have higher dropout rates and lower levels of student achievement. DeYoung and Lawrence (1995) found that most "chronically poor counties in the U.S. are located in rural areas" (p. 106). In order to overcome these problems, higher expectations, better instructional opportunities, equal funding for all schools, and greater community and parental involvement to address these students' diverse needs are essential.

Maslow's hierarchy of needs suggests that certain aspects of a child's life must be fulfilled in order for that child to have the safe haven needed to achieve academically. Parental, community, and educational support must all be present in order to ensure that a child's most essential needs are met. Children from urban and rural areas who are often classified as at risk must be provided with intervention strategies, facilitated by all community members involved.

Content and organization of academic courses and exercises shape students' school experiences. Multicultural education efforts are essential in providing both urban and rural youth with the knowledge they need to succeed in the diverse society that America will be in the next century. Core curriculum courses, as well as exploratory courses, must foster higher order thinking, relevancy, and active student engagement. These efforts should focus upon the development of content that relates to students' current interests and life experiences and that can be facilitated by successfully combining vocational with academic tasks to prepare students for real world experiences.

Multicultural Education

Welton and Mallan (1996) identified multicultural education's intent as "to develop a sense of pride, understanding, and respect for the various groups that make up American society" (p. 76). They suggested that the characterization of America as a melting pot society is no longer applicable. Rather, America is and always has been composed of a multitude of cultures.

As a new century begins, both beginning and experienced teachers continue to face cultural challenges in the classroom. Perhaps the most significant of these challenges is related to the increased diversity of students from many cultures. In order to maintain quality education, stronger connections have to exist between the students and their learning. An educational program that respects student differences relative to racial, cultural, gender, disability, social class, and language differences can be successful. The program of inclusion of multicultural concepts and strategies must incorporate the experiences of all.

Multicultural education should guide all students to develop an understanding of their own cultural group's identification. Students have the opportunity to see their culture reflected in the curriculum in order to develop more positive attitudes toward school and education.

At the 1994 Annual Meeting of the National Council for the Social Studies in Phoenix, Geneva Gay, a noted expert on multicultural education, responded to this question from the audience: "What does successful multicultural education look like?" She began her response with the statement, "Maybe there is no model, but many models." Gay suggested that successful programs include recognition of multicultural differences, interaction among students by placing emphasis upon the teaching-learning process rather than on content, and infusion versus inclusion.

Gay believed that multicultural education was a mandate and that it could be a "philosophy or tool." Multicultural education "demands change and accountability. It must penetrate all content and puncture the architecture." She implied that numerous obstacles such as a moralistic agenda, the incompetence of Americans in human relations, competition, and individualism have all harmed the overall structure of multicultural education. Her strongest point may have been made when she clearly stated, "We must desocialize the resocialized education." It appears that as society examines the recreation of the American public school, a great focus must be on working toward a functional definition and program of multicultural education that is recreated with the goal of educational equity.

In 1981, James Banks, in his text *Multicultural Education: Theory and Practice*, noted that multicultural education was an educational reform movement concerned with providing educational equity for cultural and ethnic groups. He saw clearly that equity in education must be central to the multicultural movement. Banks believed that much of the problem with multicultural education had been the lack of a total school or total educational movement, and that this would change as education becomes recreated in the twenty-first century.

Nationwide, educators must teach the principles and practices of social responsibility and participatory citizenship in a democratic environment in order to arm children with skills to participate in their political, social, and cultural institutions. Equity pedagogy requires teaching practices that respect diverse learning styles within cultural and ethnic groups. It mandates that teachers present materials in ways that enhance learning opportunities for all students. Empowerment promotes gender, racial, and socioeconomic class equity.

Prospective teachers must acknowledge the cultural specifics of all children in the class and determine how to develop teaching styles that meet the learning style needs of students from a variety of cultural backgrounds. Cooperative learning strategies have been used to build upon student strengths. This changes power relationships in the classroom and, therefore, shifts the responsibility for learning from the teacher to the student. When the pluralistic cultural backgrounds of students are acknowledge and valued, children will feel permission to relate their personal experiences to broader perspectives and understandings. Educators should consistently examine the various methods of cooperative learning in order to use the strategy effectively.

The standards of a national curriculum should include goals for multicultural education. McGuire (1992) maintained that America 2000 goals may have been misplaced and did not address the magnitude of problems that students face daily. In addressing the goals of America 2000, she stated that educators needed to incorporate the goals of social studies and participatory democracy focused around civic education.

Young people who fail to graduate from school may lead lives of poverty, desperation, and crime. Society has changed; schools have not kept pace with the change. Local schools must have the ability to make decisions by promoting teacher empowerment. In addition, American schools need economic equity in order to offer a quality education to every child. Many Americans believe that children in schools are investments that must receive top priority (Geiger, 1991).

Stewart (1991) stated that the image of the U.S. as a melting pot is perhaps romantic. He believed an emphasis on multiculturalism is needed because, although multiculturalism maintains that Americans are many peoples with different histories, those stories overlap and interact. Differences need to be recognized in schools. Multiculturalists feel that focusing on diversity should take precedence over finding common cultural ground.

Global Impact on Children

The United States may still be the superpower of the world in political terms, but in terms of how American students compare to students around the world, we are sorely lacking. Upon review of the standards of countries whose students test at the top internationally, the areas of disparity were obvious and ones which American educators must address. Reconsideration of testing criteria, curriculum development, and other concerns is necessary if American students are to become world class competitors again.

An agenda to address these concerns must be created and implemented if desired outcomes are to occur. First, clear, consistent, and concise public standards must be established to help students achieve higher performance levels. Second, tracking and grouping practices must be designed relative to the needs of specific schools and populations served. These practices must reflect goals of the school, community, and the students. Exams should test what students have been asked to learn and not some arbitrary material that is presented differently from how students learn. Exams should test students on all levels of expected mastery and should require that students attempt demanding and complex tasks.

One national effort to ensure the technological literacy of all students is found in the Educational Technology Initiative: Technological Literacy for the 21st Century. The goals of this program are to provide access to modern computers for all teachers and students, and connect every school in America to the Internet. In addition, researchers are being encouraged to develop effective software in all subject areas.

Implementation of this effort will ensure that every teacher will receive the training needed to assist students with technology. All of the nation's classrooms will be wired to have access to the Internet through the creation of an Educational Technology Fund, a private/public technology "matching" fund.

Finally, higher standards for states, school districts, teachers, and students will be the focus for implementing the initiative.

Another attempt at national reform was the Elementary and Secondary Education Act of 1965. This was designed primarily to help disadvantaged children, focusing on improvements in teaching in more than 50,000 schools. This act increased school flexibility in utilizing federal aid and helping all of America's children to prepare for participation in a competitive global marketplace. Therefore, principles of global education must be taught in the elementary schools today and in the future.

Attempts to educate America's youth on the issues of poverty, pollution, disease, natural resource depletion, hunger, war, and human rights are of extreme importance. Students must become more acutely aware of the world and be able to make effective decisions on how to lead a productive life as adults. Incorporating this into the school systems will be a challenge of the twenty-first century that teachers must address. Global education, defined as "an approach to schooling reflecting a belief that there is a critical need for schools to prepare young people for life in their world increasingly characterized by pluralism, interdependence and change" (Kniep, 1989), may be the answer to this need.

The word *world* needs to be stressed because, until the 1980s, limited discussion about educating children in political, economic, and social issues occurred beyond the United States. Controversy concerning whether global issues should be incorporated into the elementary school curriculum arose during this period. Global education has been both supported and criticized in education because of the new direction that it has introduced into the classroom. If implemented correctly, global education can make children more aware of the greater world community.

Those who oppose teaching global education see several roadblocks in adding it to the curriculum. Budgetary limitations, time allocation, inadequate preservice and in-service training programs for educators, and the limited availability of appropriate teaching resources are but a few examples of problems that have hindered the complete integration of global education into the curriculum. School budgets seem to be well-established for providing the needs of students within the traditional curriculum. Many educators believe that changing this structure and adding more materials and resources will be an inappropriate use of funds. They believe that school scores have dropped on national measures and that schools have not excelled with the resources already available. So they question the need to buy more materials to continue doing the same.

Urch (1992) found that time allocation appeared to be the biggest issue in implementing global education. The question commonly asked was, "How can teachers who are already pressed for time to teach their regular disciplines add any more subject matter into their day and expect their students to receive a full education?" Critics believed that students have no extra time to discuss global issues and asked, "How can teachers teach the material if it involves complex issues where they have limited knowledge?" In addition, teacher preparation, historically, has not included studies involving global history and current events. Including global studies in the curriculum will require additional training and in-service, which in turn will cause inconvenience to teachers and additional funding requirements for the school system.

Evans (1992) described global education as a means to develop the knowledge, skills, and attitudes that are needed to live effectively in a world possessing limited natural resources and categorized by ethnic diversity, cultural pluralism, and increasing independence.

Schools must provide students with the opportunity to gain background information necessary to understanding issues throughout the world and help them to develop a value system of tolerance and respect for ideas, beliefs, values, and customs different from their own.

Historically, the subject of social studies was the only subject that dealt with different countries and studies of cultures and values. But over the past several decades, multicultural education has been implemented into the schools. Urch (1992) found that global educators have begun to ask teachers to extend their knowledge and understanding of multiculturalism beyond the boundaries of the United States. Urch believed multicultural education should be taught in all subject areas.

Cohan (1987) maintained that the business world has become more internationalized, and so must the American public schools. Students must be introduced to global issues and be prepared to learn how these global issues will affect their lives as adults. Teachers must integrate this learning into all areas of study so students can acquire the knowledge and understanding to become not only citizens of local, state, and national communities, but citizens of the international community as well. Educators who do not acknowledge the need for global education teach the concepts effectively. Teachers who can effectively teach global education should have a positive feeling about themselves and a world view which is appreciative of other cultures. They should know how to confront a constantly changing world through their own scientific knowledge and inquiry.

Teachers should upgrade their skills and behaviors related to global education in productive workshops and seminars. Professional travel is also a means to gain knowledge and experiences. Global education, however, was still not very widespread throughout the United States in the late 1980s. At that time, approximately 20% of elementary school teachers indicated that global education was important for students. Speculation was that the attitudes of teachers toward global education varied according to the grade level they taught. Unfortunately, teachers of elementary grades considered global education a low priority. Global education must become part of the elementary program (Cogan, 1987).

Global education programs can make a difference in the future. Effective programs can have positive effects on the ways children view other nations, their people, and their cultures. This will not reduce the students' view of the

United States but, instead, enhance that view. Through global studies, students should gain a significantly more comprehensive view of the United States and its relationship to other countries.

Students must prepare for becoming global citizens because they have a responsibility as they grow to help solve the problems of the world, to understand and care for others, to protect and use natural resources wisely, and to promote an attitude of peaceful cooperation and resolution of global concerns. Educators must have the goal of creating culturally and globally diverse educated students.

In the area of global development and its relationship to education, the implications for education are profound. Michael Marien (1992) suggests key changes need to be made to ensure improvement of the schools of the future. He believes that greater attention must be given to family planning and greater regard to ethnic and cultural diversity, that global education is needed for building a global economy, and that technology can be supported by adaptations in the workplace.

In order to better prepare children for the global world, growing cultural diversity must be taken seriously and perhaps even celebrated. Banks & Banks (1997) assert the importance of teaching not only tangible traits, but intangible traits such as cultural attitudes and beliefs about specific behaviors as well.

NEW CHOICES EMERGING

Today's parents try to juggle work, family, and personal goals and aspirations while being effective nurturers. As a result of changing family structures and competing obligations, opportunities to nurture may be limited. Ensuring that children get the proper foundation they need to achieve their fullest growth and development begins with a quality child care or preschool facility. Currently, many educational options are available to parents. When children are ready to begin school, the options that face parents can be overwhelming and make selection difficult. Public education is a service and an investment in a child's future.

Information, competition, and choice among public schools should be the rule, not the exception. Parents who are dissatisfied with either their child's or the school's performance should have the opportunity to choose a school that will better accommodate their child's physical, cognitive, social, and moral needs. Unfortunately, many schools have not implemented the changes that are needed to address the growth and evolution of our children and our society. Teachers continue to lecture and take attendance. Students still mechanically perform at the chalkboard, read outdated textbooks, and push pencils. Some futuristically oriented schools, however, have recognized these methods and materials as unyielding and have begun to incorporate technological advances, even including talking computers.

In addition to regular public schools, parents can now choose to send their children to year-round schools, open-enrollment schools, magnet schools, hub schools, or provide education at home. Each type of alternative school setting has advantages and disadvantages. Parents must intelligently weigh these options in selecting the best environment for their children. In the meantime, competition for public schools becomes more fierce.

Year-round schools (available in some states, including California, Florida, North Carolina, Nevada, Texas, and Utah) provide an alternative for some working parents. Children attend school for 60 consecutive weekdays, followed by 20 "vacation" days three times per year. All legal holidays are observed. The year-round school allows for sustained learning. Since there is no summer-long vacation, the fall semester becomes a vehicle for new learning rather than a review of material learned the previous spring. Year-round schools also allow the maximum use of school buildings and facilities; however, this also means higher costs for air-conditioning and longer teacher contracts. Another disadvantage for families with more than one child is that of scheduling dilemmas when their children are on different rotations.

Open enrollment schools (found in Iowa, Minnesota, and New York) allow students to go to any school within the district as long as ample space is available and the schools remain balanced in race, ethnicity, and gender. Student assignment to these schools is based upon a lottery system. The greatest advantage of this type of system is that parents have the opportunity to select the school they feel will provide the most appropriate education for their child. Disadvantages of this system include the rapid filling of "better" schools, lack of funding for poorer schools, issues of transportation, and possibilities of favoritism and politics overriding lottery assignments.

Magnet schools are public schools that attract students by focusing upon a particular theme, such as the arts, science, or technology. While attending magnet schools, students are able to develop their personal interests, aptitudes, and skills. This specialization, when properly balanced between basic curriculum and the specialty area, can stimulate accelerated learning. However, if not properly managed and maintained, magnet schools may be more image-focused than instructionally concerned. Also, imbalances may occur between core curricula and specialty areas.

Hub schools are schools through which assistance is provided to neighborhood families via education, health, and human service programs. Advantages include the availability of health and human services and before-school and after-school programs. In order to be successful, hub schools require whole community participation, coordination, and appropriate location sites.

All 50 states will soon enact charter school laws. Charter schools are public schools created and managed by parents, teachers, and administrators. Accountability is held through a performance-based contract with a local school board, state, or other public institution. Federal funding is available to support local efforts to establish new charter schools.

Even with the variety of school choices, some parents still are dissatisfied with current educational programs and opt to assume the responsibility of educating their children at home. Some states such as New Hampshire and Wyoming require no special permission for home schooling. Other states— Arkansas, California, Illinois, Kansas, Kentucky, Maryland, Minnesota, Nebraska, North Carolina, North Dakota, Tennessee, Texas, and Virginia— require regulation of home schooling or its incorporation in the private school sector. Certified teachers are required for home schooling in Alabama, Florida, Iowa, Michigan, and North Dakota.

SUMMARY

Families of all sizes and income levels in our society face tremendous challenges and daily stresses. Today there are more mothers in the workforce who have young children and more single households. Teenage pregnancies have been on the rise in the past three decades. Poverty and violence have been on a steady increase. The prevalence of the typical nuclear family has declined, and this family structure has been replaced by several single-parent structures.

In the last decades of the twentieth century, America evolved into a truly multicultural society. With a greater diversity of cultures, the need for multicultural education became necessary. Special populations of students with physical, mental, emotional, social deprivation, and other handicaps entered the regular classroom—often unwanted by regular teachers incapable of meeting their needs. While inclusion is occurring in classrooms across America, educational leaders and citizens in general are warning the schools to become globally oriented. Some of these changes have been met with acceptance, while many remain challenged.

Changes in child development and how child development is viewed will continue to evolve as we enter the next century. Realization of the changing dynamics of America's population is essential for parents and educators of future children. Special populations of children have developmental needs specifically different from those of the norm. Parents and educators must be knowledgeable of appropriate instructional strategies to meet the needs of these children.

Inclusion practices will increase in the twenty-first century as more students with varied limitations and learning differences are better identified. The practice of inclusion for special populations will continue to provoke heated debates about the best school environment for students with physical, behavior-emotional, and cultural limitations. Improvements must continue to occur in the way schools can best educate special student populations in the future.

1. Discuss how the 1950s and the 1990s compared relative to changes in family structure. What were the most interesting and most significant changes?

2. Using statistics found in this chapter to justify your response, describe characteristics of child, home, and family which appear to have the most significant impact on school success. Select characteristics based upon the percentage of children impacted rather than intensity of impact. What role can the school play in minimizing the negative effect of some characteristics and to accentuate the positive impact of others?

3. What impact might the increased pool of options available to parents in selecting an educational path for their child have on the institution of public education?

❖ ❖ ❖   CLASS ACTIVITIES

1. In small groups select and research one school choice option—home schooling, charter schools, magnet schools, hub schools, year-round schools, open enrollment schools, private schools. Identify the pros and cons of the school choice your group selected. Predict what segment(s) of the population might find that option appealing. After sharing small group results with the class, obtain consensus as a class on the two options that have the greatest potential to negatively impact the institution of public education and the two options that have the greatest potential to positively impact public education.

2. Prepare a presentation of the above choice option using technology such as Microsoft PowerPoint®, HyperStudio, or color visuals and present your choice option to a real or mock school board.

❖ ❖ ❖   REFERENCES

Banks, J. A. (1981). *Multicultural education: Theory into practice.* New York: Allyn & Bacon.

Banks, J. A., & Banks, A. M. (1997). *Multicultural education: Issues and perspectives* (3rd ed.). New York: Allyn & Bacon.

Bennett, W. (1988). *American education: Making it work*. Washington, DC: U.S. Department of Education.

Block, M. E. (1994). The pocket reference: A tool for fostering inclusion. *Journal of Physical Education, Recreation and Dance, 66*(3), 47–51.

Boyer, E. (1991). *Ready to learn*. Princeton, NJ: Carnegie Foundation for the Advancement of Teaching.

Campbell, P. R. (1994). Population projections for states by age, race, and sex: 1993–2020. U.S. Bureau of the Census. Washington, DC: U.S. Government Printing Office.

Carnegie Corporation of New York. (1994). *Starting points: Meeting the needs of our youngest children*. New York: Author.

Children's Defense Fund. (1996). *The state of America's children: Yearbook 1996*. Washington, DC: Author.

Cohan, J. J. (1987). Expanding our horizons on global issues. *Social Education, 51*(5), 326.

Crosby, E. A. (1993). The at-risk decade. *Phi Delta Kappan, 74*(8), 598-604.

DeYoung, A. J., & Lawrence, B. K. (1995). On hoosiers, yankees, and mountaineers. *Phi Delta Kappan, 77*(2).

Eddowes, E. A. (1994). Education of younger homeless children in urban settings. *Education and Urban Society, 25*(4), 381–393.

Evans, S. (1992). Decision making: Developing a global perspective. *International Journal of Social Education, 7*(2), 10–16.

Friend, M. (1993). Inclusion. *Instructor, 103*(4), 52–56.

Gay, G. (1994). Keynote address at Annual Meeting of the National Council of the Social Studies. Phoenix, AZ.

Geiger, K. (1991). School, society, and the economy: Better childhoods. *Vital Speeches, 57*(8), 562.

General Accounting Office. (1993). *U.S. Bureau of the Census*. Washington, DC: U.S. Government Printing Office.

Goodlad, J. I. (1990). *Teachers for our nation's schools*. San Francisco: Jossey-Bass.

Hamburg, D. A. (1992). *Today's children: Creating a future for a generation in crisis*. New York: Times Books.

Hartshorn, R. L., & Nelson, R. L. (1990). Hands-on science instruction in the rural elementary school: A strategy to reduce the high school dropout rate. Paper presented at the Rural Education Symposium of the American Council on Rural Special Education, Tucson, AZ, Mar. 18–22, 1990. ERIC Document Reproduction Service No. ED337328.

Joseph, B. P. (1986). The changing American family. *Social Education*, 50(6), 438–463.

Kniep, W. M. (1989). Education about development: Lessons learned. *The American Forum for Global Education*. New York: United States Agency for International Development.

Lockwood, A. L. (1993). A letter to character education. *Educational Leadership, 51*(3), 72–75.

Marien, M. (1992). Education and learning in the twenty-first century: Promoting a healthy, democratic, sustainable society. *Vital Speeches, 58,* 340–349.

Martin, J. R. (1992). *The schoolhome: Rethinking schools for changing families.* Cambridge, MA: Harvard University Press.

McChesney, K. Y. (1993). Homeless families since 1980: Implications for education. *Education and Urban Society, 25*(4), 361–380.

McGuire, M. (1992). Whose voices will be heard?: Creating a vision for the future. *Social Education, 56*(2), 129–130.

McMillen, M. A. (1993). *Dropout rates in the United States.* MPR Associates. Washington, DC: U.S. Government Printing Office.

National Center on Child Abuse and Neglect. (1992). *A coordinated response to child abuse and neglect: A basic manual.* U.S. Department of Health and Human Services. McLean, VA: The Circle, Inc.

National Center for Children in Poverty. (1995). *National center for children in poverty: A program report on the first five years.* New York: Columbia University School of Public Health.

Population Reference Bureau for the Center for the Study of Social Policy. (1992). *Challenge of change: What the 1990 census tells us about children.* Washington, DC: Author.

Rich, D. (1987). *Schools and families: Issues and actions.* Washington, DC: National Education Association.

Roberts, T. W. (1994). *A systems perspective of parenting: The individual, the family, and the social network.* Pacific Grove, CA: Brooks/Cole Publishing Company.

Rubin, L. J. (1989). *Critical steps in educational reform.* Washington, DC: Association for Supervision and Curriculum Development.

Rubin, L. & Borgers, S. B. (1991). The changing family: Implications of education. *Principal, 71*(1), 11–13.

Semmel, M. I. (1991). Teacher perceptions of the regular education initiative. *Exceptional Children, 58*(1), 9–24.

Stewart, T. (1991). E pluribus what? *Fortune, 123*(1), 45.

Stoler, R. D. (1992). Perceptions of regular education teachers toward inclusion of all handicapped students in their classrooms. *Clearing House, 66*(1), 60–62.

Tyree, C. (1997). Teaching values to promote a more caring world: A moral dilemma for the 21st century. *Journal for a Just and Caring Education, 3*(2), 215–26.

Urch, G. E. (1992). Global education: The time is now. *Educational Horizons, 71*(1), 15–17.

U.S. Bureau of the Census. (1992). *Current population survey.* Washington, DC: U.S. Government Printing Office.

U.S. Bureau of the Census. (1993). *Statistical abstract of the United States.* Washington, DC: U.S. Government Printing Office.

U.S. Bureau of the Census. (1995). *Statistical abstract of the United States.* Washington, DC: U.S. Government Printing Office.

U.S. Department of Education. (1994). *Adult literacy in America*. Washington, DC: Government Printing Office.

U.S. Department of Education. (1991). *America 2000: An education strategy*. Washington, DC: Government Printing Office.

U.S. Department of Education. (1994, November). *Community update*. Washington, DC: Government Printing Office.

Welton, D. A., & Mallan, J. T. (1996). *Children and their world: Strategies for teaching social studies*. Boston: Houghton Mifflin.

Weston, W. J. (1989). *Education and the American family: A research synthesis*. New York: New York University Press.

✥ ✥ ✥   SUGGESTED READINGS

Adler, M. J. (1990). *Reforming education: The opening of the American mind*. New York: Collier Books.

Carnegie Council on Preadolescent Development. (1989). *Turning points: Preparing American youth for the twenty-first century*. New York: Carnegie Corporation.

Carnegie Task Force on Teaching as a Profession. (1986). *A nation prepared: Teachers for the 21st Century*. New York: Author.

Edmonds, B. C. (1992). The convention on the rights of the child. *Social Education, 56*(6), 205–207.

Hodgkinson, H. (1993). American education: The good, the bad, and the task. *Phi Delta Kappan, 74*(8), 619–623.

Johnson, M. L. (1993). *Education on the wild side: Learning for the twenty-first century*. Norman, OK: University of Oklahoma Press.

Lewis, A. C. (1997). Learning our lessons about early learning. *Phi Delta Kappan, 8*, 591–592.

Lieberman, A., & Miller, L. (1990). Restructuring schools: What matters and what works. *Phi Delta Kappan, 71*, 759–764.

Longstreet, W., & Shane, H. (1993). *Curriculum for a new millenium*. Boston, MA: Allyn & Bacon.

Ozmon, H., & Craver, S. (1999). *Philosophical foundations of education* (6th ed.). Upper Saddle River, NJ: Merrill/Prentice Hall.

Postman, N. (1995). *The end of education: Redefining the value of school*. New York: Alfred A. Knopf.

Rubin, L. (1977). *Curriculum handbook: Administration and theory*. Boston, MA: Allyn & Bacon.

Sadker, M. P., & Sadker, D. M. (1992). *Teachers, schools and society*. New York: Simon & Shuster.

Schlechty, P. C. (1990). *School for the 21st century.* San Francisco, CA: Jossey-Bass.

Sizer, T. R. (1984). *Horace's compromise.* Boston, MA: Houghton Mifflin Co.

U.S. Congress, Office of Technology Assessment. (1988). *Power-on! New tools for teaching and learning* (OTA-SET-379). Washington, DC: U.S. Government Printing Office.

U.S. Department of Education. (1997). *A call to action for American education in the twenty-first century.* Washington, DC: U.S. Government Printing Office.

Wilson, K. G., & Davis, B. (1992). *Redesigning education.* New York: Henry Holt.

PATHWAYS FROM THE PAST TO THE FUTURE

❖ ❖ ❖

3

EDUCATIONAL MODELS, PHILOSOPHIES, AND TRADITIONS

Chapter Objective and Focus:

A comparison of how educational philosophies
have influenced curriculum decisions in the
formation of educational models

Developing a personal philosophy of education requires educators to confront issues of fundamental significance to humankind and to discern the meanings or truths in life itself. The study of philosophy in education is imperative as it gives a basis or vocabulary from which problems may be solved. Philosophers are observers of human behavior. Through serious inquiry and reasoning, insight into the human condition may be gained. It is this insight that gives educators inspiration, knowledge of the thinking process and nature of ideas, and a perspective of the role of education in society. By studying various educational philosophies and their responsive curriculum models, educators may acquire a valuable tool in assessing the quality and purpose of education. Philosophy does not, however, offer one final solution to cure the ills of society. Certain debatable issues may not have one correct answer or one solution to a problem. Of great value to educators is to be knowledgeable enough to sort through the debate to reach an intelligent understanding of the modern educational system.

In this chapter, the dogma of the various philosophies, the historical conditions from which they rose, and the leaders of each belief system will be presented. Many of the tenets of each philosophy are present in more than one belief structure. The interplay of the philosophies often leads to an eclectic formation of a philosophy that fits the economical, cultural, ethical, and social status of a particular era. The influences of each philosophy and resultant educational model are easily observed in the American school today.

Ornstein and Behar (1995) described curriculum design by noting that philosophy is the standard by which the purpose, means, and ends of curriculum are decided. Values determine the purpose of the curriculum, process and methods represent the means, and the ends are the facts, concepts, and principles of knowledge or behavior that are expected to be learned.

A wide spectrum of philosophies and viewpoints exists in education. Most of these viewpoints, however, can be grouped together within paradigms or models. People who hold similar beliefs and adhere to similar value systems can often be grouped together under the umbrella of a paradigm. A paradigm describes a collection of basic beliefs shared by a group, within which some differences of interpretation or application may exist as long as the basic tenets of the paradigm hold true.

College professors, graduate students, and philosophers debate, often seriously, the boundaries and factors included in any given philosophy and related educational models. At present, they can remain matters of classroom debate. This text and this chapter, particularly, present the major focus of existing philosophies still observed in educational practice in a framework of five common models: Perennialists and Essentialists, Progressivists, Existentialists, Reconstructionists, and Futurists.

THE PERENNIALISTS AND ESSENTIALISTS

The perennialists and essentialists view education as being properly concentrated on the cultural inheritance which has survived through time. As more conservative in their thought, they believe that the chief task of education is to conserve the best of the past for it is through this that the present will be examined. One essentialist, Robert Hutchins, held that education consisted principally of studies that focused on the rules of grammar, reading, rhetoric and logic, mathematics, and the great books of the Western world.

One of the problems with the perennialist and essentialist position is that it fails to recognize modern scientific studies and the changing state of knowledge. It assumes that the best exemplars of the past, the permanent studies, are valid for the present and all time.

Another problem of this conservative position, especially from the perennialist perspective, is its fundamental premise that the sole purpose of education should be the education of the intellect, and that only certain studies have this power. This position embraces the long-refuted doctrine of mental discipline and rejects any consideration of the interest and needs of the learner or the treatment of contemporary problems in education on the ground that such concerns are temporal and detract from the school's mission of cultivating the mind.

Perennialists focus on a set of perennial truths and values and espouse the idea that education should liberate and fulfill students by developing their common essence, their ability to think and to choose. They suggest this aim is achieved by providing each person with a liberal education that cultivates rational thought and responsible choice. One method of doing this is to provide students with the opportunity to study the works of outstanding writers in all fields. Through this approach, students are introduced to the wisdom of the past and to the truths and values they need. The purposes of this exposure are to allow students to think critically, prepare them for life and its accompanying duties, and enable them to contribute to society as citizens.

Perennialist teachers must be accountable for their students' rational development. Reading, writing, computing, and other subjects are taught in the lower grades. As students mature, they raise provocative points, design stimulating exercises, question unexamined assumptions, discuss conflicting theories, and initiate critical analyses. Perennialists also focus attention on permanent values, pass on perennial truths, demand reasons for opinions, insist on evidence for conclusions, and impart a love for precise thinking. For them, education is a cooperative enterprise that sharpens a person's rational powers and stimulates each student's potential for making good choices.

The responsibilities of teachers, however, cannot readily be realized unless students choose to develop and utilize their intellectual capacities. That is, students must assume partial responsibility for their own learning. According to the perennialists, the student becomes educated by choosing to use the resources of school and society to cultivate his or her intellect.

Kuhn (1996) went to some length to discuss the importance of the textbook as a pedagogical tool in fields that are paradigm-based, such as the natural sciences. He avowed that textbooks interpret the body of accepted theory, illustrate its successful applications, and compare these applications with theoretically sound observations and experiments. Not until the very last stage of education of the scientist, observed Kuhn, is the textbook supplemented or replaced by the actual scientific literature upon which the textbook has systematically organized the knowledge of the field. Kuhn did not contend that the textbook is the only proper pedagogical device or that it is immune from abuse. Instead, he suggested that it is a key means of initiation to the systematic organization of knowledge and paradigms in mature fields of scholarship.

Another variety of conservative thinking is essentialism, which encourages schools to get "back to the basics." Essentialism, sometimes referred to as "back to the basics," was clearly defined as an educational philosophy in a paper presented to a group of educators by William C. Bagley in 1938 (Collins, 1991).

This type of conservatism focuses, in the most simplistic fashion, on the three Rs: reading, writing, and arithmetic.

Collins (1991) suggested that the philosophy of essentialism slows down educational change in an ever-changing society. The conservatives argue that modern influences are included in this type of educational model.

The essentialists demand that child-centered and activity-oriented classrooms be abandoned for a return to the basics of the three Rs. In support of this position, the National Defense Education Act (NDEA), passed by Congress in 1958, resulted in approximately $1 billion being granted over a four-year period to upgrade materials and teachers' understanding of content material (Cohan, Ellis & Howey, 1991).

This conservative paradigm of educational thought emphasizes schools as the vehicles for transmission of traditional moral values and knowledge to students so that they may become model citizens. A healthy respect for authority, hard work, responsibility to others, and the practical nature of education in life are instilled in the conservative belief structure.

As the primary educational paradigm, the essentialist model waned during the late 1950s and 1960s. During this time, education critics such as Admiral Hyman Rickover, an essentialist, argued that American education had become soft and needed to return to basic studies of math and science. Rickover blamed the decline of America as the top technological society on John Dewey's progressive educational beliefs. As a conservative, Rickover saw evidence that the American culture was slipping into an apathetic state, and that without a true commitment to basic skills, our human resources were being squandered and pulled down to average standards.

The educational aim of both the perennialists and the essentialists is that education should serve the current structure of American society. Schools should not attempt to reform society, but they are expected to prepare functioning citizens to perpetuate current values. Only when students are able to show a prescribed degree of mastery will they be promoted to the next grade level. William Bagley suggested an increase in core classes, longer school days, a longer academic year, and more challenging text materials to help students develop a high degree of mental discipline. By totally controlling students' studies, time, and practice, these conservatives believed that the high level of skill development gained would be transferable to life outside the school.

Critics of the perennial and essential educational models believe that educators with these beliefs do not address the needs of all children. It is worth noting that, as in the past when reform efforts failed for many differing reasons, educators readily return to the familiar conservative rigor or back-to-basics education. Critics of perennialism and essentialism see these schools as teaching a regimented body of knowledge that must be memorized to pass a series of courses. These schools do not teach students how to solve problems, to reason, or to learn through experiences; however, many segments of American society demand a return to this approach to education.

THE PROGRESSIVISTS

Theorists with a more societal perspective began to look for educational models that could be more child-centered without losing a sense of overall coherence. The works of John Dewey and later Jean Piaget were influential among theorists looking for a model that took into account the development of the child. Progressivists believe in the innate thinking of children and use this as a tool, along with the guidance of the teacher, to facilitate learning. The student is no longer an empty vessel waiting to be filled, but a partner in a learning enterprise. "The learner is seen as an experiencing, thinking, exploring individual" (Johnson, 1967, p. 399).

The roots of the moderates are found in the works of John Dewey, Jean-Jacques Rousseau, Johann Heinrich Pestalozzi, and Johann Friedrich Froebel. During the 1920s many educators believed that American education did not reflect the values of a democratic society or advances made in technology and natural sciences. Progressivist thought was viewed as a practical response to this issue. Progressivists believe that the classroom should be student-centered, stressing learning through experience. They suggest that educators should be aware of the interests and motivations of students as well as the individual environmental background of each student. Moderates who are considered progressivists center instruction on relevant experiences, interests, and abilities of students. Lessons are planned to motivate students and increase curiosity to push students to a higher level of knowledge. Reforming the classroom atmosphere to create a social environment allows students to utilize previous personal and group experiences to solve new problems. Therefore, while students are learning from their own experiences they are able to interact with other students to develop tolerance for varying viewpoints.

Progressivists emphasize the study of the natural and social sciences and courses that stress progress and change as fundamental forces in life. New technological advances, scientific discoveries and social reforms are studied in a democratic curriculum. The contributions of women and minorities, topics in vocational education, and a core of academic courses were integrated to teach students that the education process encompasses the totality of life.

For John Dewey, change was not an uncontrollable force but a natural occurrence that could be directed by human intelligence. His biological conception of the human was one of an adaptive organism who strove to adapt to a given environment. He believed that intelligence is something that grows and that through the development of the intellect, the environment is reshaped. In his open embrace of change, Dewey sought to change American society through the reformation of schooling. He believed that by altering the educational system to promote democratic ideals, society would become more open, democratic, and free-thinking. Dewey taught teachers to promote experiential learning and the use of the scientific method when solving problems. He established a method for solving problems that began with awareness of the problem. After the problem was defined, students proposed various solutions, examined consequences, and tested a chosen solution. Following his own five-step approach to problem solving, Dewey created the Laboratory School in 1896 at the University of Chicago to test his progressive educational theories. His school was designed for experiential learning and included laboratories, art rooms, a kitchen, and a carpentry shop. The teachers used such instructional strategies as role playing, simulations, dramatizations, and field trips while avoiding the use of rote memorization and excessive lecture. Dewey's Laboratory School was successful in becoming an extension of the community, and he worked to make that environment a true representation of life.

Dewey's theories developed from the work of Jean-Jacques Rousseau (1712–1778) who saw a distinct connection between nature and experience. His conception of the child was as a developing organism, not a miniature adult. Rousseau believed, like Dewey, that a child's interests and developmental stages should guide education. Johann Heinrich Pestalozzi (1746–1827) agreed and promoted the idea that children learn through their senses and that their natural development should serve as a guide to their training. Friedrich Froebel (1782–1852), another experiential philosopher who is known as the father of kindergarten, felt that children progressed through constructive play. These theorists believed that education should focus more on the child than the content.

THE EXISTENTIALISTS

The search for meaning of human existence in an indifferent universe, the quest for personal significance in an age of impersonal technology, and the need for individual awareness in an age of the mechanical mass led to the resurrection of existentialism thought during the second half of the twentieth century.

The plight of the lonely individual in an uncaring universe has become an overwhelming theme in literature. This concern and the search for authentic personal identity also became central in the writings of a number of theorists in the field of psychotherapy.

The liberal-minded existentialists believe that since the universe is indifferent to man, man must assign to himself the meaning of his own existence. Man cannot find such a meaning in religious dogma, social philosophies, or science. Man is absolutely worthless in the cosmos, so he must find his absolute worth through himself. By finding the meaning of his own existence, man is freed to choose what he is and will become, and he can find his authentic self through the full awakening of his spontaneous human powers. One's own need to be free must be reciprocal; it must thus recognize the need for another person to be free.

Existentialism is actually a way of viewing the world that rejects the notion of a self-contained system of educational thought and practice. This thinking is characterized by themes such as "humans are free to create themselves" and "life appears to be meaningless in terms of rational explanation" rather than by systematic and confined opinions. Experiencing, accepting, and appropriating truth as part of one's personal beliefs are important. Passively accepting beliefs and values as given is not important. Values, they argue, are worthwhile only if they are good for others as well as for oneself. Freedom and choice do not lead to moral anarchy but to personal and social responsibility.

In one sense, to the existentialists, the aim of schooling is to facilitate the development of truly authentic people. Authentic people are individuals who recognize their freedom, utilize their options, and accept their responsibility. At the same time, authentic people reject an exclusively objective, impartial, rationalistic, deterministic, logical, and scientific philosophy of life.

Existentialists have not generally addressed educational theory and practice. They are nonetheless clear on a variety of educational issues. First, their educational aim is well defined—to cultivate the authentic person. Second, the curriculum in the school is conceptualized as a tool for the student's self realization. Perhaps the most useful studies for this purpose include dialogues, discussion, and discoveries about such existential concepts as authenticity, love, freedom, responsibility, death, values, conformity, alienation, and meaninglessness.

Obviously, teachers are not autonomous in the eyes of existentialists. They enjoy freedom but are more concerned with the responsibility to facilitate the growth of the student toward an autonomous life. In creating environments that enable students to become more authentic, they value person-to-person interaction (Myers and Myers, 1995).

The belief that one can discover the fundamental truths of one's own existence comes from the works of Danish philosopher Søren Kierkegaard (1813–1855) and the German thinker Friedrich Nietzche (1844-1900). These theorists believed that the physical universe has no meaning to man. In other words, there exists no natural scheme to nature so man owes nothing to nature.

Choices of not *the* way but rather *my* way are part of becoming. The hardest choices to make are those between alternative goods. Whatever choice one makes, one will face the consequences of actions taken. One makes meaning in the world by the choices made. How does the teacher, who believes that each student must make himself, conduct a classroom? To begin, a teacher must not impose discipline but ask each student which discipline he deems worthwhile. Truths, those found by many to be true, are examined by the student. Whether or not the student agrees with a truth is his or her prerogative. A student who rejects a truth will discuss it with the teacher.

The human condition is another concern for existentialism and other liberal-oriented models. Experiences such as death, guilt, and conflict are part of one's existence. One must try to understand these conditions and respond to them with wisdom (Collins et al., 1991).

Existentialism stresses the education of the whole person, the development of self-awareness, and the promotion of creativity and imagination. In an environment of self-paced learning, students develop individual contracts with teachers because a fixed curriculum does not exist. Students are given a wide range of possible courses from which they can choose their own path of learning. The humanities are given precedence in the curriculum, and vocational education is offered only to help students explore possibilities for their future, not to train them for future careers.

The best-known example of a liberal curriculum in practice is that of A. S. Neill's school "Summerhill" in England. Students had the freedom to choose which classes they attended, or even whether they wanted to attend, the theory being that students will not learn if they do not want to learn and therefore should not attend classes.

This more liberal theory contrasts dramatically with the philosophy of the traditionalists. Education, according to existentialists, should be developed with the wishes of the student in mind. No educator can presume to know what is best for the student; the student knows what is best for himself or herself and therefore must be allowed to study what he or she wishes. This theory is decidedly non-authoritarian, even anti-authoritarian.

THE RECONSTRUCTIONISTS

Educators adhering to a much more radical perspective view schools as entirely inadequate and misguided. They want to completely remake schools. Their purpose is to create a new world order and they see education and schools as the means by which to achieve this purpose. The leading thinkers behind this paradigm, George S. Counts, William O. Stanley, and Theodore Brameld, believed that this new order must be founded upon democratic principles and patterns of government in order to avoid the self-destruction of humankind. The reconstructionists are more radical in their beliefs.

Henry Giroux is a more recent proponent of educational reconstructionism. He viewed schools as vehicles for social change, calling teachers to be transformative intellectuals who participate in creating a new society. His view may not seem quite as radical as that of Postman (1994) who foresaw an ending to the present form of education.

Radicals see a need for the school to play a more direct role in reconstructing society for a democratic social order. The discipline-centered curriculum is regarded as irrelevant to the social situation. However, the call is not to reconstruct the curriculum along the lines of experimentalist thinking but to pursue radical alternatives in education. The reconstructionists view the school as a chief means for building a new social order. They believe that contemporary national and global problems of war, poverty amidst affluence, crime, racial conflict, unemployment, political oppression, environmental pollution, disease, and hunger all serve to give cause for social reconstruction.

Obviously, educational models must be geared to the transformation of the rising generation so that they embrace the goals and develop the means needed for collective social reconstruction. Aside from the ethical question of whether the public school should take it upon itself to effect this reconstruction and to impose such a mission upon children and youth is the practical question of whether our society is committed to such a reconstruction. Implementing experimentalist ideas in the curriculum would constitute a revolutionary transformation. Americans look to education as a key institution for social improvement. Their tendency to lend an open ear to every attack on the schools that comes along during periods of social "crisis" stems from their great expectations of the role of the school in correcting social problems and not from a lack of faith in education. At the same time, the American public has resisted radical proposals for education models, whether it be the abandonment of the comprehensive secondary school in favor of the dual European model or the use of the school for imposing reconstructionist ideology upon children and youth. Radical education reforms have been left to alternative schools that are on the periphery of mainstream American education.

Although reconstructionists embrace democracy as the appropriate goal of education, experimentalists see the educational means of reconstructionism as inculcating prescribed beliefs in the learner. History is replete with utopian schemes for education and society. Yet, however noble and admirable may be the utopian visions of reconstructionists, the history of utopian schemes reveals unmistakable absolutism.

In a radical education reform, contemporary critics could embrace the tenets of romantic naturalism, although they rarely acknowledge that their ideas have earlier record in modern history. The reaction against the pursuit of academic excellence beginning in the mid-1960s brought forth a number of best-selling books that condemned the schools as being responsible for every conceivable failure and evil and that proposed a variety of formulas for freeing pupils to learn. At that time, a number of college students were embracing activism and self-sensationalism while rejecting reflection and self-discipline. "Doing your own thing," the situational ethic of the ghetto street, became fashionable on the college campus.

Relevance is the key doctrine of the reconstructionists. The teacher's role is indirect, that of the guide and facilitator who must get out of the way of children. John Holt (1981), radical educator and author, contended that given a variety of real world experiences in the classroom setting with guidance as requested and a listening ear when needed, children can be trusted to be responsible for their own learning.

Some radicals who oppose mere superficial change suggest that revolutionary change, which alters everything down to the very foundation of American schooling, must be made. These radicals question everything and perceive that their role is not to successfully participate in society, but to dramatically alter it. Many have called for a deschooling of America or the abolishment of schooling as an institution. The ideas of these radical reformers had their impetus in the 1960s and 1970s. The sweeping changes they prescribed have not occurred. However, their zeal advanced the question of what was wrong with schools and has prompted numerous national reports on the failure of education in America.

Holt (1981) felt that schools taught students to learn only what was assigned to them or what they would be expected to know on an exam. This is not far removed from the practices of the 1990s, where teacher accountability for student progress has resurged. Holt wrote numerous books, including *How Children Fail* and *How Children Learn*. His newsletter for parents, *Growing Without Schooling*, brought national attention to homeschooling. Holt's aim was to break down the barriers that separate children from the work and concerns of adults (Holt, 1976).

THE FUTURISTS

Educational thinkers throughout history have been interested in the influence of the school upon the future. However, only recently has a group of thinkers known as futurists made an impact upon educational policy and practice. Similar to the radicals, futurists wish to fully reform education, yet they tend to take a less radical approach. They see the history of education in this country as a basis upon which to build, and from which educators can learn how the educational system has functioned and should continue to function. They agree with the radicals that a total transformation is necessary, that mere improvement of our educational system will not suffice (Schlechty, 1990). For them, however, the task is to transform the purpose of education while still preserving the existing purposes of education. Future students still need to know the basics of reading, writing, and arithmetic; they still need to learn about and understand the American culture and political system; and they still need to have marketable skills. However, they must also learn how to continue to acquire and apply knowledge in the future; they must learn to become lifelong learners and thinkers because "in the information society, knowledge and the ability to use it are power" (Schlechty, 1990, p. 40). For the futurists, the task of schools now is to rethink their purpose and better prepare students for the fast-paced, ever-changing world of Alvin Toffler's *Future Shock* (1991a) and *The Third Wave* (1991b). Toffler, Shane, and Theobald imply that the person of tomorrow must be intellectually and emotionally capable of living in a strange new world (Myers & Myers, 1995).

While understanding the past, controlling the present, and shaping the future are aims expressed by both pragmatists and reconstructionists, futurists move beyond this position to argue for another proposition—namely, that the person of tomorrow must be intellectually and emotionally capable of living in a strange new world, requiring adaptation and survival skills.

Some futurists stipulate that schools should constitute and promote participatory democracy both through what they teach and by their example as operating institutions. Rather than prepare students for a past that no longer exists or a present that is rapidly disappearing, teachers should, by their teaching and their example, prepare students to live in a democracy with many unknowns. Students, in order to live satisfactorily in this future, must acquire strategies for adaptation and survival. Adaptation, in particular, will require that students learn to think for themselves. Independent thought by the adult of tomorrow involves, among other abilities, thinking ethically and creatively.

According to the futurists, the school that cultivates independent thinking should also stimulate autonomous decisionmaking. More than ever before, the future will belong to people who think and choose for themselves. This aim, developing tomorrow's thinkers and choosers, is partly an outcome of schooling that attempts to produce both liberally educated people and highly trained specialists. It is aided by students who recognize both the autonomy and the responsibility implied by the concepts of studying and learning. Students who learn to think independently, live democratically, choose ethically, interact tolerantly, and act wisely offer hope and promise for the future.

Futurists are attempting to develop a philosophy of dealing with the rapidly changing present that will have vast future implications. The world of the future will demand that people be able to deal with the exploitation of resources, the pollution of air and water, warfare, a rapidly increasing population, the unequal use of natural resources, and the rising incidence of violence. Futurists hope to educate students to be able to make healthy choices about the future. Students will not predict the future, but they will be able to select a desired vision for the future and the choices that will help them realize their vision. Harold G. Shane (1973), a social reconstructionist who is now viewed as a futurist, believed that all people shape their destiny. He taught that if future trends are studied and students have access to all the pertinent facts, they will be able to create a desired future.

The futurist educational model can be organized into multidisciplinary seminars of integrated learning through which students meet to discuss research that will have future implications, such as new technology, scientific innovations, and societal goals. The role of the school from a futurist perspective will be to prepare students for change by involving them in scenario writing. Students will respond to predicted events and changes by projecting themselves into the steps leading to a best-result scenario.

In thinking and planning for the future, futurists believe that it is imperative to prepare children to deal with rapid change. The reasoning behind this philosophy is that change may become so accelerated that many will not be able to handle difficult situations that change brings.

The author divides futurists into two categories: the soft futurists and the hard futurists. In the extremes, the soft futurists believe that the school of the

From a futurist point of view, the role of the school will be to prepare students to deal with rapid change.

future must incorporate the best elements found in present-day schools and move the reform efforts more toward the goals of adaptation and survival. At the opposite extreme, the hard futurists maintain that society must experience a revolution and demolish the school and start a new creation model for the future. Emphasis is still on adaptation and survival. Only the process varies. Most futurists fall in the middle. Myers and Myers (1995) argue that the person of tomorrow must be intellectually and emotionally capable of living in a strange new world. According to futurists, the school that cultivates independent thinking should also stimulate autonomous decisionmaking; the future will belong to people who think and choose for themselves. Developing tomorrow's thinkers and choosers is partly an outcome of schooling that attempts to produce both liberally educated people and highly trained specialists. It is aided by students who recognize both the autonomy and responsibility implied by the concepts of studying and learning. Students who learn to think independently, live democratically, choose ethically, interact tolerantly, and act wisely offer hope and promise for the future.

In the technological systems of tomorrow (Toffler, 1991a), machines will deal with the flow of physical materials; men with the flow of information and insight. Machines will increasingly perform the routine tasks; men the intellectual and creative tasks. The technology of tomorrow will not require lettered men, but men who can make critical judgments, who can weave their way through novel environments, and who are quick to spot new relationships in the rapidly changing reality.

Every school and community should create a "council of the future," that is, a team of men and women devoted to probing the future in the interest of the present. This movement will pursue three objectives: to transform the organizational structure of the educational system, to revolutionize its curriculum, and to encourage a more future-focused orientation. For generations, it was assumed that the proper place for education to occur was in a school. But as the nation moves toward knowledge-based industry, some parents may pull their children out of the public education system, offering them home instruction instead. These children might continue going to school for social and athletic activities. Toffler appears to have predicted the future correctly. Home schooling in the 1990s is growing at a rapid rate.

According to Shane (1973), the future is a new discipline concerned with sharpening the data and improving the processes through which policy decisions are made in various fields of human endeavor such as business, government, and education. The purpose of the discipline is to help policy makers choose wisely, in terms of their purpose and values, among alternative courses of action that are open to leadership at the given time.

The significance of education in the future can be summarized in four points. First, education is significant because it can provide a direction for clarifying values for a changing society and because schools can prepare children to participate more effectively in continued efforts to bring about better ways of life. Second, basic problems can be attacked through education once a sense of purpose is rediscovered. Third, education can prepare citizens to implement the social decisions to bring about the best of all possible futures. Fourth, the improvement of the psychological and social climate of the school can promote a new significance for education in the next decade.

In the United States, educators must look at three major changes that are necessary for future education. Educators must (1) create new goals, (2) develop new structures or organizational patterns for the school, and (3) be skilled in the proper selection of content and processes to be taught to students.

The development of new educational futures for young learners does not imply any loss of respect for substantive content. No research proposes a substitute for being able to read and to interpret the nuances of the printed page. However, research does imply need for changes in the climate of learning as well as new and expanded approaches to content. Futurists advocate that children should have experiences, beginning with birth, that promise to create desirable cumulative cognitive input, with methodical schooling beginning no later than age three. They suggest an emphasis on a "personalized" program that concentrates on the learner's optimum development rather than merely focusing on attempts to bring him up to group norms and careful efforts to build in the student a positive view of himself. They propose the development of a suitable future-focused role image (FFRI) to motivate the learner to conceptualize the options available in working toward a life-role that brings satisfaction and promises self-respect and dignity. Futurists also advise that educators and community leaders identify ways in which children and youth can increase their value to the community through work-service programs and utilize the community itself as a huge teaching aid. This implies making the community environment not an alternative school but a more meaningful adjunct to schooling. This approach is more aligned with soft futurists because the emphasis is on reformation and renewal rather than on demolition or revolution.

In 1997, Dr. S. Colum defined futurism as the study of possible futures. Futurism, as described by Livingston in 1973, is more of an art than a science in that a forecast of the future is the informed opinion of an individual who interprets the data. Forecasting for the future is considered exploratory and normative. *Exploratory* means discovering changes, opportunities, and problems of the future, and *normative* implies discovering goals or norms for the future and analyzing costs-benefits of alternative courses of action and new options. The serious study of the methodologies of forecasting as a science began in the 1960s (Hencley and Yates, 1974).

There are numerous forecasting methods. Contextual mapping is one. A contextual map is a conceptual plan offering direction. It relies upon societal, economic, cultural, and technological trends. A set of hypotheses and relationships among these trends is used to forecast whether or not these trends are likely to continue, and whether or not these trends promote change patterns when combined.

Some trends include school building construction and design, media trends in teaching, trends in school financing, and trends in systems of teaching. An advantage of contextual mapping is that it provides a basis on which to plan. Acceptance of a possible future by a school district will allow teachers to plan activities, plan programs, budgets, and involve higher education in training programs.

Futurism has the potential for a massive impact on the development of curriculum as it is known. Futurist theorists look back over the history of education and see a variety of goals and purposes for education that were appropriate for the society of the time. Schlechty (1990) categorizes these as (1) the school as tribal center, (2) the school as factory, and (3) the school as hospital. During colonial times the purpose of the school as tribal center was to promote morality and develop the required degree of literacy to fulfill one's civic duties. As immigration to America became more diverse and society became more industrialized, the view of the school as factory became more prevalent. The goal of this model was to prepare the immigrant child to fit into the urban factory system. However, almost as a reaction to the situation brought about by rapid industrialization and urbanization, the school as hospital has also now become a popular viewpoint. In this perspective, education is used to redress many social wrongs, "to serve social reform purposes as well as political, economic and cultural ends" (Schlechty, 1990, pp. 17–18).

Futurists, therefore, see how education has responded to the environment of the time and modeled itself accordingly. It seems to them that the purposes of education are not guided by philosophical understandings of reality, but rather by the environment within which the nation finds itself at a certain time. This indeed would fit the pragmatic perspective. The futurist's main point now is that the present educational system is laden with a legacy from previous periods in history that no longer bear any relevance to the situation in which students find themselves. It is now time to shed these old perspectives and completely reexamine the purpose of education in a new society.

The world of the future is one that is information-based. The information flow will constantly grow and change. Successful citizens will be those who know how to acquire and apply information. Schools must prepare students to be successful in this future society. To do this, students must not learn just the basics, they must also learn to use all available resources and to think, to do what Schlechty (1990) calls "knowledge work" (p. 39).

It is still to be seen how futurist schools will look. Indeed, they may have many different faces. What is clear, however, is that they should have a common underlying, an educational philosophy, a common purpose, that will fit the needs of the future society and the future citizens of that society.

To build the bridge to the next century and beyond, futurists believe that the schools have to be recreated. Faulty curricula, ineffective teaching, and poor communication between the home and school are all elements of education that must be changed. One vehicle for bringing about this change is technology. Technology can be one tool the schools make use of to educate children and give them the skills necessary for living in the next century.

Futurists believe the education system is not changing to meet the needs of the future. They assert that the people of tomorrow should have the skills to live in a completely different world. They argue that today's system of education was designed more than a century ago to satisfy the needs of an emerging industrial society. The mission was well accomplished and succeeded in placing America at the top of the world. The agriculturally based structure was replaced by a new industrial society. People remained in the same job until retirement. Workers did not need many different skills. Physical strength and the ability to follow a few directions were more important than mental aptitude. Most companies were locally owned by one family or individual. Schools tended to mirror the functioning of industry. Therefore, the raw materials to be assembled en masse were the students who would be processed by teachers who were the workers in a concentrated factory, the school. The products of these schools would fit perfectly into the rigid industry. Schools were not for everyone. The schools were generally homogeneous and designed for the privileged few who could get in. Only the smartest and hardest working students would graduate. The schools lacked individualization, the teacher was a dictator—always having the last word, and everything was standardized (Toffler, 1980).

In the world today and tomorrow the only thing that is standard is the rate of change. Everything is changing at an accelerated pace, causing disorientation in many people because of the requirement for fast, high-level decisions. The old saying that knowledge is power is more true today than ever before, because what is true today will not hold true for tomorrow. Some futurists called theses times the *"Information Era,"* the *"Space Age,"* the *"Global Village,"* or the *"Super-Industrial Society."* Whoever gets and manipulates the information first to his advantage will control the world (Toffler, 1990). So why, if this is true, are schools still a hopeless anachronism? Why is the use of high technology in the schools not the norm but the exception? Why are outdated teaching standards still being used?

The answer may lie in the uneasy feeling the future brings. People do not feel secure about the future and some people believe futurists to be prophets or fortune tellers. However, future studies and research today may help to answer questions about the philosophy and visions of the futurists and legitimize their work (Shane, 1973).

The futurists are attempting to obtain a consensus in identifying trends most likely to impact society, to analyze the social and educational consequences, and to develop and assist in the implementation of actions that will give youth the skills necessary for the future in this fast-changing society through the process of future research. As Shane (1973) explained it, future research is a discipline that examines data to direct effective decisionmaking among different alternatives at a given time. It differs from conventional planning by placing more emphasis on the different choices instead of on linear projections. Conventional planning projects a tomorrow that is better than today; future research envisions different images of the future. Finally, the intention of future research is not on the reform of the past, but rather in the designs of a "probabilistic environment" in which different consequences and possibilities are studied very carefully before decisions are made.

Future research as described by Shane (1973) has been in place since World War II. Olaf Helmer, a futurist research scholar, observed in 1967 that policy planners and others concerned with the future were beginning to develop a new attitude toward the future as intuitive gambles were being replaced by systematic analysis of the opportunities the future offers. Companies like RAND Corporation, the Bell Telephone Laboratories, General Electric, and Singer Company began using different methods of planning, such as PERT (Program Evaluation and Review Techniques), the Delphi Methodology, and Trend Extrapolation, to develop new products. For example, RAND staff wrote a document in which they predicted developments like the heart transplant and events like the moon landing. The tools futurists use to plan are human reasoning power, computers, mathematical models, three-dimensional models and other analysis methods.

Using such tools of reasoning power, models, and computers, theorists in the 1970s anticipated that women would continue to be a significant growing segment of the workforce; that racism would continue to decline and cross-ethnic marriages would increase; that a minimum standard of living would be established before the beginning of the next century; that new methods of public transportation would come into use; that the status of minorities would improve; and that cable TV would increase cultural exposure. All have been proven accurate (Shane, 1973).

Shane and some members of the National Education Association (NEA) observed that mankind was undergoing a human revolution, and they foresaw a number of developments very likely to impact living in the twenty-first century, including an increase in the rate of change and level of complexity of living, closure to the hydrocarbon age, continuing cries for an increase in human equity, and increased participation by Third World countries in a new economic order (Shane, 1977).

Next, Shane questioned the responsibility of schools for preparing children for the future. He advocated four roles schools must undertake. First, since schools are a reflection of society, schools should prepare children to find means to improve ways of life. Second, society should work toward solving most of the basic problems of contemporary society through education. Third, schools should put into practice the best choices for the future. Fourth, schools should create a sense of inner security.

Educators need to feel that they can contribute to the future. Futurists feel optimistic about the ability of society and educators to reform the schools. Their main concern is that red tape does not allow the basic changes to take place as quickly as needed. Some focal points of these reform recommendations are to clarify the goals and make necessary changes in the organization of the schools and in the courses taught. To accomplish this, futurists suggest that children should start schooling no later than the age of three; that educators should place emphasis on a personalized program, raise self-esteem, and prepare students to conceptualize a personal role in the future; and that educators and the community together should determine how community resources can be most effectively utilized. Futurists also recommend that the infrastructure of education should be streamlined to eliminate red tape and that teachers should use more imagination and relate better to students' needs (Shane, 1973).

In 1977, Shane, in conjunction with the NEA, recommended 28 premises to improve teaching and learning for the next century. Highlights of some of these ideas include the creation of a sense of global community, a search for world peace, attention to the environment, and cultivating the view that learning is a lifelong process that prepares the learner for tomorrow. Premises that impact the organization of a system of schooling include flexibility in programs based upon individual aptitude and societal needs; embracing early childhood, adult, and senior education as integral parts of the education process; and coordination with community resources of student services. Premises that impact the way instruction is delivered in the classroom include development of an attitude and a practice that teachers and students can learn from and teach each other; the use of technology as a tool in acquiring new knowledge and making decisions; utilization of instructional methodologies appropriate to the content and the learner; increased attention to communication skills; and increased problem-solving and interdisciplinary learning.

To accomplish these premises and make it possible for education to be a truly lifelong learning process, the child needs to be born as defect-free as possible. For this to occur, the educational process needs to start before birth to identify problems and find solutions for them (Shane, 1977).

The super-industrial society will need three basic skills: learning, relating and choosing.

- Learning: The school of the future must teach the students to learn how to learn—how to choose the data and how to manipulate it to solve problems. Students need to change as the information base changes and make high-quality decisions.

- Relating: People need to learn how to relate to each other and understand friendship formation.

- Choosing: As information becomes more available, the number of decisions to be made increases. Students need to be able to adapt to a wider number of choices and learn how to select the best one.

All these can be summarized as "life know-how" skills that students need to learn (Toffler, 1970).

TECHNOLOGY AND THE FUTURE

Technology, especially the computer, must be utilized in order to prepare children for the future. Almost every home in America has some type of electronic device such as a radio, television, telephone, video recorder, CD player, fax, or computer, but not every school is equipped with these technological tools.

The goal must be that every child have access to a computer. Mary A. White (1987) in *What Curriculum for the Information Age?* shares that the computer not only allows wide and quick distribution of information but also facilitates learning to manipulate, analyze, synthesize, and recombine to create new knowledge. Use of technology can enhance acquisition of knowledge and skills. For example, in reading and writing the opportunities are numerous. A student can access original scripts, practice writing with three-dimensional graphics, use word processor editing options, share original writing with the world, research topics, and publish an electronic newspaper. The possibilities are as diverse and numerous as the imagination can create. In mathematics, the student can manipulate numbers to project different outcomes, create graphics to illustrate concepts, conduct analyses to assess effectiveness, or apply alternatives to create different scenarios.

A Report on the Effectiveness of Technology in School, 1990–1994, authored by Jay Sivin-Kachala and Ellen R. Bialo (1994), states that students who use computers are better readers and grasp abstract math concepts more easily than nonusers. Additionally they found that those who use computers in writing become more sophisticated writers and perform better than nonusers in measures of verbal creativity.

In general, futurists believe that schools are malfunctioning. Schools must make radical changes to meet the needs of an uncertain future. The system is too rigid to respond to the diverse variety of learning styles, cultural experiences, and socio-economic backgrounds that children bring to school with them. If schools want to provide the types of knowledge and skills students will need to be contributing, responsible, and self-fulfilled citizens in the future, they must break away from monopolistic practices and establish a true democratization of classrooms. Schools need to function under the rules of a free market in which buyers and sellers come together to set prices.

There are those who believe that the schools are doing an adequate job. They suggest that the reports don't reveal the whole story and are using numbers to create a crisis that really doesn't exist. David C. Berliner and Bruce J. Biddle (1995), in *The Manufactured Crisis*, attempt to provide a fair assessment of the job schools are doing. They described this belittling of schools as the "Socrates Syndrome." More than 2500 years ago, Socrates complained about the lack of discipline and knowledge of the Greek youths who felt that adults always viewed the next generations as inferior to the former one. It is like the pessimist slogan: A pessimist is an optimist about the past. However, it is not necessary to condemn today's schools in order to engage in debate about what is needed for tomorrow.

These same individuals and groups argue that, although the tests that rank American schools lower than schools in other developed countries are not supported by evidence, this does not mean that all American schools are doing well. They also attack with evidence some of the myths about education:

1. College-student performance has recently declined in America.
2. American schools fail in comparative studies of students' achievement.
3. America spends a lot more money on education than other countries.
4. Money is not related to school achievement.
5. Cost in education has skyrocketed wastefully.
6. American schools are generally incompetent.
7. American schools do not produce workers with good technical skills (Berliner & Biddle, 1995).

SUMMARY

Statistics are like witnesses—they will testify for either side. All players in the debate over school effectiveness acknowledge that improvements are needed to reach every student. For a country to fully develop, it must use all of its resources effectively, and the most powerful resource is people. If children are taught to teach themselves how to "learn to learn," the opportunity to solve present and future problems is increased. It is difficult to visualize the future, but the nation, individually and collectively, must participate in its shaping. The journey will be long and not without roadblocks and obstacles, but by developing a new map for directions and with the mutual support of other individuals on the journey, a safe and productive arrival will be possible.

❖ ❖ ❖ DISCUSSION QUESTIONS

1. Describe the major elements found in the five different philosophical and potential curriculum models: Perennialist and Essentialist, Progressivist, Existentialist, Reconstructionist, and Futurist.

2. Develop a personal philosophy of education, and indicate the curriculum paradigm with which your teaching style would fit best. Compare beliefs with other class members.

3. Two major events that caused a crisis in education, the launching of *Sputnik* and the revelations of *A Nation at Risk*, forced the schools to get "back to the basics." What would the Perennialists and Essentialists, Progressivists, Existentialists, Reconstructionists, and Futurists have suggested for the curriculum in those times of political and social unrest?

❖ ❖ ❖ CLASS ACTIVITIES

1. How can philosophy direct the organization of a school curriculum?

2. What instructional materials would a Perennialist or Essentialist utilize? A Progressivist? An Existentialist? A Reconstructionist? A Futurist? What methods of teaching would a Conservative utilize? A Moderate? A Liberal? A Radical? A Futurist?

3. Futurists are concerned that our students may face a losing battle if the schools do not begin to concentrate on the future. What suggestions does the class have for adding future studies to the curriculum?

4. How may futurism affect preservice teachers and teacher education in general?

5. *Scenario Writing*. Predict the classroom of 2020 by describing the classroom organization, instructional strategies, curriculum, teacher characteristics, and the role of education in the society.

6. *Projecting.* In pairs, pretend it is the year 2010. You are writing a curriculum textbook on the history of curriculum change. Prepare a hyperstudio presentation that depicts your predictions of the influences of futurism, the presidency, technological advances, and the environmental crisis on schooling in America after the year 2010.

❖ ❖ ❖   REFERENCES

Berliner, D. C., & Biddle, B. J. (1995). *The manufactured crisis: Myths, fraud, and the attack on America's public schools.* New York: Addison-Wesley.

Boyer, E. L. (1995). *The basic school: A community for learning.* New Jersey: The Carnegie Foundation for the Advancement of Teaching.

Cohan, J. J., Ellis, A. K., & Howey, K. R. (1991). *Introduction to the foundations of education* (3rd ed.). Upper Saddle River, NJ: Prentice Hall.

Collins, H. C., Dupuis, V. L., Johansen, J. H., & Johnson, J. A. (1991). *Introduction to the foundations of American education.* Boston: Allyn & Bacon.

Fiske, E. B. (1995). *Smart schools, smart kids. Why do some schools work?* New York: Simon & Schuster.

Gerstner, L. V., Jr. (1995). *Reinventing education.* New York: The Penguin Group.

Hegener, H., & Hegener, M. (1994). *Alternatives in education* (5th ed.). Washington, DC: Home Education Press.

Hencley, H. P., & Yates, J. R. (1974). *Futurism in education: Methodologies.* San Francisco: McCutchan Publishing Corporation.

Holt, J. (1976). *Instead of education: Ways to help people do things better.* New York: E.P. Dutton.

Holt, J. (1981). *How children fail.* New York: Delta.

Johnson, M. (1967). Definitions and models in curriculum theory. *Educational Theory 17*(2), 127–140.

Kuhn, T. S. (1996). *The structure of scientific revolutions* (3rd ed.). University of Chicago Press.

Myers, C. B., & Myers, L. (1995). *The professional educator: A new introduction to teaching.* Nashville, TN: Wadsworth Publishing Co., ITP.

Ornstein, A. C., & Behar, L. S. (1995). *Contemporary issues in curriculum.* Boston: Allyn & Bacon.

Postman, N. (1994). *The end of education: Redefining the value of school.* New York: McGraw-Hill.

Schlechty, P. C. (1990). *Schools for the 21st century: Leadership imperatives for school programs.* New York: Macmillan College Publishing Co.

Shane, H. G. (1973). *The educational significance of the future.* Bloomington, IN: Phi Delta Kappa Educational Foundation.

Shane, H. G. (1977). *Curriculum change toward the 21st century.* Washington, DC: National Education Association Publication.

Sivin-Kachala, J., & Bialo, E. R. (1994). *Report on the effectiveness of technology in schools, 1990–1994.* ERIC Document ED371726.

Toffler, A. (1991a). *Future shock.* New York: Bantam Books.

Toffler, A. (1991b). *The third wave.* New York: Bantam Books.

Toffler, A. (1990). *Power shift.* New York: Bantam Books.

White, M. A. (1987). *What curriculum for the information age?* Newark, NJ: Erlbaum.

✣ ✣ ✣ SUGGESTED READINGS

Astuto, T. A. , Clark, D. L., Read, A., McGree, K., & Fernandez, L. (1994). *Roots of reform: Challenging the assumptions that control change in education.* Bloomington, IN: Phi Delta Kappa Educational Foundation.

Barth, P., & Mitchell, R. (1992). *Smart start: Elementary education for the 21st century.* Golden, CO: North American Press.

Carnegie Council on Adolescent Development. (1989). *Turning points: Preparing American youth for the twenty-first century.* New York: Carnegie Corporation.

Combs, A. W. (1991). *The schools we need.* New York: University Press of America.

Committee for Economic Development. (1995). *Investing in our children.* New York: The Carnegie Corporation.

Cremin, L. A. (1961). *The transformation of the school: Progressivism in American education, 1876–1957.* New York: Alfred A. Knopf.

Crosby, E. A. (1993). The at-risk decade. *Phi Delta Kappan, 74*(8).

Delpit, L., Gates, H. L., Kohl, H., Zinn, H., et al. (1995). *Rethinking school.* New York: The New York Press.

Department of Education. (1997). Third International Mathematics and Science Study. Washington, DC: U.S. Government Printing Office.

Eisenhart, M. (1995). Perspectives on a changing world: A return visit with Alvin Toffler. *MicroTimes,* 1995.

Fiske, E. B. (1995). *Smart schools, smart kids: Why do some schools work?* New York: Alfred A. Knopf.

Fitch, R. M., & Svengalis, C. M. (1979). *Futures unlimited: Teaching about worlds to come.* (ERIC Document Reproduction Service No. ED 174 539).

Goodlad, J. I. (1966). *Changing school curriculum.* New York: The Georgian Press.

Goodlad, J. I. (1975). *The dynamics of educational change: Toward responsive schools.* New York: McGraw-Hill.

Goodlad, J. I. (1976). *Facing the future.* New York: McGraw-Hill.

Henderson, J. G., & Hawthorne, R. D. (1995). *Transformative curriculum leadership.* Englewood Cliffs.

Hodgkinson, H. (1993). American education: The good, the bad, and the task. *Phi Delta Kappan*, *74*(8), 619–623.

Jackson, P. W. (Ed.). (1992). *Handbook of research on curriculum: A project of the American educational research association.* New York: Macmillan.

Johnson, J., Collins, H., Dupuis, V., & Johansen, J. (1988). *Introduction to the foundations of American education.* Boston: Allyn and Bacon.

Johnson, J. A., Dupuis, V. L., Murial, D., Hall, G. E., & Gollnick, D. M. (1996). *Introduction to the foundations of American education* (9th ed.). Boston: Allyn and Bacon.

Johnson, M. L. (1993). *Education on the wild side: Learning for the twenty-first century.* Norman, Oklahoma: University of Oklahoma Press.

Kauffman, D. L., Jr. (1976). *Futurism and futuristic studies.* National Education Association of the United States.

Livingston, D. (1973). Schooling up for a future with the futurists. *Media & Methods*, p. 26–28.

New Scientist meets the controversial futurologist. (1994). Alvin Toffler: Still shocking after all these years. *New Scientist* (March, 1994).

Pierce, T. M. (1987). *Imperatives of lasting public school reform.* Alabama: The Truman Pierce Institute for the Advancement of Teachers Education.

Postman, N. (1995). *The end of education: Redefining the value of school.* New York: Alfred A. Knopf.

Power, E. J. (1982). *Philosophy of education: Studies in philosophies, schooling and educational policies.* Upper Saddle River, NJ: Prentice Hall.

Reese, W. J. (1986). *Power and the promise of school reform: Grassroots movements during the progressive era.* Boston: Routledge & Kegan Paul.

Sarason, S. B. (1990). *The predictable failure of educational reform.* San Francisco, CA: Jossey-Bass Publishers.

Schlechty, P. C. (1990). *Schools for the twenty-first century: Leadership imperatives for educational reform.* San Francisco, CA: Jossey-Bass Publishers.

Sizer, T. R. (1984). *Horace's compromise.* Boston, MA: Houghton Mifflin Company.

Smith, G., & Kniker, C. (1975). *Myth and reality.* Boston, MA: Allyn and Bacon.

Tanner, D. & Tanner, L. (1995). *Curriculum development: Theory into practice* (3rd ed.). Upper Saddle River, NJ: Merrill/Prentice Hall.

Toffler, A. (1996). (*Http://www.startribune.com/digage/toffler4.htm.*). Star Tribune.

U.S. Department of Education. (1997). *A call to action for American education in the twenty-first century.* Washington, DC: U.S. Government Printing Office.

Willie, C. V., & Miller, I. (1988). *Social goals and educational reform.* New York: Greenwood Press.

Wilson, K. G., & Davis, B. (1992). *Redesigning education.* New York: Henry Holt.

Wright, N. (1993). *Assessing radical education.* Philadelphia, PA: Open University Press.

✥ ✥ ✥

4

HISTORICAL AND SOCIAL INFLUENCES

Chapter Objective and Focus:

An examination of the historical and social context
in which contemporary issues of curriculum
development have been made

The history of American education, when placed in a broad cultural, political, social, and economical context, reveals a basic relationship between educational thought and society. Throughout history the pervading focus of education has varied from schooling as preparation for future involvement in society to schooling as a vehicle for changing society. Initially, European educational ideology prevailed in North America. As a result of the frontier lifestyle and revolutionary impulses, a uniquely American education system was formed. The basic institutions of common schools, high schools, and universities evolved through significant historic events such as the Civil War and subsequent Reconstruction, the era of industrialism, the depression of the 1930s, and World Wars I and II. In the affluent times following World War II, Americans experienced efforts to achieve civil rights and the tensions caused by the Cold War. The Soviet launching of *Sputnik* caused Americans to increase educational support and reevaluate the role of education in society. Protests of the 1960s and resultant reform movements gave way in the 1970s and 1980s to revived conservatism. Recent reports on the decline of American education urged reform efforts to raise academic standards and accommodate the future technological needs of society.

COLONIAL EDUCATION

As possessions of the British empire, the colonies were an extension of British society, politics, culture, and economics. The familiar educational institutions and instructional methods of Great Britain were imported to the colonies along the Atlantic Coast. The accepted European structure of vernacular and Latin grammar schools stressed the importance of religion and the ideals of classical humanism. The vernacular schools were established for the purpose of teaching the skills of writing, reading, spelling, mathematics, and basic religious doctrine to the common children. Once these children completed an elementary or primary school, their studies ended and they entered the world of work. The Latin grammar schools and colleges were designed to educate the sons of the privileged classes. While these schools prepared boys in the study of Latin and Greek languages for future coursework in college, they also stressed the basic religious doctrine of the Protestant Reformation.

The New England colonies of Massachusetts, Connecticut, New Hampshire, Vermont, and Rhode Island designed their schools to create adults who would continue the religious, social, political, and economical beliefs of the society. The students were taught a common religious belief system, that to be God-fearing and engage in diligent work gave meaning to life. The Puritans in these colonies based their religious theology on the teachings of John Calvin, a French reformer who believed in Predestination. He believed that God had chosen an elect who were destined for salvation. These elect lived by a strict code of behavior that included hard work, frugality, good conduct, and the worship of a stern God. Calvin stressed that illiteracy was the sign of idleness, ignorance, and evil. To the Puritans, education was important in the battle against sin. Students were viewed as evil creatures who must be taught a better way of life and to avoid the influences of Satan. Therefore, children were active in school or in an apprenticeship through which they learned to read and write and to incorporate religion into everyday life. Laws were passed in Massachusetts in 1642 that required children to be enrolled in a school or appointed to an apprenticeship master. Following this law, the "Old Deluder Satan Act" was passed in 1647 to prevent ignorance. It required Massachusetts towns of fifty families or more to provide elementary education and towns of one hundred or more families to provide Latin preparation for boys entering college. Children in New England contributed to the economic well-being of their families by performing household chores and laboring on the farms. Therefore, vocational training was not included in the formal curriculum of the schools. Serving as an extension of the church, the school was to teach reading, writing, spelling, mathematics, and the basic tenets of religion. This uniform purpose of schooling was quite different from the purpose of the diverse Middle Atlantic colonies.

The settlers in the Middle Atlantic colonies were of a wide, culturally diverse, ethnic, religious, and linguistic background. The plurality of the region prevented a singular focus to schooling. Each ethnic and language group strove to teach their children to perpetuate a singular lifestyle related to their heritage. The Puritans were doing the same thing, yet they did not have to contend with the diverse populations that existed in New York, Pennsylvania, Delaware, and New Jersey. The rise of parochial schools in the Middle Atlantic colonies was a direct result of religious groups such as the Quakers, the Anglicans, the Puritans, the Moravians, the Anabaptists, the Irish and German Roman Catholics, and the Jews' desire to educate their children to become active adult members of their religious community. Along with the varied religious groups, ethnic and language groups such as the Dutch, English, Norwegian, Irish, German, Scotch-Irish, Scotch, French, and Swedish also established schools to transmit cultural identity, history, and language. The parochial and private schools emphasized teaching religious doctrine and language which continued to make the colonists a part of the Old World.

In Pennsylvania, the Quakers found a place to worship in a very personalized manner far from the persecutions of England. This interesting group who settled in the Middle Atlantic colonies stressed literacy and viewed the child as possessing a divine power from God. The Quakers did not feel that they had to train children to become divine or to educate them out of a preexisting sinful state. Abhorring violence, the Quakers did not utilize corporal punishment nor did they bear arms. The belief structure allowed for anyone to testify or preach the message sent by God. Children were freed from memorizing religious admonitions or catechism questions and answers and learned instead through direct experience. William Penn, the colony's governor, was interested in the education of children in practical subjects and direct application of knowledge. He felt that this would create motivated students and that this education should be open to all children.

Pietist groups known for their heart-felt religious beliefs and practices also came to the New World to escape religious persecution. The Pietist groups were mostly German-speaking worshippers including the Moravians, the Mennonites, the Amish, the Dunkers, the Shakers, the Anabaptists, and the Seventh-day Adventists. These groups often isolated themselves within self-supporting agricultural communities where they taught their children to work using rewards rather than punishment.

In the Southern colonies, single families owned large areas of land and cultivated a single crop with the use of slave labor. This mode of plantation agriculture dominated the area and placed the region in opposition to the Northern colonies from the start. Because of this plantation and slave system, the population in the Southern colonies was small and spread over a vast amount of land. The isolation of the self-supporting plantations and the cultural and economic diversity found in the Southern colonies prevented the formation of many established schools. Plantation owners trained their sons to become plantation owners and often employed tutors for a time in this effort. Poor white farmers taught their children how to farm and become active members in the family enterprise of subsistence farming. African slaves were isolated from their own ethnic groups to prevent rebellion. Often they were forbidden to learn to read and write.

Colonial education established the foundation of schooling in America. Religion served to shape the educational focus of schools along with a desire to transmit cultural and ethnic knowledge of heritage from the Old World. A dualistic educational system was formed, giving opportunity for education to many, yet restricting higher education to those belonging to a wealthier social class.

REVOLUTIONARY EDUCATION

In 1776, when revolution broke out in the colonies, the impulses of the Age of Reason or the Enlightenment bolstered the desire for self-government and individual freedom. The ramifications of Thomas Jefferson's Declaration of Independence on education lie in the rights of all men to seek happiness. Since anyone can lead and govern, all should be taught to do so. Education became imperative for civic competency in that the choices regarding government must be made by an educated populace.

Enlightenment theorists saw the human being as an inherently good creation capable of being perfected. The perfection of mankind or societies in general relied on the discovery of natural laws. Scientific reasoning and study of the sciences were emphasized in an effort to discover these natural laws and perfect society. The Enlightenment moved Americans toward a more secular orientation of schooling with civic education, science education, and the use of schooling as a means of teaching American identity.

In developing an inherently American educational system, unique proposals were made by Benjamin Franklin, Thomas Jefferson, Benjamin Rush, and Noah Webster. Benjamin Franklin used trial and error to test scientific inventions. He stressed practical skills to be taught in English and that true knowledge can only come from experience. Franklin proposed that education should aim to prepare citizens to make useful and practical contributions to society. Thomas Jefferson, an Enlightenment theorist and political leader, believed that people must be educated to make wise civic decisions and elect capable leaders to represent them in the state legislatures and in Congress. Jefferson sought to establish state-controlled schools, schooling for every citizen, and schools focused on civic rather than religious aims. Jefferson also worked to create the University of Virginia as a school without any restrictive religious affiliation and reorganized the curriculum of the College of William and Mary to include more modern subjects. Benjamin Rush also attempted to create an educational system that promoted American nationalism; however, he disagreed with Jefferson's ideas that religion interfered with scientific reasoning and research. Rush encouraged the integration of religion, science, and nationalism in educating American children. Noah Webster, like Rush, recommended reform in education to include an emphasis on nationalism along with very contemporary ideas such as increased teacher training, low class size, and interesting presentations to motivate student interests. Webster wrote textbooks and a dictionary void of British influence.

Influenced by the Enlightenment and revolutionary ideas of government, education moved toward a more secular orientation with emphasis placed on science, civic responsibility, and the development of an American identity.

EARLY NINETEENTH CENTURY EDUCATION

Industrialism, the emergence of the middle class, and philanthropic support for schools influenced the continuing search for an educational system that would be appropriate for America. The Industrial Revolution and a growing class of industrialists, entrepreneurs, and various other professionals supported education for children of lower socioeconomic classes. It was beneficial to educate all children because it was successful in maintaining the status quo. Monitorial methods of education provided literacy to a larger number of students at a relatively lower cost. In the monitorial method, a master teacher trained teaching assistants to teach a basic skill to students. Students were homogeneously grouped by ability and efficiently taught lessons by one of the teaching assistants. Monitorial schools began to decline due to the atmosphere which became quite factory-like, and opposition was raised as to the qualifications of the assistants who often did not have knowledge of the complete educational process.

In opposition to the monitorial method of education, William Maclure developed schools of industry for the working classes. Maclure's schools of industry taught that research in science could be the framework for agricultural, industrial, and economical development. Maclure was also responsible for introducing the Pestalozzian method of education to the United States.

Maclure later worked with Robert Owen, a socialist who was in favor of utopian communities and an ideal society based on cooperation. Owen's conceptualization of communitarian education involved teaching students the value of common ownership and the happiness achieved from involvement in cooperative relationships. In an experimental community in New Harmony,

Indiana, Owen and Maclure joined together to achieve a communitarian system of education. Pestalozzi's principles of learning from the senses and presenting new information from concrete to abstract or specific to general drove the instruction. The schools were open to all of the community's residents and were a place of love and emotional security where social reform could begin. The monitorial system, Robert Owen's communitarian ideology, and William Maclure's industry schools set the stage for public schools.

MID-NINETEENTH CENTURY EDUCATION

The common school movement or public school movement placed emphasis on education in the basic skills and subjects for all. The basic premise of common schools was to educate all social classes and to instill a common core of knowledge. This educational movement followed the political reforms and popular democratic ideals of the time. Progress in commerce and transportation paired with the common man entering politics pushed government to define its role in improving education for the common man. The organizational leadership for the common school movement came from the state level. One of its leading proponents was Horace Mann, who is often referred to as the father of the common school movement. He served as secretary of the Massachusetts Board of Education and as a Massachusetts Senator. While in college, Mann was exposed to Transcendentalism and the belief in the inherent goodness of mankind. He, like other transcendentalists of the age, believed in human and societal perfection.

The successes of the common school movement varied; however, the end result was an established elementary education made available to large numbers of students and the basis of public education in the United States. The common schools valued hard work, morals, economic contributions, and civic and political involvement. Finally, the common schools also established the state government as the locus of control over schools.

Prior to the Civil War, the American secondary schools progressed through several stages of development. The Latin grammar schools were replaced by academies, private institutions operated under the auspices of specific religious denominations. The academies offered three major curricula: the normal curriculum for students preparing to teach in elementary schools, the English-language curriculum for students who would end their schooling after the academy, and the college preparatory curriculum for students entering college. Uniform standards and accrediting agencies did not exist. This meant that the academies could offer varying programs with no real check on the quality. After the Civil War, the American high school began to replace academies and connected the link between the public elementary schools, or common schools, to the state-supported universities and colleges. As the American high school

This reconstruction of a Civil War era schoolhouse allows students to envision what life was like in an earlier time.

developed as an institution, the enrollment grew at an advanced rate. By the 1920s the curriculum was organized into a college preparatory program, a business program, an industrial program, and a general academic program. This four-fold curricular organization developed along with the emergence of intermediate or junior high schools. Junior high schools were created as a response to the need for a gradual transition between elementary school and high school and to offer a curriculum that matched the middle adolescent child.

POST–WORLD WAR I EDUCATION

During the 1920s Americans prospered. Many discovered ways to make quick fortunes through investment in the stock market. Inventions such as automobiles, airplanes, electric lights, and radio signaled the advancement into a modern era. Education served to prepare students to participate in the world of business and enjoy an individual portion of the new prosperity.

A more permissive attitude toward children existed along with an increase in the period of social adolescence. Child-centered teaching based on learning through interests and experience allowed for expressive creativity without fear of censorship. The lengthening of adolescence grew from the compulsory attendance laws and the increased number of students attending and completing high school.

The Great Depression had profound effects on social, economic, political, and educational attitudes. In many schools, teachers were fired, class size increased, and the number of course offerings decreased. Adolescents dropped out of school in unsuccessful attempts to find work, while many children suffered from malnutrition. The depression also caused great debate over educational ideology. The essentialists believed that schools transmit knowledge to students who will become active members of society, while the progressive movement argued that through education children can change society.

POST–WORLD WAR II EDUCATION

Following World War II, the American middle class increased and the socioeconomic gap between the upper and middle classes began to close. This widespread affluence became apparent in the growth of suburban communities and in the rapid increase in population or "baby boom." The suburban school districts began to grow and prosper due to the increasing tax base while inner city schools suffered from a lack of support from the business community. The middle class and more affluent students attended the suburban schools, while the economically disadvantaged students and black students attended the neglected inner-city schools. Segregation existed along racial and economic lines and relegated to inner-city schools few resources and an uneven educational opportunity. Legal action was finally taken to end the segregation of public schools in 1954 in *Brown v. Board of Education of Topeka* in which the Supreme Court overturned the separate-but-equal ruling of *Plessy v. Ferguson* of 1896.

By the end of the 1950s, heated debates over the curriculum of American schools were being fought. A conservative group questioned studies in life skills and warned that Dewey's progressive approach would lower standards and cause the United States to fall behind other nations with respect to education. Critics such as Arthur Bestor, Hyman G. Rickover, and Max Rafferty agreed that academic standards were falling, that the purpose of schooling was no longer clear, and that the curriculum should consist of basic traditional skills. When the Soviet Union successfully launched *Sputnik* into orbit around the earth, education in the United States shifted its curricular emphasis to science, physics, mathematics, and chemistry. Americans began to believe that something was wrong with its schools and quickly enacted the National Defense Education Act (NDEA) to develop students' technical skills. NDEA also provided funding for the curricular areas of math, science, and foreign languages to bolster the national defense.

THE 1960S

The 1960s will always be known as a decade of great discontent and subsequent call for active change. The controversial Vietnam War and a general call for activism created a subculture of young people who rejected the values of their parents, often used drugs to "raise" consciousness about social order, and put aside the American work ethic. Schooling was seen by this counterculture as conditioning for life in a society rather than fueling personal interests. So while those providing funding from NDEA and educational conservatives were calling for higher standards and studies of basic skills, many others in the 1960s were searching for major reform. These new reformers criticized the bureaucratic, formalized, restrictive classrooms and called for a greater degree of flexibility to enhance creativity. The result of this criticism was a movement toward humanistic education, abandonment of excessive rules and routine, and the use of open education. The open education movement was partially successful when schools were built to accommodate the open environment. However, open schools like many other reforms of the 1960s gave way to the desire in the 1970s and 1980s for a stabilized society.

THE 1970S

The energy crisis, inflation, and recession in the 1970s caused great economic upheaval and enduring educational ramifications. Reports on the poor condition of American education placed the blame for educational decline on the country's economic crisis. The United States was no longer the preeminent economic world leader and, paired with the internal migration of the population to the Sunbelt states, schools suffered from a declining tax base in the North and overcrowding in states such as North Carolina, California, Texas, Florida, and Georgia. Economic and political changes in the United States promoted educational reform in many areas. One area in particular was the recognition of the educational rights of special learners. Congress passed the Education for All Handicapped Children Act in 1975 which ensured that all handicapped children between the ages of three and twenty-one would be guaranteed public education designed to meet their special needs.

Throughout the 1960s, 1970s, and 1980s, programs were federally funded to help the nation's disadvantaged students. The Head Start program was created for preschoolers to make up for the lack of educationally simulating experiences in the home. Funding continued for lunch, medical, vocational, bilingual, and gifted programs until the mid-1980s. In the 1970s, teacher education programs included student teaching and higher standards for accreditation.

Teachers in the 1970s developed learning centers and extended the use of audiovisual materials. Inquiry learning and concept learning were utilized and can be traced to Dewey's reflective thinking process.

THE 1980S AND BEYOND

The 1980s marked a return to a more conservative political and educational ideology. The Reagan administration promoted the back-to-basics study of essential skills which had been popular only on a state level during the 1970s. During the 1980s, an influx of reports on education which shared the basic theme of alarm over the declining quality of American education were published. These reports all urged reform and a return to basic education as a means of raising academic standards. Many of these reports pointed to the permissive nature of schools as the reason for the societal ills of teen pregnancy, drug abuse, increasing numbers of single-parent families, and increasing violence. The report of the National Commission on Excellence in Education entitled *A Nation at Risk: The Imperative for Educational Reform* attracted national attention and prompted debate over the condition of American schooling. Just as the essentialists of the 1930s and the reformers of the 1950s believed, the authors of the report compared American education with other countries and found American performance to be inferior. The report specifically highlighted the high rate of illiteracy, the decline in SAT scores, and the need for college remedial courses.

By identifying the problems inherent in American education, the writers of these reports sought to expose the cause of the problems and offered several suggestions for improvement. Many called for teacher training, increased salaries for educators, and a reorganization of leadership. Communities were recommended to amend their budgets to include funding for educational improvement and utilize professionals to guarantee the resourceful use of these funds. Recommendations were also made to increase the academic rigor and attendance requirements, to eliminate all nonessential or "soft" curricular courses, and to require an objective method of testing teachers and schools for quality of instruction (Tanner & Tanner, 1995; Meyers & Meyers, 1995).

Ernest Boyer (1983) and Theodore Sizer (1984) examined the condition of the American high school and offered suggestions for curricular change. Boyer sought to create a clear sense of purpose for American high schools and designed goals for students which would be met in a common core of learning. Critics argued that this created high schools that singly prepared students for college and dismissed the vital need for vocational education. Sizer's report recommended raising expectations and achievements in a flexible atmosphere. He did not agree with Boyer's prescribed list of courses as he stressed teaching concepts of learning rather than isolated subjects. Sizer's model included spheres of learning where students would develop intellectual skills, the ability to transmit knowledge, and questioning skills.

Sizer's idea for integrating learning moves education away from treating each subject as an isolated discipline. This trend of integration is likely to continue as many middle schools in the United States are successfully teaming teachers to offer students a related core curriculum. The impact of computers and various forms of educational technology will promote computer literacy as a basic skill along with the traditional skills of reading, writing, and arithmetic. Flexible scheduling and the integration of learning in high schools may thwart the predicted decline of vocational programs in schools.

❖ ❖ ❖   SUMMARY FOCUS ACTIVITY

What are your thoughts?

Listed below are several statements of actions that many citizens and educators throughout history have thought America should take to improve the education of its children and youth. Many of these areas have not been discussed at this point, but are included in future chapters. However, examine these from the perspectives of the time periods discussed within this chapter. Which of these actions were imperative in the improvement of education in each historical time frame and in the future? Place a plus sign (+) in the space by the statement if you agree, a minus sign (–) if you disagree, a question mark (?) if you are unsure, and N/A if not applicable. Make a response sheet for colonial education, revolutionary education, and so on. Be sure to add the 1990s and the future decade.

___ 1. National standards and measurements must be set at the average, not the minimum, levels. States and local school districts must develop specific guidelines and procedures for implementation of national standards. The failure of local school districts to meet these standards within two years should result in the takeover of the system by the state.

___ 2. America needs and should design a national curriculum as has been done by other developed nations.

___ 3. If a national curriculum is developed, it should be implemented at the state and local levels.

___ 4. Each state should limit the number of institutions offering teacher certification in order to provide more consistent training and tighter quality control.

___ 5. National teacher licensure procedures and standards should be developed. Educators who achieve national certification must be recognized and rewarded.

___ 6. Standards for admission to teacher education programs must be improved. Education professors must hold teacher licensure and be assigned for a portion of their professional time to working with children and/or teachers in the classroom.

___ 7. A large portion of the money that business and industry uses to retrain new employees should be used to fund additional teacher positions to lower teacher-pupil ratios. Business/school partnerships in which businesses provide personnel to assist directly with instruction must be established.

___ 8. School boards across America must reduce central administrative positions to a minimum. Moneys saved through this action should be redirected to instructional support. Each remaining centrally based administrator and staff member must spend a portion of the year working directly with students.

___ 9. Tenure for principals and teachers must be discontinued and replaced with initial two-year contracts for beginning teachers and three-year contracts for new principals. After the initial contract period, local school districts can base contractual terms upon market conditions. Contracts should not exceed five years.

___ 10. Teachers and principals who are not doing their jobs, either through neglect of duty or incompetence, must be removed.

___ 11. Parents must get directly involved in the instruction of their children. This process must begin at conception through birth with the practice of good prenatal care.

___ 12. As a child develops during the infant, toddler, and preschool years, parents must actively pursue the role of the child's first teacher. Critical to these periods of the child's life is being read to daily. The child should be provided opportunities to explore and experience many aspects of his/her home and community and engage in manipulative games and activities. Parents as teachers must gain proper instructional knowledge and techniques for all aspects of growth and development including cognitive and social development.

___ 13. Parents must support schools by being positive about school, teachers, and learning. Additionally, parents must ensure that their children complete homework, get to bed early, and become responsible for all of their actions.

___ 14. Educators must view parents and students as full instructional partners. Parents must take an active and on-going role in instructing their children in all aspects of formal and informal schooling. Children must be encouraged to explore, inquire, and problem solve at school and at home.

___ 15. The role of educational leadership must expand from the principal's office to include teachers and parent representatives. Leadership must be practiced in the form of site-based management which includes the daily operation of the school and allows teachers and parents to have input into decisions of policy, procedure, and curriculum alignment. It is imperative that teachers receive appropriate training in team building and decisionmaking.

___ 16. Local curriculum alignment teams composed of teachers and specialists must be created to establish instructional guidelines.

___ 17. Teachers currently in the field must be provided in-service opportunities in the skills of curriculum and instructional alignment.

___ 18. Students must be held accountable for the skills of group interaction, cooperative problem solving, and the democratic process.

___ 19. Students must be held accountable for academic subject matter, application of content, and the use of critical thinking skills.

___ 20. Citizenship education, character development, and responsibility development should be included within the context of curriculum and instruction.

___ 21. Every classroom must be designed to be inviting to every child regardless of cultural background, creed, or degree of impairment of any type.

___ 22. Teachers must be provided with the resources and training needed to be successful with students of varying cultural background, creed, or degree of impairment of any type.

___ 23. Corporal punishment must be outlawed in every state.

___ 24. Discipline programs which focus on fear techniques or habitual rewards and which are used to control the student externally must be replaced with programs that are internally oriented and require students to be responsible for their own actions. Logical and reasonable consequences should be used to assist students to self-correct their actions.

___ 25. Each school system must design and establish alternative schools at all levels for students who cannot function or who have extremely disruptive discipline problems. Parent/guardian involvement must be a requirement for continued involvement in the program.

___ 26. States must pass laws which make the presence of a weapon in the school a felony. Verbal threats and physical aggression toward teachers should also be considered as acts of felony and given appropriate legal consequences.

___ 27. The school year must be tailored to address individual student needs in an ever-changing society. Extended school days in which students focus on such things as the arts, physical fitness, or remediation should be established in every school.

___28. America's challenge is to convince every citizen that every child must have an equal opportunity to be successful in school.

___29. The United States can accomplish a mission of academic success for all students through government, private enterprise, family, and community partnerships with the schools.

___30. Educators must act as the catalyst for change through a professional mission to create a system of public instruction which gives every child in this diverse society an equal opportunity to be successful.

___31. Classroom teachers should be involved in all aspects of curriculum development and not just the areas of classroom instruction and management.

___32. Curriculum is best developed at local grass roots levels, but successful curricula and programs should be duplicated at the state and the national levels.

❖ ❖ ❖   DISCUSSION QUESTIONS

1. To succeed in an information-based society, students should graduate with the ability to acquire and apply new knowledge. Reality is ever-changing; our understanding of the world and of our lives must continuously adapt as new things are discovered or learned. How will this affect schools? How will it change the classroom in the future?

2. The educational system of the twentieth century does not fit the needs of the twenty-first century. Describe your vision of a more appropriate system of education.

❖ ❖ ❖   CLASS ACTIVITIES

1. *Pendulum Shifts.* Trace the changing historical and philosophical view of the child in education. Where do the educational experiences and opportunities of your parents and grandparents fall on this continuum? Compare findings in small groups and share with the class at large.

2. *Impacts.* As a class, select one historical event other than the launching of *Sputnik* or the publication of *A Nation at Risk* that the class thinks had a significant impact on the elementary curriculum and defend that position.

3. Prepare a video production of the various roles of teachers in the elementary school with relatives and friends who attended school during the last half of the 1900s. Share the video with your class and present a composite description of the teacher's instructional role for every decade from 1950–2000. What will the composite be in the decades to come?

❖ ❖ ❖   REFERENCES

Boyer, E. L. (1983). *High school: A report on secondary education in America.* New York: Harper & Row.

Meyers, C. B., & Meyers, L. (1995). *The professional educator: A new introduction to teaching.* Nashville, TN: Wadsworth.

National Committee on Excellence in Education (1983). *A nation at risk: The imperatives for educational reform.* Washington, DC: U. S. Government Printing Office.

Sizer, T. R. (1984). *Horace's compromise: The dilemma of the American high school.* Boston: Houghton Mifflin.

Tanner, D., & Tanner, L. (1995). *Curriculum development: Theory into practice* (3rd ed.). Upper Saddle River, NJ: Merrill/Prentice Hall.

❖ ❖ ❖   SUGGESTED READINGS

Cohan, J. J., Ellis, A. K., & Howey, K. R. (1991). *Introduction to the foundations of education* (3rd ed.). Upper Saddle River, NJ: Prentice Hall.

Collins, H. C., Dupuis, V. L., Johansen, J. H., & Johnson, J. A. (1991). *Introduction to the foundations of American education.* Boston: Allyn & Bacon.

Gutek, G. L. (1986). *Education in the United States: An historical perspective.* Upper Saddle River, NJ: Prentice Hall.

Ravitch, D., & Vinovskis, M. A. (1995). *Learning from the past.* Baltimore, MD: The Johns Hopkins University Press.

❖ ❖ ❖

5

THE PROCESS OF CURRICULUM DEVELOPMENT

Chapter Objective and Focus:

Curriculum definitions and the processes used
to develop and organize curriculum goals
and standards

CURRICULUM: A MATTER OF DEFINITIONS?

Curriculum, perhaps the most disagreed-upon term in educational literature, gives the basic direction for what is to be taught in schools. The basic definition one would find in the dictionary might be as follows:

> "Curriculum, from a Latin term, literally means running a course." (Webster, 1996, p. 285)

Within the educational community curriculum is defined in a more functional manner. Definitions center upon purpose, objectives, and organization of content. Hilda Taba (1962) viewed curriculum as a plan for learning and stated that all curricula (plural form of curriculum), "no matter what the design, are composed of certain elements. A curriculum usually contains a statement of aims and of specific objectives; it indicates some selection and organization of content; . . . " (p. 10).

One of the first writers on curriculum, Bobbitt (1918), perceived the term to be a "series of things which children and youth must do and experience" to grow up to be productive in adult life (p. 42).

Mauritz Johnson, Jr. (1967) explained his definition of curriculum in an article in *Educational Theory* as a systems approach. He believed that curriculum was a "structured series of intended outcomes" (p. 130). He viewed the curriculum development system as an input into an instructional system.

Beauchamp (1975) viewed curriculum as a "written document." Bestor (1956), an essentialist, believed that curriculum included "intellectual training" in the fundamental disciplines. Caswell and Campbell (1935) thought that curriculum included "all the experiences" which are guided by the classroom teachers.

Many curricularists view curriculum as product-oriented, that is, having specific outcomes, blueprints for instruction, or a plan for instruction. Other curricularists believe curriculum to be more process-oriented, that is, to include instruction. Many educators view curriculum and instruction as being the same.

Oliva (1997) summarized the various interpretations that depended on philosophical beliefs. He listed these interpretations as follows:

- Curriculum is that which is taught in school.
- Curriculum is a set of subjects.
- Curriculum is content.
- Curriculum is a program of studies.
- Curriculum is a set of materials.
- Curriculum is a sequence of courses.
- Curriculum is a set of performance objectives.
- Curriculum is a course of study.
- Curriculum is everything that goes on within the school, including extra-class activities, guidance, and interpersonal relationships.
- Curriculum is everything that is planned by school personnel.
- Curriculum is a series of experiences undergone by learners in a school.
- Curriculum is that which an individual learner experiences as a result of schooling. (p. 4)

As one can easily see, definitions tend to have a philosophical flavor and vary greatly. It is important that future teachers be aware of the varying definitions and the instructional implications. One may end up in schools or systems that prefer one approach over another. However, in the recent past a more eclectic approach has been used.

The author, as a futurist, views curriculum as society's requirement of the formal educational process to prepare the next generations for adaptability, acceptance, diversity and survival in an unknown world.

Choosing a curriculum design has always been controversial. Of the several different approaches to designing curricula, many are diametrically opposed to others philosophically. Various definitions and beliefs related to curriculum have been presented. Special focus will be given to how philosophy affects curriculum planning, design, and implementation. Educators must equip their students with new skills, because the very nature of society, the students, and the teaching profession will be in constant change.

PATTERNS OF CURRICULUM ORGANIZATION

The author believes that most states and school systems use some form of three distinct levels for curriculum development. Historically, these progress from a broad, general goal to specific, behavioral objectives.

Level I: Curriculum Goals

Curriculum goals are generalized as major student outcomes. These goals usually originate from state and/or local school board action. Ultimately, decisions are guided by a belief system that explains a group's purpose of education and which answers the most important question of all: What is it that students should achieve during their formal education years in the public schools? Educational philosophies can guide the creation of these broad goals, and one could conclude that these constitute a de facto Level I. Although there are several different belief systems, all are derived from one of three philosophical camps, or paradigms—the internal paradigm, the external paradigm, and the constructivist paradigm.

The internal paradigm is based on the work of such philosophers and theorists as Rousseau, Erikson, and Freud. This model concerns itself with the innate aspects of the person. Internalists think of education in terms of maturation, the natural unfolding of one's personality, and how best to enhance that process. This paradigm is most closely associated with the educational philosophies "romanticism," "naturalism," and "existentialism." It is also referred to as "humanism." Internalist educators are far more concerned with the needs of the student than facts and figures of a particular subject area.

The external paradigm, more commonly called the "behavioralist" paradigm, can be viewed as the exact opposite of the internal. It is based on the work of such philosophers and theorists as Skinner, Bruner, and Adler. This model concerns itself strictly with the observable aspects of a person. Although it does not deny the existence of the internal aspects of students, it contends that the personality is best dealt with from the outside, what the person does, not what he thinks or feels. External paradigms are scientifically measurable and professional in nature. This paradigm is most closely associated with the educational philosophies "perennialism," and "essentialism." Externalists argue that internalism is both inefficient and ineffective. They propose that there is a core of knowledge that is timeless and crucial. It is the duty of the school to impart this knowledge from one generation to the next. Therefore, the facts and figures of a course of study take precedence over the individual needs of students. They view people as driven by goals. If the right "carrot" can be found, students will work to learn in order to receive the prize.

The third paradigm is sometimes erroneously referred to as a combination of internal and external paradigms. Although elements of both do exist in it, the constructivist paradigm is a unique philosophy. Often paired with "progressivism," it is based on the work of such philosophers and theorists as Piaget, Dewey, Ward, and a host of others.

Constructivists assert that from the dynamic interplay between the innate self and the environment a person organizes and reorganizes (or "constructs") his or her view of the world and his or her self. Constructivist educators insist that what is taught should be made relevant to the student. The more abstract the means of instruction, the less a student will feel that it relates to his needs. A classic example of this is found in the teaching of math. Following traditional methods, mathematical formulae are learned first, then word problems are begun. To the constructivist, this is backwards. By beginning with the word problems, the student can see how math relates to his or her world and own needs. Constructivists think of students as "little scientists." Learning is based on the student's innate need to know.

Level II: Curriculum Translations into Specific Programs

During this phase, the school system (or in some cases, the school) develops procedures to interpret and to specify goals set in Level I. Level II curriculum translations are more specific than curriculum goals, in that the structure of the curriculum is more clearly defined. Often Level II goals are referred to as specific programs or program classifications. These could include the math program, science program, integrated elementary program, etc. How these Level I goals are "translated" or "interpreted" can vary widely based upon the program planners' belief system, management style, and understanding of the curriculum goals. Subject specialists, representative classroom teachers and central office personnel usually develop Level II program goals and objectives.

Level III: Curriculum Pacing and Content/Process Alignment for Instruction

During this phase, the "behavioral objectives" or standards are mapped out. These are actual objectives for instructional use. What is meant by "behavioral objectives"? Care must be taken not to confuse behavioral objectives with the behaviorist philosophy. Behavioral objectives are based upon what the instructor wants the student to be able to do at the end of the lesson. Wiles and Bondi (1997) make the point that assessing whether or not a student has learned has to be based on observable, quantifiable actions that the student can demonstrate. Attempts at judging whether a student has learned something based solely on instructor intuition are neither effective nor professional. For example, if an objective was "the learner will be able to operate a microscope," the intended outcome is clear cut and the means of assessing whether or not the student can successfully operate the microscope is easily observable. However, an objective such as "the student will understand photosynthesis" is insufficiently clear. This objective can be refined by restating it as "the student will be able to draw a simple illustration and explain the process of photosynthesis in his/her own words." This second example is transformed into a behavior or action that the student can perform.

Unfortunately, the planners at Level II may not be totally clear on the Level I goals. Subsequently, Level III planners are even further in the dark about the original aims that they are to carry out (Wiles and Bondi, 1997).

Another way of restating levels of curriculum organization is by breaking them down into "macrocurricular" and "microcurricular" considerations. Macrocurriculum is the "big picture," or "long-term planning." At this level, drafters must be keenly aware of state and local guidelines. They must break down subjects into units of instruction. They must take into account the textbook issued for a particular course of study (Borman and Levine, 1997). Equally important is the task of integration. Today's system of schooling is still suffering from the work of Bruner and others who insisted that all academic subjects must be completely separate. Blending together learning from two different fields of study was forbidden. Most educators now see the folly in such an approach, but its legacy haunts educators today and perhaps will continue into the future. Those concerned with macrocurriculum should strive to find ways of connecting learning from various subjects in order to assist students' cognitive development. Macrocurriculum is closely associated with Levels I and II of Wiles and Bondi.

Microcurriculum is the "little picture," or "short-term planning." It concerns itself with instructional units, specific lesson plans with content, skills or processes. Step-by-step learning outcomes are plotted and daily routines are established. This is closely associated with Level III of Wiles and Bondi.

Looking at Wiles and Bondi's (1997) model, one might assume that teachers are not involved with macrocurriculum. Such is not the case. Both long-term and short-term objectives should be in the forefront of teachers' thinking. Unfortunately, teachers often neglect or actively ignore macrocurriculum. Perhaps becoming bogged down in the day-to-day struggles of instruction causes them to lose sight of this crucial element of education. Equally likely, many teachers may simply say that "macrocurricular concerns are not in their job description."

In their book *Curriculum Development: Theory into Practice*, Daniel and Laurel Tanner (1995) created a list describing three levels at which teachers function. The lowest of these is Level I, which includes teachers and administrators who merely maintain the established curriculum (microcurricular).

Level II describes those who refine the established curriculum (also microcurricular). Educators in this group are aware of the need for change and innovation, but do not go far enough. They still tend to compartmentalize subject areas. Theory and practice continue to remain separate. The final and most desirable position is Level III, which describes those who take an integrated view of curriculum and seek to continually examine and rework it in its entirety (macrocurricular). They strive to connect theory and practice and frequently consult professional literature for recent educational research.

Tanner and Tanner (1995) are quick to point out that these levels are not sequential. In other words, first-year teachers do not start as Level I teachers and progress to Level III through years of experience. Rather, this list reflects teachers' attitudes toward their profession. Ideally, a first-year teacher should start his or her career at Level III, despite lack of experience. This rebuts the work of Dona Kagan, who maintains that preservice teachers should concern themselves with establishing daily instructional routines. Kagan maintains that combining educational theories with these established routines can be done later through professional development and experience. Tanner and Tanner and John Dewey contend that beginning teachers should establish instructional practices that are supported by current research. Teachers, like all humans, are creatures of habit. Too often routines can become rooted into a teacher's mode of instructing and remain there even after updated professional development shows that the established routine is not educationally sound. Conversely, an educationally sound system that, for whatever reason, isn't working with a particular group of students is just as ineffective as one that isn't educationally sound. Therefore, taking the attitude that the curriculum should be in a constant state of evolving should be standard fare for the beginning teacher as well as the more experienced one. Unfortunately, most educators operate at Level I or II, not Level III.

One problem the author has with Tanner and Tanner's (1995) assertions is that the microcurricular aspect of teaching is almost always treated as something to avoid. As can be clearly seen through the work of Wiles and Bondi (1997), there is a division of labor. Educational leaders and curriculum specialists must be more concerned with macrocurricular issues than individual teachers. Consequently, teachers must deal with more microcurricular issues, but should not be completely left out of macrocurricular decisions. Nevertheless, both groups should be far more aware of what is going on at all levels. Otherwise, we have a classic "tale of two cities" with insufficient communication.

BALANCING SUBJECT CONTENT AND PROCESSES

To begin this section, it is essential that the author clarify what is meant by the terms "content" and "process." Process is often defined as being synonymous with the term "implementation." The way in which a curriculum is utilized, the implementation or "processing" of curricula over time, was not included in the definition for this chapter. Rather, the intention can be summed up in the words of Marilyn Jager-Adams:

> Process is about interpretation and understanding. Content is about knowledge. Knowledge without the ability to explore its relations is useless. And cognitive theory makes clear that understanding without knowledge is not merely impractical, but psychologically impossible. (cited in Costa, 1991, p. 2)

To paraphrase Evelyn Sowell (1996), content can be thought of as the "raw material" for the curriculum (p. 154). To the exogenist, it is the very essence of the curriculum. It is a well-thought-out list of knowledge and skills that the student is expected to learn.

The researchers' working definition of processes is the *cognitive* and *maturational* processes of the child, the child's needs and abilities. Herein lies the age-old battle of "the child versus the subject content." Which is more important, the developmental needs of the child or the learning of the information and skills that will be needed in life? It is essential that educators do not think of content and processes as merely diametrically opposing needs. Rather, they should be thought of as compatible components of the curriculum. Discovering individual biases about the priorities and the point of balance between content and process is very useful in helping educators design curricula.

There are various notions of curriculum design. In 1949, Ralph W. Tyler created a curriculum paradigm that is perhaps the single most influential paradigm of its kind. Entitled *Tyler's Basic Principles*, but better known as the Tyler Rationale, it states that there are three sources of content: the needs and interests of the learners, the needs of the society, and the educational disciplines or subjects. Bearing Tyler's work in mind, Longstreet and Shane (1993), have proposed four concepts of curriculum design:

1. The society-centered curriculum.
2. The child-centered curriculum
3. The knowledge-centered curriculum.
4. The eclectic curriculum.

The society-centered curriculum focuses on the needs of the society. It becomes the number one consideration when designing a curriculum. The other two factors are important, but secondary. Concerning itself primarily with the needs and interests of the learners is the child-centered curriculum. Society is best served by assisting the child's pursuit of self through developmentally appropriate techniques. As the name implies, the knowledge-centered curriculum exalts the time-honored knowledge, embodied in the various educational disciplines, above society or the learner. The last is the eclectic curriculum.

This represents the de facto state of American curricula now in use. From the author's perspective, it is a compilation of the various philosophies stuck together in a haphazard, ineffective manner.

Consumers of Content

Given that America is a capitalist society, the culture is dominated by consumerism. Knowledge of what type of people purchase or "consume" specific goods and services is crucial to predicting market trends. To quote futurist Alvin Toffler (1997), "consumer research has been able for years to tell us in mind-numbing detail what the average American automobile purchaser or soap user is like, what he earns, how many bathtubs, television sets, or educational degrees he has and where his warts are located" (p. 25). In his book, *The Culture Consumers*, Toffler (1973) also contends that individuals are "consumers" of things other than consumer goods—namely the arts. Following this line of thinking, the author contends that education has its consumers and producers as well. Obviously, the consumers of education are the students. It is for their benefit that the curricula were designed. It is a growing market. In the course of their lives, practically every American at some time or other is a consumer of education. The content of the curriculum is decided upon for the benefit of the student consumer.

Just as consumers themselves are different and their needs for soap and cars change from time to time, students are individuals and their needs change as well. Corporations must be keenly aware of changes among their consumers and adjust themselves accordingly. Yet educators seem content to create curricula without the slightest regard for their consumers and their changing needs. It is as if Ford Motors would say, "We only make one kind of car. We've made 'em just like this for the last 30 years. If you don't like it, then walk!"

Considering the billions of dollars spent by the United States government (and foreign governments as well) and the millions of dollars invested and reaped by companies that make educational supplies, it should come as no shock to hear students referred to as "consumers."

Producers of Content

Tyler (1949) concluded that there are three sources of content: the student, the society, and the subject. In contrast, Sowell (1996) listed five sources of content. These are: (1) recommendations of professional organizations, (2) state guidelines, (3) textbooks and related materials, (4) alternatives to textbooks, and (5) teachers' knowledge bases.

Many people are involved in determining the content of curricula. Traditionally, administrators in the central office have been responsible for deciding upon the content of the curriculum. The momentum towards placing more power in the hands of educators in individual schools in the late 1980s and the 1990s created another option. This is known as "site-based curriculum design" and will be dealt with in greater detail later in this chapter. In this design, the teachers themselves are responsible for creating the curriculum.

Beginning at the End

In designing curricula, it may seem odd at first to talk about beginning at the end. Yet, it is in fact the most logical way. When someone takes a trip, the first step is determining the destination. It is the same with curriculum design. First, the intended outcomes should be established. The second step is to determine what skills must be learned in order to accomplish these educational outcomes. The third step is to determine what skills must be learned in order to be proficient in the skills required in step two and beyond. Every skill is based on other skills that were previously learned. By working backwards from the final goal, planners can create a sequence of objectives that have to be met to make the final goal possible.

Implementing a Subject-Centered Curriculum

ıla, or in Longstreet and Shane's (1993) words, knowl-
a, espoused by exogenists, are static in nature. New
l, but the core curriculum from the turn of the century
ʒenist tenets of behavioral psychology view the child
. that is a *tabula rasa* or a blank slate. That is to say, the
e child are present at birth, and the child begins to fill
ith the sensory experiences that surrounds it (Green,
nting the subject-centered curriculum is a matter of fill-
ⱱhat the school system deems important for students to

fluential writers about subject-centered curriculum was
ꞅ. Skinner. Skinner contended that teaching was not an
onsidered successful implementation of the curriculum
s: controlling the learning environment and using effec-
ⱱen that students are goal-oriented, one of the teacher's
inding out what will motivate them to learn. The sticker-
chool children of today give a clear example of this
n are reinforced to continue studying in order to keep
ιy complex learning task can be broken down into simple
ⱡte work was viewed as time-consuming but effective for
ιg.

Skinner also developed a machine that was the forerunner of individualized computer learning. Called "the teaching machine," it utilized rolls of paper with questions on them and a crank. Skinner strongly advocated individualized learning in this manner. His insistence that all instruction should end in a clearly definable purpose is perhaps his best legacy. Although far from the first to advocate such, he prescribed a clear scientific manner of doing so.

There are some disadvantages to a subject-centered curriculum. Critics are quick to point out that this approach leads to knowledge but not thinking; it results in knowledge of facts without the skills to reason. The "back to the basics" drive begun in the mid- to late-1970s led to a drop in thinking and writing skills. It ignored one of the fundamental aims of American education—exploration. By treating teachers as technicians rather than artists, the status of teachers was lowered both in the eyes of administrators and the public. Exogenism often seeks to make curricula "teacher proof," implying that because the teacher is only a technician, the well-built curriculum should be able to work effectively even if the teacher is incompetent.

Consumers of Processes

Just as the consumers of content were the learners, so it is with the consumers of processes. Children have cognitive and emotional needs. To thrive in the future, they will need flexible thinking skills.

Due to the enormity of the data, it would be impossible to cover everything in school. More importantly, with the mountain of new learning pouring into the culture, the child will need skills to interpret and understand these changes and what it means to adapt and survive in society. Learning to adapt to an ever-changing world will be vital to success.

Producers of Processes

Two of the chief producers of processes for the child are role models and the society at large. Society has grave and pressing needs. Whereas content tends to be subject-centered, processes tend to be child- or society-centered. More specifically, the endogenists strongly advocate concern for the maturational and cognitive processes of the child based upon the needs of the child or society. The progressivists tend to advocate for the child as a member of the society and are concerned with the child's needs from the society and society's needs from the child.

Beginning at the Beginning

One of the major complaints about "beginning at the end" is that the process of curriculum building can become very mechanical. In that no two schools are exactly alike, just as no two students are exactly alike, many child-centered educators are concerned about the curriculum drafted at the central office and distributed to all the schools in the district. To some, working from end to beginning is permissible as long as the goals are not so specific that teachers are prevented from molding the curriculum to their students' needs. To others, planning the curriculum in advance will invariably prevent curriculum building by teacher and student. In 1917, when the child-centered curriculum was in its prime, a laboratory school named the Modern School was begun at the

Lincoln School of Teachers College, Columbia University. To progressivists, it represented a highly successful school whose teachers worked tirelessly to build curricula in this manner. Based on thorough research conducted on the school by Dewey in the 1930s, Lincoln School students excelled in regular achievement tests. Yet, from its beginning until its demise in 1941, the Lincoln school never had a written curriculum.

Some progressivists point to the accomplishments of the Lincoln School to illustrate the advantages of building curriculum from the beginning. However, despite the wonderful accomplishments there, it must be pointed out that the Modern School was a small, laboratory school on the grounds of a college campus. Translating this to the public schools of an entire district may be more difficult. The average classroom teacher has neither the time nor the training to build curricula in this manner. Curriculum building by individual teachers or schools also has the potential for creating gross inconsistencies between schools with competent curriculum innovators and those without. Most curriculum specialists today and of tomorrow should not support this manner of curriculum building.

Implementing a Process-Centered Curriculum

In a very real sense, part of implementing processes is educational democracy in action. Unfortunately, the typical school of today has many teachers who are incapable or refuse to support a democratic system within their classroom. Dewey asserted that school was "democracy in microcosm." The child must be a "citizen" of the school, a decisionmaker and an accepted member of the student body.

CAUTIONS AND WARNINGS

There are many pitfalls to avoid in the process of curriculum development. With regard to the three sources of curriculum embodied in the Tyler Rationale, it is imperative that the balance between these three sources be maintained. In regard to Dewey's way of thinking, these were essential to the whole process. Dewey taught that none of the three could be deleted or ranked according to importance because they were all equally vital. Not only did he feel that the three sources of curriculum were of equal weight, he also insisted that how the three relate to one another was of the utmost importance. He warned that if this advice was not heeded, problems were sure to follow.

Knowing that a teacher's own performance is judged by the success rate of his or her students, there is a strong temptation to make the behavioral objectives too simple. Although this would assure high success rates, it will not enable the students to accomplish what they will need in the next phase of their academic life.

INTEGRATING THE CURRICULUM WITH CONTENT AND PROCESSES

Subject area content has always been a part of the curriculum. The key to integration, therefore, is to ensure that content is in part guided by awareness of the child's age-appropriate cognitive processes. Students cannot be expected to function ahead of what their own mental development will allow.

Additionally, the author contends that the traditionalist view that the purpose of school is to pass down core knowledge to the next generation will be insufficient in the future. The curriculum should reflect the need of the child to interpret and understand the desired knowledge and to use the wealth of new knowledge attained in the future.

Above all, the individual subject areas should be integrated. Strict separation of educational disciplines should be abolished. This will, in effect, promote the use of cognitive processes. Democratic education must not stop at learning the Pledge of Allegiance. It must be an integral part of the functioning of the school. In this way, the student gains not only knowledge of democracy but understanding of it as well.

THE CHALLENGES OF ASSESSING CURRICULUM PACING FOR CONTENT AND PROCESSES

As Skinner pointed out, his behaviorialist approach to education was easy to assess, and progress was simple to track. If all children were the same, establishing a speed at which material was covered would be a small matter. Naturally, children are different, and their mental and emotional processes and the pace at which they can digest new material varies greatly. Recognition of this often presents the teacher with a dilemma. While the teacher has learning objectives that the students must meet, one cannot teach faster than the students' ability to comprehend. If too much time is spent maximizing students' understanding of a particular point, the class may lack time to complete other educational goals.

Part of this problem can be resolved by "flexible pacing" as advocated by Daniel and Cox. In flexible pacing, students are grouped according to their ability rather than their age. In this way, students can advance through the curriculum at their own pace. However, flexible pacing cannot be used exclusively and for all subjects. Tanner and Tanner (1995) stated, "There are many desirable educational experiences and outcomes that do not lend themselves to a system of self-paced instruction" (p. 126).

MISSION STATEMENTS AND VISION STATEMENTS

These two terms are often used interchangeably. However, each has a unique purpose. A mission statement is a declaration of the unique goals and focus of a school or school district. Mission statements should be broad, simply worded, and as brief as possible. These should never exceed one page in length and must coincide with the mandates set down by the state or locality.

Vision statements, on the other hand, can be seen as a vision of the future for individual schools or districts. Vision statements work hand in hand with mission statements. These seek to give direction to the desired goals espoused in the mission statement. The vision statement does not in any way attempt to alter the mission statement. Rather, it seeks to fulfill and/or maintain these goals into the future. Once adopted, the contents of a mission statement should not be changed for an extended period of time.

Although Jerry J. Herman (1989), in his journal article *Site-Based Management: Creating a Vision and Mission Statement*, contends that the vision statement must be created first, the author tends to disagree and finds the planning model created by the College of DuPage in Illinois to be a more logical progression. In this model, the first step is to create the mission statement. In that the vision statement's purpose is to help direct the implementation of the mission statement and keep it on track in the future, it does not seem sensible for the vision statement to be created first.

Mission statements and vision statements are easier to write than they are to implement and maintain. Obviously, those most affected by these statements—faculty, students, parents, and the community—should be included in the creation process. This will engender a sense of ownership among these groups. This feeling that the vision and mission statements, in a sense, belong to them is crucial for implementation. The mission and vision statements should be the foundation of all school activities, particularly with regard to curriculum planning. Otherwise, these statements will lose the power to guide.

THE CHANGING ROLE OF TEACHERS IN CURRICULUM DEVELOPMENT

Originally, teachers were responsible for what is often termed the "processing" of curriculum, that is, the implementation or instruction of curriculum, not its creation. Generation was not the concern of teachers; it was the responsibility of the school board and/or the central office. Because of this, teachers were not trained in the skills of curriculum design and development. There was no need for them to have such training unless they wished to become a curriculum specialist. However, many teachers, particularly those who were more child-centered, complained that the curriculum decisions determined by the central office were out of step with the needs of their students. A growing number felt that the teachers themselves should have a voice in designing the curriculum.

Since the late 1970s, there has been a movement in the schools toward "site-based management." Site-based management (SBM) is a means of "powering down" or the devolution of certain powers from the central office to the schools themselves. Often coupled with SBM, but not always, is site-based curriculum design. Site-based curriculum design (SBCD) is the specific power granted by the state or central office for schools to create their own curriculum. More teachers are finally having a say in curriculum design, including design of the curriculum to fit the needs of their students.

On the other hand, this new "freedom" has created a great many problems. First of all, even though this duty has fallen to them, many teachers are still not adequately trained to design curriculum. Secondly, teachers are often forced to "make time" during the day or after school to meet to discuss and design various components of the curriculum. Thus, teachers are forced to do double duty, both creating and implementing curricula with insufficient time and training. Finally, one of the great concerns of many local educators is that, after building the curriculum, there might be insufficient funding to carry it out for implementation and further improvement.

CURRICULUM DESIGN TEAMS

In order to enact SBCD, schools establish teams of educators who are responsible for formulating the curriculum. Frequently, this is done by having teachers experienced in a specific subject area devise the curriculum for their particular discipline. In elementary schools, teachers of the same grade level meet and devise the curriculum for their program or grade level. The obvious problem with these approaches is a lack of macrocurricular perspective. There is scant integration of the various disciplines. There is inadequate farsightedness with regard to the curriculum progressing from grade level to grade level.

To counter this, some schools create a committee of teachers whose responsibility is to make sure that this integration and flow is taking place in the curriculum. Needless to say, the work of such committees would require a great expenditure of time. Considering the already hectic schedules of many classroom teachers, SBCD seems more burdensome than necessary.

Perhaps the most serious problem is the lack of competent curriculum specialists involved in the curriculum development process. This results in a disparity between the curriculum and what is actually taught in the classroom. One local school district relied heavily on curriculum specialists who traveled from school to school assisting curriculum design teams throughout the district. Unfortunately, due to financial cutbacks the number of specialists was sharply reduced. Design teams with insufficient training were forced to finish the work with minimal guidance. Needless to say, the results were not as good as had been expected.

BALANCING CONTENT WITH PROCESSES

Florante and Cecilia Parrenas (1990) assert that, due to the ever-increasing base of knowledge and information, the content taught to today's children will be outdated by the time they get to high school. Thus, content and process must be equally emphasized. They maintain that tomorrow's students will be more producers of knowledge. They urge educators to make the necessary changes in methods of instruction, regardless of how drastic, to help students be able to do just that.

In order to do this, it is essential that educators concentrate on HOW they expect students to learn as well as WHAT they are to learn. Subject matter and learning activities cannot be separated. Learning is inhibited by traditional methods that require students to mindlessly recall data they have read in textbooks or heard from the teacher but that does not tap into the students' thinking abilities. Students must be given sufficient opportunity to share their opinions and USE the data they have collected and analyzed.

FUTURISM AND A GREATER SENSE OF COMMUNITY

Educational futurism is a society-oriented philosophy. As its name implies, futurism is concerned about the future of society and education's power to impact it. Futurists are keenly aware of the great changes that have befallen civilization due to the ever-accelerating pace of technological advances. Societal changes once occurred over the course of a century; now they are happening in a handful of years. The traditionalist reaction to this is to cling to the standards and practices that have guided society for centuries. The futurists reject this as narrow-minded and, perhaps, even dangerous. To paraphrase futurist Harold

Shane, the industrial society may be on the verge of major changes that could rearrange the world as we have known it with incredible abruptness. With such unprecedented changes on the way, reliance on "tried and true" methods seems to be rather myopic. Successfully weathering this change will require a populace that is prepared to make a myriad of difficult decisions.

This is where "the greater sense of community" comes into play. Futurism is chiefly concerned with keeping society together. However, this desire is coupled with the knowledge that only a flexible, cooperative society can weather the changes that will surely confront it. The best way of achieving these ends is through education. To quote Longstreet and Shane, "the school's role is to develop skills and useful knowledge so that the members of the society can participate in the future directions of society as decision makers."

Unfortunately, curriculum designs currently in use do not prepare students for a future that is significantly different from the present. There is an almost innate tendency toward maintaining the status quo and denying the ability to have an effect upon it. Shane and Longstreet refer to this as "cultural inertia." It is this cultural inertia that could stifle the whole process of creating innovative strategies for coping with future societal changes.

The author believes strongly that flexible thinking, predicting, and cooperative decisionmaking ought to be made a part of school curricula. This would be particularly fitting for a nation, such as the United States, that prides itself on being guided by democratic principles.

THE AUTHOR'S OPINION

The philosophy underlying curriculum design is rarely explicitly stated or understood by the practitioners who practice under one or another of the paradigms described in this chapter. A wide range of educational philosophies are practiced in the schools of today. Identifying and understanding these will clarify the forces at work in the schools. One must also bear in mind the historical and social issues that have helped form some of these educational philosophies or affected how these belief theories have been interpreted and applied.

Because the philosophical bases for action in schools are often not apparent, conflicting theories often coexist, resulting in confusion of purpose and goals. The desire is strong now to better understand the educational purpose of the system of schooling and, therefore, to clarify the educational goals so that education in the United States can be restructured to best achieve those goals. The author believes the reform and restructuring that is required must be radical to fit the future. Education must change now to address the imminent needs of the future.

A SEMESTER ACTIVITY

A Futurist's Model is illustrated below. Much of the material is in outline format, and a limited number of examples are given. The idea of integrated threads or themes are interwoven throughout the model. As a class activity, complete the model, making modifications the class views as necessary. More detailed skills will be built in later chapters. Refer to these for assistance. Feel free to use other sources in completing the model.

Futurist's Model

Philosophy

As futurists, we believe we are moving from a centralized industrial age into a highly technological age focused on information and the individual. We feel that children should gain the necessary tools to discover their unique abilities to assist them in this new time period. These abilities include adaptability/flexibility, ability to identify and solve problems, and acceptance/diversity.

Adaptability/Flexibility

Children need to learn how to appraise and correctly assimilate new technologies and ways of thinking into their lives. At the same time, they need to remain resilient enough to refuse to accept all changes without estimating the consequences, but be flexible enough to test ideas that seem valuable.

Ability to Identify and Solve Problems

Being able to identify and solve problems is imperative in our ever-changing society. Students first need to gain the knowledge to recognize problems, then develop sound, qualitative and quantitative solutions. They must learn how to solve problems in any context and live with the outcomes to the best of their ability.

Acceptance/Diversity

Today's schools comprise students from diverse cultures. In order for students to be successful in school and in the everyday world, they need to learn how to accept differences and recognize the diverse backgrounds of others. Through multicultural teaching in subject areas, students will be exposed to many cultures and people. By learning about each other's similarities and differences, they will achieve greater understanding of themselves and each other.

Mission Statement

Our vision is to guide students along the career paths that best suit their aspirations and evolving individual skills. We hope to fulfill this through a multidimensional, multicultural, and pluralistic program and environment that will be adaptable to an ever-changing society.

Vision Statement

It is our vision to grow together to where our school structure becomes the model for the schools of the Twenty-first Century.

Level I Goals

Goal One: Adaptability

Upon completion of Grade 12 at Queen City Secondary School, the student has demonstrated the ability to adapt to a constantly changing environment in an ever-evolving world.

Goal Two: Higher Order Problem Solving

Upon completion of Grade 12 at Queen City Secondary School, the student has demonstrated:

1. the ability to identify the source of a problem in his or her environment and/or within himself or herself;
2. the ability to create realistic, adaptable solutions to problems facing him or her in a vastly changing world using sound judgement; and
3. the successful execution of a problem that shows applicable and quantitative results in which the effectiveness of the solution can be measured.

Goal Three: Acceptance/Diversity

Upon completion of Grade 12 at Queen City Secondary School, the student has demonstrated acceptance of and gained the desire to understand the diversity of various cultural backgrounds.

Level II Goals

Program Goals

Upon completion of each program area, the student has demonstrated the following:

IA. *Adaptability (Content)*   The ability to select and learn appropriate content

IIA. *Higher Order Problem Solving (Content)*   The ability to integrate the content and processes of each program area into a higher level of understanding

IIIA. *Acceptance/Diversity (Content)*   The ability to contrast and compare without bias the values and traditions of other cultures to his or her own

IB. *Adaptability (Social)*   The ability to adapt to and accept other points of view in an ever-changing society

IIB. *Higher Order Problem Solving (Social)*   The ability to recognize and analyze social issues in order to create equitable solutions

IIIB. *Acceptance/Diversity (Social)*   The ability to respond to various opinions through the development of diplomatic skills

IC. *Adaptability (Individual)*   The ability to adapt to various situations

IIC. *Higher Order Problem Solving (Individual)*   The ability to analyze and discover one's true identity

IIIC. *Acceptance/Diversity (Individual)*   The ability to accept the many cultures of a diverse society while continuing to focus on one's own individuality

Instructional Goals

In accordance with the program goals, students will:

IA. *Adaptability (Content)*
1. Develop skills in evaluating and analyzing content
2. Develop mastery of a variety of learning strategies and/or styles such as:
   a. Discussion
   b. Computer
   c. Inquiry
   d. Textbooks
3. Develop diplomatic/debating skills
4. Work cooperatively in a group using such skills as:
   a. Listening
   b. Play

        c. Procedure following

        d. Diplomatic behavior

        e. Debate

IIA. *Higher Order Problem Solving (Content)*

1. Develop the ability to decide which content skills and processes are best suited to particular problem solving contexts. Some abilities needed to perform:

    a. Ability to draw from previously learned skills and knowledge

    b. Ability to perform previously learned skills and knowledge

    c. Knowledge of several different content areas

2. Become adept at using skills from other content areas in new and different situations. To be able to do this, students should already:

    a. Understand how skills are interchangeable

    b. Have practiced overlapping content areas

3. Develop the ability to understand, learn, accept, and then integrate new information as part of a whole knowledge system.

IIIA. *Acceptance/Diversity (Content)*

1. Be able to identify personal and/or learned stereotypes and their sources. Skills needed include:

    a. Ability to distinguish between fact and fiction

    b. Ability to replace old stereotypes with new, accurate information

2. Develop investigational skills needed to reveal all angles of a situation. Included are the following:

    a. Library/Media research

    b. Interviewing

    c. Community involvement

3. Develop sound judgmental skills. Needed to perform sound judgment:

    a. The ability to see different points of view

    b. The ability to distinguish between fact and fiction

    c. Empathy

    d. A sense of fairness

IB. *Adaptability (Social)*

1. Develop skills to adapt to various points of view.

2. Develop acceptance skills to get along with and form relationships with those different from themselves. These skills include:

    a. Listening

    b. Questioning

    c. Understanding

    d. Planning

IIB. *Higher Order Problem Solving (Social)*   Develop analytical skills to create quantitative and qualitative solutions through the following skills:
    1. Mathematical
        a. Problem solving techniques
        b. Procedures
        c. Inquiry
        d. Discussion

IIIB. *Acceptance/Diversity (Social)*
    1. Develop skills that adjust and respond to different points of view through:
        a. Listening
        b. Discussion
        c. Cooperation
        d. Questions

IC. *Adaptability (Individual)*
    1. Develop skills in adapting to different situations, such as:
        a. Being exposed to many common situations
        b. Learning how to handle oneself in different situations
    2. Develop a mastery of different disciplines. Students should do as many of the following as possible:
        a. Enroll in academic classes
        b. Enroll in vocational classes
    3. Develop the ability to listen to those who are different from oneself

IIC. *Higher Order Problem Solving (Individual)*
    1. Develop skills to analyze different situations and learn how to create proper solutions.
    2. Learn about various career choices in order to be able to skillfully choose a good career path for oneself

IIIC. *Acceptance/Diversity (Individual)*
    1. Learn about the various cultures in our society. Skills needed include:
        a. Research and exploration skills
        b. Ability to replace previously learned stereotypes with new, accurate information
    2. Develop skills for discovering oneself, such as:
        a. Understanding one's true cultural background
        b. Understanding how one's cultural history interacted with other diverse groups' histories
    3. Develop skills to stand up for one's individuality. These skills include:
        a. Participation in debates
        b. Voicing one's opinion while respecting those of others

❖ ❖ ❖

SUMMARY

Various educational philosophies can guide and influence one's views of curriculum design. Patterns of design typically move from broad overall goals to very specific daily learning outcomes that the teacher endeavors to realize. Although macrocurriculum is traditionally the realm of the central office and microcurriculum that of the teacher, it is time for teachers to take a macrocurricular look at their work as well.

Subject content and processes are equally important entities. Striking a balance between them is crucial for successful instruction. Elevating one over the other generates a unique set of problems.

The role of the teacher is now in a state of change. This role must change to accommodate the great changes that are occurring in the society. Teachers are being asked to take stronger leadership roles and to become more team oriented with regard to their colleagues.

❖ ❖ ❖ DISCUSSION QUESTIONS

1. Discuss the difference between macrocurricular and microcurricular aspects of teaching. Is one more important than the other? What is the balancing point between the two? What sort of considerations would you categorize as macrocurricular or microcurricular?

2. If you were dean of the education department of a university, what courses would you require education students to take to prepare them for teaching in the twenty-first century?

3. Unfortunately, there are often differences between curriculum and how it is actually implemented. What are the reasons behind the discrepancy? What can be done to close the gap?

4. In what ways can we assure that we are not merely teaching the facts of a subject area, but also helping the students to become flexible thinkers and problem-solvers as well?

5. Interview a candidate running for the local school board. Have the candidate identify the three most critical needs for change in the school district. Ask him or her to describe how these changes can be accomplished.

6. Longstreet and Shane (1993) wrote, "the school's role is to develop skills and useful knowledge so that the members of the society can participate in the future directions of the society as decision makers." How must schools change in order to fulfill this responsibility?

7. How do you see yourself as a future teacher trying to meet the needs of students in a school structure that lacks direction and purpose?

❖ ❖ ❖   CLASS ACTIVITIES

1. Differences sometimes exist between the curriculum and how it is actually implemented. Make a collective list of the reasons for this discrepancy. Recommend what can be done to close the gap.

2. In what ways can we assure that we are not merely teaching the facts of a subject area, but also helping the students to become flexible thinkers and problem-solvers as well?

3. Pretend the class is composed of parents who have gathered to formulate five or six goals for the local school system. Construct these goals without using educational jargon.

4. Design a curriculum model based upon a chosen model and design a website for schools and teacher education programs.

❖ ❖ ❖   REFERENCES

Beauchamp, C. A. (1975). *Curriculum theory* (3rd ed.). Chicago, IL: Kagg.

Bobbitt, F. (1918). *The curriculum*. Boston: Houghton Mifflin.

Borman, S., & Levine, J. (1997). *A practical guide to elementary instruction: From plan to delivery*. Boston, MA: Allyn and Bacon.

Caswell, H. L., & Campbell, D. S. (1935). *Curriculum development*. New York: American Book.

Costa, A. (1991). *Developing minds: Programs for teaching thinking*. (Report No. CS 010 589). Alexandria, VA: Association for Supervision Curriculum Development. (ERIC Document Reproduction Services No. ED 332 167)

Green, M. (1989). *Theories of human development: A comparative approach*. Upper Saddle River, NJ: Prentice Hall.

Herman, J. (1989). *Site-based management: Creating a vision and mission statement*. NASSP Bulletin, National Association of Secondary School Principals. Reston, VA. (73 [519] 79–84).

Johnson, M. (1967). Definitions and models in curriculum theory. *Educational Theory, 17*(2), 127–140.

Longstreet, W., & Shane, H. (1993). *Curriculum for a new millenium*. Boston, MA: Allyn & Bacon.

Oliva, P. (1997). *The curriculum: Theoretical dimensions*. New York: Longman.

Parrenas, F. Y., & Parrenas, C. S. (1990). *Cooperative learning, multicultural functioning and student achievement* (Report No. UD 028 300). Chicago, IL. (ERIC Document Reproduction Services No. ED 337 540)

Sowell, E. (1996). *Curriculum: An integrative introduction*. Upper Saddle River, NJ: Merrill/Prentice Hall.

Taba, H. (1962). *Curriculum development: Theory and practice.* New York: Harcourt Brace Jovanovich.

Tanner, D., & Tanner, L. (1995). *Curriculum development: Theory into practice* (3rd ed.). Upper Saddle River, NJ: Merrill/Prentice Hall.

Tanner, L. (Ed.). (1988). *Critical issues in curriculum: Eighty-seventh yearbook of the National Society for the Study of Education.* Chicago, IL: University of Chicago Press.

Toffler, A. (1973). *The culture consumers: A study of art and influence in America.* New York: Random House.

Toffler, A. (1997). *Learning for tomorrow: The role of the future in education.* New York: Bantam Books.

Tyler, R. W. (1949). *Basic principles of curriculum and instruction.*

Webster's Collegiate Dictionary (10th ed.). (1996). MA: Merriam-Webster, Inc.

Wiles, J., & Bondi, J. (1997). *Curriculum development: A guide to practice* (5th ed.). Upper Saddle River, NJ: Merrill/Prentice Hall.

❖ ❖ ❖ SUGGESTED READINGS

Begler, E. (1993). Spinning wheels and straw: Balancing, content, process, and context in global teacher education programs. *Theory into Practice, 32,* 14–20.

Behar, L., & Ornstein, A. (1995). *Contemporary issues in curriculum.* Needham Heights, MA: Paramount Publishing

Brouillette, L. (1996). *A geology of school reform: The successive restructuring of a school district.* Albany, NY: State University of New York Press.

Buckland, M., & Dye, C. M. (1991). *The development of electronic distance education delivery systems in the United States: Recurring and emerging themes in history and philosophy of education.* Paper presented at the Mid-Western Educational Research Association, Chicago, IL.

California Distance Learning Program. (1997). (Available on-line: http://www.cdlp.rssd .k12.ca.us/.)

Christiansen, E. (1997). *Education alternatives: Home schooling.* (Available on-line: saludos.com.ed.homeschl.html.)

College of DuPage. (1993). *College of DuPage planning process: The foundation for decision making* (Report No. JC 930 268). College of DuPage, Glen Ellyn, IL. (ERIC Document Reproduction Services No. 357 786)

Christa McAuliffe Academy. (1997). (Available on-line: http://www.cmacademy.org.)

Doll, R. C. (1996). *Curriculum improvement, decision making and process* (9th ed.). Boston, MA: Allyn & Bacon.

Doll, W. E., Jr. (1993). *A post-modern perspective on curriculum.* New York: Teachers College Press.

Ediger, M. (1992). *Play as education in the school curriculum* (Report No. SO 022 277). (ERIC Document Reproduction Services No. ED 359 084)

Garrison, D. (1989). Distance education. In S. B. Merriam and P. M. Cunningham (Eds.), *Handbook of adult and continuing education* (pp. 221–232). San Francisco, CA: Jossey-Bass.

Hellgren, P. A. (1992). *Developing academic professionals through the Finnish teacher education curriculum* (Report No. SP 034 038). Helsinki Univ., (Finland) Dept. of Teacher Education. (ERIC Document Reproduction Services No. ED 350 269)

Henderson, J. G., & Hawthorne, R. D. (1995). *Transformative curriculum leadership.* Upper Saddle River, NJ: Merrill/Prentice Hall.

Hoffman, B. (1997). *Distance education: The elusive definition.* (Available on-line: http://www.distance-educator.com /hoffman,html.)

Holmberg, B. (1985). *Status and trends of distance education.* London: Croom-Helms.

Keegan, D. (1986). *The foundations of distance education.* London: Croom-Helms.

Lemlech, J. K. (1998). *Curriculum and instructional methods for the elementary and middle school* (4th ed.). Upper Saddle River, N.J.: Merrill/Prentice Hall.

Lieberman, A., & Miller, L. (1990, June). Restructuring schools: what matters and what works. *Phi Delta Kappan, 71,* 759–764.

McKenzie, J. (Ed.). (1992). *The fine art of paradigm busting and flexidigm breeding.* (Available on-line: http://fromnowon.org/FONNov.92.html.)

McNeil, J. D. (1990). *Curriculum: A comprehensive introduction.* HarperCollins Publishers.

Nathan, J. (1996). *Charter schools: Creating hope and opportunity for American education.* San Francisco, CA: Jossey-Bass.

Posner, G. (1995). *Analyzing the curriculum* (2nd ed.). New York: McGraw-Hill.

Rogus, J. (1990). *Developing a vision statement: Some considerations for principals.* NASSP Bulletin, National Association of Secondary School Principals; Reston, VA. *74*(523) 6–13.

Stahl, G. (1995). Adapt locally: Software assistance to locate and tailor curriculum posted to the internet. *Computer and Education, 24*(3), 237–246.

Steiner, V. (1997). *What is distance education?* (Available on-line: http://www .fwl.org/edtech/distance/html.)

Toffler, A. (Ed.). (1972). *The futurists.* New York: Random House.

Verduin, J. R., & Clark, T. A. (1991). *Distance education: The foundations of effective practice.* San Francisco. CA: Jossey-Bass.

PATHWAYS TO PROGRAMS

❖ ❖ ❖

6

THE ELEMENTARY SCHOOL: EARLY GRADES

Chapter Objective and Focus:

To present content and processes that are taught in Grades K, 1, and 2 in traditional and nongraded environments

---

Many of the recent reform efforts have focused on preschool and early childhood education. Educators realized that if students were allowed to move into the upper elementary grades without a strong foundation in reading, writing, and mathematics, opportunity to develop these critical basic skills later was significantly diminished. Although initial reaction to *A Nation at Risk* focused upon the plight of poorly prepared high school graduates, it was soon acknowledged that intervention must begin early. For some children, kindergarten may be too late.

THE HISTORY OF EARLY CHILDHOOD EDUCATION

Popular universal education had its beginnings five hundred years ago. Although the primary impact of the sixteenth century Reformation was religious, it had a lasting educational impact as well. Martin Luther (1483–1546), the father of the Reformation, believed that the authority of the Bible was supreme to the authority of the Catholic Church. He believed that each person should be free to work out his own salvation through a personal interpretation and understanding of the Scriptures. Luther, therefore, advocated that each person learn to read the Bible in his native tongue in order to establish individual beliefs. This marked the beginning of teaching and learning in the people's native language and the onset of support for popular universal education.

John Amos Comenius (1592–1670), a Moravian minister, also held educational convictions that arose from his spiritual beliefs. Comenius believed that it was one's duty to be educated to the fullest extent possible in order to understand religion. If education was so important, he concluded, it should begin when a child was young and most malleable to the positive influences of his parents and the church. Another of his fundamental spiritual beliefs was that people were essentially good. Therefore, Comenius believed that education should be a positive experience that encouraged autonomy and self-regulation. He also believed that education should follow the order of nature. Just as a young bird could not be persuaded to fly before it was ready, neither should a child be forced to learn before he was capable or before the necessary precursory learning was acquired. This belief was reflected in the later work of Montessori and Piaget and in the never-ending debate over school readiness. Another educational conviction that Comenius espoused was that learning was best achieved when the senses were involved and that, therefore, sensory learning was the foundation of all learning. This principle was also reflected and refined in the later work of Montessori and Piaget and in contemporary programs that stress manipulation of concrete objects.

John Locke (1632–1704) conceptualized the blank slate or *tabula rasa* view of children, and this and other views of his greatly influenced modern early childhood education. Congruent with his blank slate view of children was his belief that experience, not innate temperament, determined the nature of the individual. Because of this belief, sensory training became a prominent element of the application of his theory to early childhood education.

Jean-Jacques Rousseau (1712–1778) asserted that natural education, the abandonment of society's artificiality and pretentiousness, promoted and encouraged such qualities as happiness, spontaneity, and the inquisitiveness that was naturally associated with childhood. He believed that since maturation was natural, educators should promote the student's learning in symphony with innate timetables.

In 1837, Friedrich Froebel, known as the "Father of Kindergarten," established the first kindergarten in Blankenburg, Germany. Froebel devoted his life to developing a system of education for young children. Although during his lifetime Froebel was not personally or professionally successful, his contributions had a significant impact on the philosophy and form of contemporary early childhood education. He believed that the educator's roles, whether that person be teacher or parent, were to observe the child's natural progression of complexity of understanding and support continued learning through nurturing of the child's innate qualities for learning. Thus, the teacher was designer of experiences and activities and facilitator of a child's appropriate engagement in these experiences and activities so that the child could become a creative, contributing member of society (Morrison, 1993).

Contemporary educators have not always heeded the lessons of history. Although most kindergarten curriculum and program designs acknowledge the value of guided play in developing a child's innate qualities of learning, school and classroom practices do not always reflect this principle. Additionally, the value of these principles of learning must extend beyond kindergarten into the first and second grade programs. Kindergarten continues to be primarily a center-oriented setting with lots of activity and sound and movement. With first grade comes less activity and some pencil and paper activities. First grade students are often taken away from a center-type environment and placed into a more traditional classroom design. By second grade, students are relatively settled into the type of traditional textbooks, pencil, and paper routine that are standard in the following grades.

Just as the pendulum swings, so does the pattern of enactment of the principles of historically shaped educational theory and philosophy. The educational pendulum appears to be swinging in the direction of acknowledgment of the early childhood principles advocated by the founding fathers of education. Current early childhood reforms recognize the need for the development of a child's innate learning characteristics in a developmentally appropriate setting and time frame. At the same time, educators acknowledge that these early experiences and activities can have an increased "academic" focus through careful planning and implementation of developmentally appropriate activities and experiences that intentionally promote the development of basic literacy skills in reading, writing, and arithmetic.

DEVELOPMENTAL NEEDS AND INTERESTS

An understanding of child development is important for all teachers and imperative for early childhood educators. The foundation for all future learning is established before a child begins third grade. If the foundation is carelessly laid or appropriate materials are not used, it will not support continued learning. This foundation is prepared by engaging students in developmentally appropriate learning activities and experiences. For example, a child can be an effective reader in third grade if his initial reading instruction and experiences are developmentally appropriate. Once basic reading skills are established, continuing practice improves fluency, strengthens comprehension, and promotes critical and creative examination of learning and life experiences. However, if initial instructional experiences are not developmentally appropriate and do not build a strong foundation, no amount of later practice can completely overcome this early deficiency.

The focus of the effective lower elementary program (grades K–2) is the developmental needs and interests of the students. Hands-on and free exploration activities are the teaching methods that early elementary teachers often use to gain student interest. With this type of teaching tool, attention is focused on the fun of the activity instead of the actual educational value. Students are learning something while they are having a good time (Zahorik, 1996). However, educators must be cautioned to assure that these fun experiences and activities have a strong developmental base which prepares students for increasingly complex, symbolic, and ultimately abstract involvement with skills and content.

Younger students are also in the process of developing and acquiring many of the attitudes about learning, work, and study that will affect their continuing experience of schooling. It is in these early years that students decide whether they will love, like, or hate school (Zahorik, 1996).

Kindergarten

Four areas must be examined when considering the developmental needs and interests of kindergarten children. These major areas include social, emotional, physical, and cognitive needs. The social characteristics of kindergarten children at most times tend to be consistent. They play well with others, including those of the opposite sex. Children tend to have one or two best friends, but friendships may change rapidly. Play groups are not highly organized and are usually small. Quarrels and fights can be frequent but short lived. Children begin to become aware of sex roles as they progress in age and development.

Kindergarten children express their emotions freely and openly. Angry outbursts are common in the kindergarten classroom, especially early in the year as students adjust to this structured social environment, with children entering a more formal learning setting for the first time. Children feel affection for their teacher and seek approval. What an adult says to a child at this stage is important and personal; praise and positive, productive criticism are crucial elements of a teacher's interpersonal relationship with students.

Physically, these children are active and enjoy activity for its own sake. They have high energy levels and need to rest often. Their muscular development surpasses their skeletal development; therefore, they tend to have less developed fine motor skills and more developed gross motor skills. It can be difficult for them to focus their eyes on small objects, and hand-eye coordination may be imperfect. Boys are generally physically bigger, while girls are relatively more advanced in all other areas of development as well as in fine motor skills. Handedness is now established in children; most are right-handed (Biehler and Snowman, 1986).

Students in grades K through 2 have many developmental needs that must be met. Exemplifying the nature of the relationship that must exist between a developmentally appropriate curriculum and instruction is the area of fine motor skills. Young children aged four through six have not yet developed adequate coordination in their fingers and hands to grasp a pencil and control it enough to write; therefore, these students should use a developmentally appropriate writing instrument (a thicker pencil, crayon or marker). Also reflective of their developing fine motor skills, students need fine motor experiences that engage not only the fingers and hands, but also the arms, shoulders, and complete upper torso. Painting at an easel, tracing a peer on a large sheet of paper as he lies on the table, and using fingerpaint on a table-top provide this practice. Blocks, modeling clay, and cut-and-paste experiences provide the opportunity to strengthen fine motor skills.

Elementary children in the early grades respond well to activities that require manipulatives or a hands-on approach to learning.

According to Piaget, kindergartners are cognitively in the preoperational stage but moving toward the concrete operational stage. In the preoperational stage, from ages two to seven, children begin to represent their world with symbols, images, and drawings. They are concretely oriented in terms of successful engagement with experiences and oriented to sensory impression rather than cognitive generalization. Language development accelerates. They internalize events and are egocentric in thought and action. They may stick to their own rules in using language and in interpreting experiences. By the end of the stage they can use symbolic representation, and they can do mentally what they once did physically (Santrock, 1995).

Grades 1 and 2

To examine the needs and development of these children, the same four areas apply. At the social level, these children are selective in choosing friends. They are likely to have a more or less permanent best friend and even an "enemy." They enjoy organized games in small groups but tend to get overly concerned with rules or team spirit. Quarrels still occur frequently, but the weapons used are more often words than physical aggression. Boys and girls play together some; however, sex role identification is becoming stronger and children tend to identify more closely with peers of the same sex. They recognize their own sex roles and notice their distinct characteristics. Playing "doctor" is a developmentally appropriate, although maybe not a socially acceptable, activity.

First and second graders are still sensitive to criticism and ridicule. They have difficulty adjusting to failure, therefore praise continues to be important. They want to please the teacher. At this age, children are becoming sensitive to the feelings of others.

The continuing physical development of these children is evident. They are still active, but energy may be released in nervous pursuits such as nail biting, hair chewing, and normal fidgeting. Children still need rest periods to balance mental and physical exertion. Large muscle control is still superior to fine motor coordination. Many children, especially boys, have trouble using a pencil. They have difficulty focusing on small objects or print. They have enormous control of their bodies and develop confidence in their skills, yet bone growth is not complete so bones and ligaments cannot control heavy pressure. These children grow up to 2½ inches per year and gain up to 5 pounds (Biehler and Snowman, 1986).

Cognitively, first and second grades are in transition from the preoperational to the concrete operational stage. The concrete operational stage lasts approximately from age seven to age eleven. Children can perform operations and internal mental actions instead of physical ones. Logical reasoning replaces intuitive thought as long as it is applied to concrete examples. Children need to have something to see or hold because they are unable to think abstractly. They are eager to learn, like to talk more than write, and because of their literal interpretations they love to "tattle." They are concretely oriented and are beginning to understand generalization and issues of reversibility. Teachers must be aware of sex differences in certain abilities and in overall experiences (Santrock, 1995).

Children go through a tremendous period of change at these three grade levels. This is a period of intense developmental maturation mentally, socially, physically, and emotionally. If children are to have an effective early formal learning experience, attention must be given to their developmental characteristics in the design of curriculum and program.

THE EARLY CHILDHOOD CURRICULUM

Early childhood teachers instill in students all the fundamental educational skills that they will need to progress in school. For example, in the lower primary grades, teachers focus on letter recognition and sounds, blends, digraphs, short and long vowel sounds, and basic sight word vocabulary. These are necessary prerequisites to successful reading. In math, students are taught basic numeration skills and number words, how to match and make numeral sets, patterning, sorting, and classifying, one more, one less, in between, and simple addition and subtraction facts.

Teachers also teach important educational values to these students. The values of responsibility, honesty, effort, and respect should be modeled and developed through the experiences children have in the classroom. Teachers accomplish this while also acting as parent, guardian, friend, nurse/doctor, policeman, disciplinarian, and social worker. Early childhood teachers have one of the most critical roles in education, that of building a strong foundation on which a successful educational "career" may be built.

National, State, and Local Direction

Several presidents have spoken in favor of national standards for education. Several national educational organizations have developed standards for their discipline. However, widespread public support for the continuing development and implementation of national standards is absent. As stated in Chapter One, in 1990, President George Bush and many state governors adopted six national education goals for the year 2000 in their plan titled America 2000. They included (1) improvements in school readiness skills, (2) higher high school graduation rates, (3) curriculum mastery, (4) greater math and science achievement, (5) improvement in adult literacy and skills, and (6) reduction in drug abuse and violence levels. The goals lacked the governmental, public, and private enterprise support that was required to give rise to real reform. In his national education plan called Goals 2000, President Bill Clinton returned these six goals and added two more: (1) providing the staff development needed to promote professional excellence, and (2) increasing parental involvement.

The United States is far behind other developed nations in achieving educational excellence. One of the contributing factors is the absence of a universally adopted national curriculum. If the United States is to make *national* gains in education, the development of a national curriculum may be necessary. However, national diversity, culturally, ideologically, and socio-economically, may forestall the development of or perceived need for a national curriculum. It will be difficult to develop a specific curriculum appropriate for and acceptable to all Americans.

National Curriculum Initiatives

Although most state and local governments have established standards of education, many educators advance the need for national standards. In the National Benchmark Goals, produced by the Department of Education (1995), all children are expected to gain competency the areas of life skills, foreign language, health, physical education, geography, art, history, language arts, math, and science. These recommendations are not as explicit as the state and local guidelines, but do outline the expectations for learning that every child in America should acquire.

The life skills standards comprise four basic areas: (1) thinking, (2) reasoning, (3) working with others, and (4) self-regulation. Thinking and reasoning are acquired through the understanding of logic and reasoning, problem solving and identifying similarities and differences, each at a level of complexity appropriate for the particular grade. Working with others stresses the ability to work within a group of diverse individuals, the demonstration of leadership skills, and cooperatively working together for a desired outcome in a setting in which everyone contributes. For a child to be self-regulated, he must set and manage goals and maintain a good self-concept. Goals for young children are general, such as brushing teeth twice a day, but achieving these goals is critical for mastery of the following, more complex goals. Life skills are a starting point for kindergarten through second grade children. Children begin achieving these goals by practicing the basics and develop more complex life skills as they grow older.

In an integrated program, the development of foreign language skills reinforces learning about diverse groups of people and how to work together with peers of different cultures. Most school systems offer one to three different foreign languages. One national goal is that citizens learn a second language. Children learn to communicate through basic vocabulary, to listen, read, and write in the target language while continuing linguistic development in their native language. Early childhood students would learn about weather, foods, and animals in the target language just as they would in the regular classroom setting for their grade level.

In kindergarten through second grade, children often learn about health in their physical education classes. At the ages of five through eight, these children focus on the development of gross motor skills then go on to master fine motor skills. They learn to play ball, catch, run, jump and do various activities that help their gross motor development. To develop their fine motor skills, children learn how to manage a bat or tennis racket to develop hand-eye coordination. They learn how to select nutritional foods in the development of healthy eating habits, wash their hands before eating, cover their mouths when coughing, and use the bathroom properly. These skills begin their journey down the road to a healthy lifestyle and are emphasized and expanded upon as they grow and progress throughout the school years.

Children are also given opportunities to develop and value artistic and musical abilities. The main purposes are to establish early an interest in the arts to assist children in developing and appreciating the connections among the various art forms and disciplines and provide a variety of means of expression of ideas, values, and experiences.

The early childhood student should learn basic movements in dance, how to sing alone and within a group, and read simple music notes. At this age, children tend to enjoy dance and music. It provides the opportunity to be creative and expressive and to give their busy minds a rest from the normal structured classroom. Children also learn how to be expressive and active through drawing and painting in the visual arts. They must learn basic symbols and colors, but, most importantly, they learn to express their creativity. Not all trees have to be green and brown. Trees can be purple if imagined that way.

Early childhood students study the basic core areas of education, geography, history, language arts, math, and science. Geography standards are simple at this level. In the early childhood grades, children learn to read a map and identify certain countries. They begin by learning about their neighborhoods and communities. Developmentally, concrete operational students need direct experiences with the subjects of instruction. Learning will expand to include the state, the country, the continent, and the world as students become developmentally ready to approach geographical concepts symbolically and abstractly. They learn about the basic structure of the earth and the environment. This learning extends to how their actions impact the environment of their neighborhood and community.

History and, more inclusively, social studies, increase students' awareness of their world, their nation, and their state, giving them fundamental understanding of their own society and others, both past and present. The ultimate goal of social studies is to provide students with a global understanding of the influence of a society's history, culture, economic structure, government, and social institutions which will impact their ability to be effective problem solvers, decisionmakers, planners, and civic participants. As with geography, learning begins within the domain of the family and extends to the community in the early childhood grades.

Language arts and mathematics are the two most essential areas of education at any level and in any form of government, local or national. The acquisition of basic literacy competency in communication arts and math prepares the student to effectively apply these basic concepts and skills to all other areas of learning.

An effective early literacy curriculum directs a program that emphasizes listening, reading, writing, and viewing skills development, language development, and appreciation for learning. The new basics are congruent with a philosophy that acknowledges that literacy is a social and linguistic process as well as a cognitive one. These basics include establishment of personal relevance for these skills and balance in curriculum design and instructional implementation. Specifically, a curriculum should be designed with the realization that a successful early literacy experience is built upon print awareness, alphabetic knowledge, and phonemic awareness which is fostered in an atmosphere that allows students to learn about the written language through active engagement in reading, writing, and discussion with others and provides practice of skills and strategies in meaningful context.

A firm mathematics foundation is built upon concrete and personally meaningful experiences. The early childhood student should experience math physically by exploring spatial relationships within the world around him, manipulating real objects to give meaning to numbers and operations, engaging in experiences that illustrate the relationships between mathematical concepts, and applying their learning in meaningful contexts. Children who internalize mathematical concepts through active engagement with real objects and meaningful experiences are prepared for symbolic and abstract application of these concepts in later grades.

The science curriculum should emphasize integration of science goals in order to prepare scientifically literate individuals. This implies an understanding of basic science concepts and the scientific processes of reasoning. Experiences should promote a positive attitude towards science and contribute to its understanding. Early childhood education focus should be upon introduction and practice of the skills that these students are developmentally prepared to master, including observation, classification, using numbers, communicating, measuring, and predicting. Emphasis should be on the areas of earth, life, and physical sciences. Learning should be integrated by including reading, writing, listening, and math experiences that complement attainment of the science goals.

National standards are now available in many content areas. A national mandate to use these standards does not exist. However, as states assess the appropriateness of state standards, the recommendations of national organizations are carefully studied and often used as the foundation for state directives. As increasing attention is given to the effectiveness of public education in preparing students for an information-based society, this author hopes standards will evolve from a futuristic philosophy that prepares children for the uncertainty the future holds.

State Curriculum Initiatives

Children in kindergarten through the second grade should learn the same basics of education that the national standards propose, but state and local requirements are much more specific. Most state school boards suggest that children in the early elementary grades receive instruction in four major areas—English/Language Arts, Math, Science, and Social Studies—along with music, physical education, art, and foreign language as supplements to their school week. Local districts use the state standards or convert the state standards to a local format. Some are detailed and thematic in nature while others closely mimic the state standards. State standards look at instruction and learning in grade strands, K–2, 3–5, 6–8, and 9–12. Some districts have used the state standards as a basis for grade level standards to ensure that students will learn and be able to perform properly at their own grade level. By setting these standards, a child's progress can be monitored not only by teachers and administration but also by their parents or guardians. Through class work, homework, projects and special assignments, the child's progress is made easier to follow.

Every state and many local school systems have requirements that must be met by students. The main focus of the K–2 curriculum lies in the area of communication literacy. This includes listening, speaking, reading, writing, and viewing. These five communication processes build upon and support one another. When students are developing skills in listening comprehension, they are also improving reading comprehension. Early experience with and mastery of these basic literacy skills are imperative for continued school success (NCDPI, 1995).

Many states strive to establish a uniform curriculum that prepares its young citizens for the future. Historically, American schools have prepared students to join an *industrialized* economy and become contributing citizens in their community. However, the challenge has become to prepare students for a rapidly changing world. Students must be prepared to function in a global economy, to understand and operate complex communication and information systems, and to apply higher level thinking skills to make decisions and solve problems. This challenge has been extended to all public and private education providers and is reaching into the arenas of preschool education and the home.

The main priorities of the state's literacy program are language development and the development of literacy skills along with the desire to use those skills that will endure for a lifetime and to promote a lifelong thirst for learning. The Standard Course of Study reflects a futuristic philosophical intent of equipping students with the level of literacy needed to participate as an informed and effective citizen in a democratic society, to function effectively in the world of work, and to realize personal fulfillment.

Language development is the first priority. Humans are uniquely able to communicate in a spoken and written language. This allows for the expression of the human spirit, the development of ethical responsibility, and the ability to interact with and influence others. The use of language in a reflective, logical, and creative manner allows one to examine and clarify values, mores, and beliefs in attempts to communicate thoughts and ideas to others.

English/Language Arts

Many states call for a balanced approach to beginning literacy instruction. In a balanced reading program, teachers should be constantly aware of students' individual needs and progress. A balanced reading program includes direct instruction to scaffold learning and support as students extend their instruction through functional reading and writing. A balance of instructional strategies and activities should exist in the classroom. The state advocates modeled, shared, guided, and independent reading experiences as well as direct instruction. Children should spend time in individual, small group, and whole group direct instruction to support literacy needs. Phonics instruction should be designed to fit individual needs, integrated into the daily literacy experiences of students, and balanced with the emphasis upon comprehension, fluency, and writing.

The formal early childhood English/Language Arts program is based upon the concept of emergent literacy. Emergent literacy includes the factors of print awareness, alphabetic knowledge, and phonemic awareness. The emergent literacy curriculum design was based upon acknowledgment that (1) literacy development begins early in life, long before formal instruction; (2) reading and writing are interrelated and develop together; (3) children learn about written language through active engagement in reading, writing, and discussion with others; (4) to help children internalize skills and strategies as an integral part of reading and writing processes, these should be practiced within a meaningful context; and (5) the functions of literacy are an integral part of the learning process.

Reading is much more than sounding out words. It is a complex process that requires the coordination of cues as sources of information: sound/symbol relationships, syntax, semantics, and context. States have developed early childhood reading standards to assure that comprehension is given a balance of attention in the early childhood classroom. As an element of the standards, characteristics of a proficient reader during the process of reading any text include engaging in reading as a dynamic, interactive process of constructing meaning. This process includes preparation, engagement, and response. Before reading, proficient readers (1) preview the text; (2) activate and build upon background knowledge; (3) set purpose for the activity; (4) focus attention on the task; and (5) make predictions about the content. During the reading process, proficient readers (1) check their understanding by paraphrasing the author's words; (2) monitor comprehension by using context clues; (3) integrate new information with existing knowledge; (4) reread and revise their purpose, predictions, and understanding; (5) use a "fix-up" strategy when they do not understand; (6) give complete attention to the task; and (7) persevere with difficult text. After reading, proficient readers (1) summarize what has been learned; (2) reflect on and evaluate the information and ideas in the selection; (3) respond and make applications of the information and ideas; (4) seek additional information, if needed; and (5) decide if they have achieved their purpose.

This comprehensive reading program for an early childhood classroom provides teachers with direction in the types of instruction they should use, the processes of reading they should teach, and the reading competencies students should learn to use effectively as a result of immersion in this program. This comprehensive model recognizes the child's development of language through both direct instruction and contextual learning, and through both selective skill activities and extensive interaction with varied print materials. Young readers must experience success in every one of the components of this model. Proficient readers process these components automatically and simultaneously. Because reading is essentially a dynamic thinking activity in which the reader interacts with text to create a meaningful understanding of the writing, good readers seek to identify meaning.

A balanced model of reading for early childhood classrooms that immerses students in literacy should include a continuum of skill and process development incorporating the following elements:

- Engagement and motivation—reasoning for appreciation of reading;
- Emergent literacy—concepts about print, letter knowledge, phonemic awareness, and understanding of the alphabetic principle;
- Word recognition—phonics, decoding, sight word development, spelling development, and appreciation of morphemes;
- Vocabulary and concept development—dictionary use, inferring meanings from context, proper usage, shades of meaning, and general knowledge;
- Comprehension—understanding narrative and expository text;
- Strategies used by good readers—developing a system for learning; and
- Fluency—automatic word recognition, good oral reading, and good silent reading.

The model should include planned direct instruction, contextual reading, and guided reading. These types of instruction are spiraled in a classroom where children experience immersion in reading and writing, and all are needed in the balanced reading program. Students should be taught to use graphophonic, semantic, and syntactic information acquiring meaning from text.

Examples of how the scope and sequence of early childhood curriculum standards were developed in the state of North Carolina are shown in Table 6.1.

TABLE 6.1
North Carolina Standards and Grade Level Benchmarks

Curriculum Standards	Kindergarten Benchmarks	First Grade Benchmarks	Second Grade Benchmarks
Decoding and Word Recognition	Recognizes most beginning consonant sound-letter associations in one-syllable words	Uses phonics knowledge of sound-letter relationships to decode regular one-syllable words when reading words and text	Uses phonics knowledge and structural analysis to decode regular multi-syllable words when reading text
Spelling and Writing	Represents spoken language with temporary and/or conventional spelling	Applies phonics to write independently, using temporary and/or conventional spelling	Correctly spells, using previously studied words and spelling patterns, in one's own writing
Language, Comprehension, and Response to Text	Connects information and events in text to experiences	Elaborates on how information and events connect to life experiences	Connects and compares information across expository selections to experience and knowledge

Mathematics

As in English/Language Arts, the Math curriculum in the early childhood grades focuses upon literacy. Mathematical literacy implies that a student is a problem solver, is confident in his or her ability to do mathematics, is able to communicate and reason mathematically, and values mathematics. Children in the early childhood grades should have opportunities to participate in activities conducive to developing mathematics concepts. The major emphases in this grade range should be placed on activities which engage the learner physically in exploring spatial relationships with the world around him, manipulation of real objects, experimentation which leads to the discovery of numerical and geometrical relationships, and applications which allow students to use numbers to solve problems.

As with the scope and sequence of English/Language Arts, the scope and sequence of the Math curriculum develops logically and in a developmentally sound manner through expanding current knowledge and extending learning into more complex related concepts. For example, in regard to Classification, Pattern, and Seriation, a kindergarten student should be able to describe likenesses and differences; sort by a given attribute and describe his reasoning for his classification; and identify and describe patterns and copy and continue simple patterns. A first grader should be able to describe objects by their attributes and compare and order those objects; sort by one or more given attributes and explain sorting rules; and copy and continue more complex patterns and translate these patterns into different forms. A second grader should be able to compare and describe similarities and differences; classify by more than one attribute and describe rules used in sorting; and identify classification and patterning in the environment.

Science

Five major program goals are generally found in science standards: (1) nature of science; (2) process skills; (3) manipulative skills; (4) attitude towards science; and (5) concepts. Teachers are expected to teach these goals in an integrated fashion. Science standards are also designed to ensure that students become scientifically literate, i.e., understand basic science concepts and the scientific process of reasoning and continue to learn and think logically. Kindergarten through second grade teachers are encouraged to integrate science within all content areas. The emphasis in kindergartens is on readiness skills that help refine and develop the child's sensory mechanisms through opportunities to observe and experience the properties of matter such as color, size, shape, texture, smell and weight through experiences with plants, animals, and numbers. In first and second grade, these same goals are emphasized and experiences become formal though still concrete.

Social Studies

The social studies goals of many states are correlated to the National Council for the Social Studies *Standards.* The primary purpose of social studies is to help young people develop the ability to make informed and reasoned decisions for the public good as citizens of a culturally diverse, democratic society in an interdependent world. At the early childhood level, the program introduces children to major concepts and generalizations from history and engages them in an integrated study of the individual and group (K), the homes and school (1st), and the neighborhoods and communities (2nd). Standards are designed to provide students with a generalized conceptual base which is relevant to their experiences that they can employ as they later engage in more sophisticated examination of the perspectives of other children in other places and times.

Excerpts from the North Carolina Social Studies Standards Framework in Table 6.2 illustrate how the major goals are considered from different perspectives, the manner in which children are exposed to increasingly complex examination of these goals, and how conceptual instruction is used to build the knowledge and experience base on which future learning is grounded.

TABLE 6.2
North Carolina Social Studies Framework

Kindergarten	First Grade	Second Grade
Goal 2. The learner will infer that individuals and families are alike and different	**Goal 2.** The learner will infer that individuals and families are alike and different	**Goal 2.** The learner will infer that individuals, families, and institutions in neighborhoods and communities are and have been alike and different
2.1 Describe aspects of the family	2.1 Describe the roles of individuals in the family	2.1 Distinguish similarities and differences between oneself and other family members
2.3 Compare one's family life with that of another child	2.3 Compare one's family life with that of a child living in another culture	2.2 Describe similarities and differences among families in different neighborhoods and communities
Goal 9. The learner will apply basic economic concepts to individuals and families	**Goal 9.** The learner will apply basic economic concepts to home and school	**Goal 10.** The learner will apply basic economic concepts to neighborhoods
9.2 Distinguish between wants and needs	9.3 Distinguish between goods and services	10.5 Distinguish between goods produced and services provided in neighborhoods

Source: North Carolina Department of Public Instruction, 1997.

MODELS OF INSTRUCTION AND EVALUATION

The Nongraded School Curriculum

The nongraded school was established in the 1930s but did not become popular until the 1950s. In a nongraded school, students progress through the curriculum at their own pace. No grade level distinctions are made in curriculum, instruction, or assessment. The basic areas of curriculum that are taught in traditional graded schools are taught, but in an intentionally integrated fashion. Students can study and achieve at their own pace, one that is more comfortable to them and not as rigid as the grade level system. This program design allows opportunity for learning to be developmentally specific to individual student needs. If a student can learn at a more accelerated pace in one subject area than another, his instructional program will reflect that. It is permissible for students to work at their own pace and complete levels of curriculum without worrying if they will pass to the next grade as in a graded system. Student progress is measured by tasks completed and the way that content and skills were learned, not by grades or a rating system. All children are placed on a level playing field because the factor of time becomes a variable rather than an absolute as is the case in graded programs (Lemlech, 1994).

This method of schooling works well for teachers because, by reason of its design, it gives teachers permission to place primary emphasis on the student rather than on the curriculum. Teachers are free to be creative and expressive in their teaching. This encourages students to be creative in their learning as well, without being restricted to the expectations of a specific grade level curriculum. Instructional materials are selected to meet students' needs, not grade level recommendations, giving more freedom to the teachers and allowing the students to use a variety of materials and teaching methods (Beach & Reinhartz, 1997).

One of the disadvantages of this system is the difficulty encountered in placing students at an appropriate starting level. Upon entry, students are given standardized math and language tests to establish individual learning plans which address their specific strengths and needs.

Statistical Advantages

- The nongraded students perform 58 percent better on academic achievement tests than graded school children.
- The benefits of this type of schooling increase the longer the children have nongraded experiences.
- Certain at-risk children (African-American boys in particular) learn better in a nongraded curriculum.
- Standardized testing results tend to favor nongrading as opposed to the normal graded school system. (Beach & Reinhartz, 1997)

Multigrade and Multiage Classrooms

Multigrade and multiage classrooms are more evident in the early childhood grades than in the upper elementary setting. A multiage classroom is defined as a setting in which students from two or more grades are taught by one teacher at the same time (Veenman, 1995). These students concentrate on their respective curriculums, but have opportunities for review or advancement by being exposed to all curriculums. Students generally spend up to three years with the same teacher. This is one of the more significant differences between a multiage classroom and a combination class, which is generally formed out of the need to limit class size when adjoining grades have memberships that do not match state-mandated student-teacher ratios. Multiage classes are formed deliberately to enhance student achievement. Multigrade classes are basically the same; however, these classes are formed for administrative or economic reasons.

There are many advantages to multiage grouping. One major advantage is that it allows students the freedom to work at their own pace and advance through the stages of academics in a fashion similar to, but not the same as, nongraded education. Instruction is individualized. Students have a chance to form relationships with a greater diversity of children, enhancing opportunity to strengthen a sense of belonging, support, security, and confidence in the development of interpersonal skills. Teacher-student relationships can have a positive impact on attitudes about learning and the continuity and intensity of instruction since, after an initial period of getting to know one another, the student-teacher relationship can focus on meeting student needs for a period of two to three years without change.

Of course, all methodologies have disadvantages. Some teachers feel that one of the drawbacks of the multiage classroom is that it requires more planning and preparation. These teachers also state that not enough time and attention is given specifically to subject area content. In a 1986 study, teachers identified the following disadvantages: increased workload, increased planning for individualized instruction, and lack of opportunity to reflect on the teaching activities of the day. In the same study, rural communities were found to be more accepting of multigrade and multiage classrooms than metropolitan communities (Veenman, 1995).

Alternative Intra-Classroom Models

Another classroom model currently in use is productive small groups, also known as cooperative learning groups. Through this instructional model, opportunity is available to provide direct instruction and guidance in small groups to facilitate the development of higher-order thinking skills, prosocial behavior, and interracial acceptance. Small groups offer opportunities for active learning that are essential for authentic achievement (Cohen, 1994).

Reciprocal teaching is another way to set up a classroom to enhance learning. Reciprocal teaching is defined as an instructional approach that features guided practice in applying simple, concrete strategies to the task of text comprehension. Studies using this method show increased comprehension in many subject areas (Rosenshine & Meister, 1994).

The most frequently used approach to enhance instruction is integration. Of the alternative models described here, this is the most commonly used model in the early childhood classroom. Integration encourages students to discern connections between the various subject areas. It also is time efficient. Given the many roles an early childhood teacher assumes, it seldom seems there is enough time for everything. Integration allows the teacher to address all curriculum areas while concentrating on a central theme. For example, if the theme were animals, the teacher would integrate all related subject area skills and content to the theme of animals. There is no "math time" or "reading time." Students are involved in a unit of instruction often initiated with a big book experience. Through the accompanying discussion, the teacher finds out what students already know about the subject matter and what they want to know. It focuses on building upon students' prior knowledge (Evertson, 1989).

Above are just a few of the many classroom models used by teachers. The best teachers employ a combination of these models to ensure success of every student.

Instructional Precautions

The most critical precaution any teacher must take is to assure that teaching and learning are not mutually exclusive ventures. Teachers must provide instruction just above the child's comfort zone without reaching his frustration level. Professional judgment based upon understanding of child development and curriculum expectations should be used when adapting and changing the instruction to meet the child's needs (Wong, 1991).

When considering the education of the early childhood student, a teacher must understand the impact of developmental readiness and behavior on learning. In kindergarten, children express emotions freely. They can be lovable and difficult, often moving from one extreme to the other.

Kindergarten through second grade children are enthusiastic and imaginative partners in learning. They direct their energy toward mastering knowledge and intellectual skills. They can be made to feel competent and successful or incompetent and unproductive. How the teacher interacts with her students and engages them in instructional experiences and activities will impact children's sense of self-worth, self-discipline, and responsibility (Santrock, 1995).

Although a teacher should be sensitive to what occurs in the classroom, she must remain cognizant of the impact of home and community circumstances on a child's school experience. A teacher must remember that to act as a positive change agent in the life of a child, she must first accept the child as an individual.

Educational Technology

Educational technology is no longer an educational novelty or a trend which will eventually be superseded by other trends. Technology is now an educational necessity. Students without daily opportunity for computer experiences are considered to be at an educational disadvantage. Computers have moved out of the lab and into the classroom where they have become a valuable teaching tool and motivator. Students and teachers can design and use graphics, data bases, and spreadsheets, "surf" the Internet, and communicate with peers and experts anywhere in the world. A more recent technology development that has become available to educators is multimedia. Multimedia simply means the presentation of material through any combination of media such as video, computor, spoken word, written word, still images, and various hands-on materials. With the addition of multi-media capability, the computer can provide a variety of opportunities in instructional presentation and alternative assessment.

Most states and many local districts have technology standards. In North Carolina, kindergarten students are expected to identify the computer as a machine that helps people to work and play, identify the major physical components of a computer, and demonstrate its correct use. First and second graders are expected to continue to develop their understanding of important issues of a technology-based society and computer ethics by identifying uses of technology at home, at school, and in the community and demonstrating respect for the computer work of others and the right of individual ownership of created computer work. These students will demonstrate increased knowledge and skills in the use of computer technology by becoming increasing familiar with special keyboard functions and terminology, demonstrating correct use of hardware and software, and demonstrating beginning word processing techniques.

North Carolina has initiated a statewide program that will place computers in almost every public school in the state. State technology standards require a minimum level of competence before a student can graduate from high school. New teachers now have to pass state level tests showing their level of computer competency in order to receive certification. Computers have become the wave of the future. These tools of technology are quickly gaining favor as important learning tools in education (North Carolina Public Schools, 1997).

Instructional Evaluation

The nongraded curriculum, multiage classroom, productive small group, reciprocal teaching, and integrated instruction provide opportunity for an evaluation technique described as nongraded. This technique moves away from the traditional system of grading (A+, 84, 76) towards a performance-based assessment in which the students apply what they have learned instead of memorizing for the test. This type of evaluation system allows students to produce, not reproduce, knowledge that is relevant to their lives through inquiry. It allows them to achieve in ways that are of value to them and society. It provides opportunity for students to participate in meaningful discussions, to present ideas to the class through a variety of media, and to work independently and with other students (Duis, 1995).

The most common form of nongraded assessment is the use of a student portfolio. This concept actually originated in the field of the arts as a means by which artists could share their talent. It has entered the academic world as a means through which students demonstrate progress towards or mastery of a concept. Portfolios allow for demonstration of not only facts but also how the students can use those facts. This vehicle of authentic assessment also includes students' reflections on the quality of their work. Portfolios contain a collection of work done over time so that students' growth can be evaluated in a variety of domains, such as writing skills, reading, language, and knowledge of content areas. This type of assessment is ongoing and evidence of change is an important element in the process (Waterhouse, 1993).

Another nongraded evaluation method available to early childhood educators for measuring performance and progress is the rubric. Rubric assessment provides *quantitative* data that are based upon selected *qualitative* criteria. A rubric is a guide for judging a student's performance or work product. A point system is derived and students receive a point as a grade. Students are assessed only on what they can do (Schmoker, 1996). Some states have designed an observation matrix for on-going assessment and end of the year evaluation of student progress in mathematics. Student proficiency is quantitatively stated based upon learning characteristics defined by a rubric. See, for example, Figure 6.1.

FIGURE 6.1
First Grade Observation Matrix for On-Going Assessment and End of Year Evaluation

Performance Indicator	**Problem-Solving**
Level IV: *Above grade level*	
• consistent performance beyond grade level • works independently • understands advanced concepts • applies strategies creatively • analyzes and synthesizes • shows confidence and initiative • justifies and elaborates responses • makes critical judgments • makes applications and extensions beyond grade level • applies Level III competencies in more challenging situations	• explores different methods of solving problems, using a variety of strategies • initiates, plans and carries out problem solving tasks, evaluating results • uses mental math and makes reasonable estimates • uses calculator as a tool • solves spatial visualization problems • describes process to solve problems • solves simple logic problems
Level III: *On grade level*	
• exhibits consistent performance • shows conceptual understanding • applies strategies in most situations • responds with appropriate answer or procedure • completes tasks accurately • needs minimal assistance • takes appropriate risks • makes applications • exhibits fluency • shows some flexibility in thinking • works with confidence • recognizes cause and effect relationships • applies models and explains concepts	• uses calculator with situations beyond computational expectations • uses visual memory; solves spatial visualization puzzles; copies simple designs accurately • estimates, suggests reasonable solutions to problems • uses models or "acts out" to solve problems • uses drawings, diagrams to solve problems • uses guess and check to solve problems

FIGURE 6.1, *continued*

<table>
<tr><td colspan="2">Performance Indicator</td><td colspan="2">Problem-Solving</td></tr>
<tr><td colspan="4" align="center">Level II: Below grade level</td></tr>
</table>

Performance Indicator / **Problem-Solving**

Level II: *Below grade level*

- exhibits inconsistent performance and misunderstandings at times
- shows some evidence of conceptual understanding
- has difficulty applying strategies in unfamiliar situations
- responds with appropriate answer or procedure sometimes
- completes tasks appropriately and accurately sometimes
- requires teacher guidance frequently
- needs additional time and opportunities
- demonstrates some Level III competencies but is inconsistent

- performs basic operations using the calculator
- solves spatial visualization puzzles and copies simple designs with some errors
- estimates are within a reasonable range when related to a specific problem
- tends to use single strategy for solving problems
- makes guesses to solve problems but neglects to check results

Level I: *Significantly below grade level*

- exhibits minimal performance
- shows limited evidence of conceptual understanding and use of strategies
- responds with inappropriate answer and/or procedure frequently
- very often displays misunderstandings
- completes tasks appropriately and accurately infrequently
- needs assistance, guidance, and modified instruction

- needs assistance in using a calculator
- has difficulty copying simplest designs depicting spatial relationships
- makes unreasonable estimates or inappropriate guesses to solve problems
- needs assistance with models, drawings to solve problems

Source: North Carolina Department of Public Instruction, 1997.

Other types of evaluation systems include checklists and anecdotal records. Both allow for students to work on a particular skill until mastered. Once mastered, it is either checked off or noted and the student moves on to another skill (Elster & Moje, 1993).

All of the above-mentioned assessment methods allow for the content (subject matter) to be integrated in many academic areas. The writing process is the most easily described example and also the most commonly assessed by the nongraded methods described in this section. The teacher maintains a portfolio to show improvement in writing processes over time, uses a rubric to assess skill level, and uses a checklist to show mastery of the specific skill.

By using nongraded assessment strategies, teachers can see growth and improvement. Teachers can see the scope and sequence (what is taught and in what order) because students are developing a skill until it is mastered. This is a very worthwhile concept; however, because it is new and many teachers do not like change, the nongraded system is often viewed with skepticism.

As with any form of assessment, the nongraded evaluation system has advantages and disadvantages. Non-graded methods allow the teacher to see students perform the learned objective through demonstrations or experiments, document continuing growth over a period of time, promote student success, and allow for advancement or review of content.

A disadvantage of nongraded evaluation, especially from a parent's perspective, is that students receive no grades to show progress. Therefore, parents question whether or not learning is occurring and whether or not their child is mastering content and working to potential (Gilman & Hassett, 1995).

It is the teacher's responsibility to determine the most appropriate evaluation tools for his or her students. Many early childhood educators are moving toward use of nongraded methods because more traditional grading methods are applied too subjectively to the experience of learning for young children.

SUMMARY

Early elementary school children, kindergarten through second grade, usually between the ages of five and eight, change developmentally. Kindergarten children start out in the preoperational stage and develop into the concrete operational stage by the second grade. These children are eager to learn and experiment. Young children become more coordinated as gross and fine motor skills are developed. During this time play is fun and often very imaginative. In the classroom children engage in mathematics, communication arts, science, and social studies experiences which bring the added benefit of opportunity for affective and social skills. Computers can assist young children in the learning process and should be readily available to every child. There are numerous ways to educate a child, whether graded or nongraded. The early elementary grades are the building blocks for a child's success. This experience will be more crucial in the twenty-first century.

As times change, so does education. Education must keep up with the demanding needs of our society. Future teachers will be greeted by an even more diverse group of students in the future. By the year 2000, one-third of students in public schools will come from minority families which are socially and economically disadvantaged (Boyer, 1988). The future holds conflicting implications for upcoming teachers.

✤ ✤ ✤ DISCUSSION QUESTIONS

1. Discuss how teachers can make learning fun and exciting for students.
2. Which class models would be more effective to ensure that every student experiences success?
3. List a few precautions to take when teaching young children.
4. How would a national curriculum impact the early childhood program?
5. How does the local curriculum compare with the state curriculum?

✤ ✤ ✤ CLASS ACTIVITIES

1. Read a selection from a novel to second grade students. The objective of the lesson is to describe the main character. Design a rubric (only three steps) to see if children have mastered the desired skills. Explain to the students that in their writing the teacher will be assessing capital letters and ending punctuation, descriptive words, and sound-spelled words. Then allow students ample time to describe the main character.
2. List the types of student assessment that are appropriate for the early years.

✤ ✤ ✤ REFERENCES

Beach, D. M., & Reinhartz, J. (1997). *Teaching and learning in the elementary school.* Upper Saddle River, NJ: Prentice Hall.

Biehler, R. F., & Snowman, J. (1986). *Psychology applied to teaching.* Boston: Houghton Mifflin.

Boyer, E. (1988). The future of American education: New realities making connections. *Kappa Delta Pi Record, 25*(1), 6–12.

Cohen, E. (1994). Restructuring the classroom: Conditions for productive small groups. *Review of Educational Research, 64*(1), 1–35.

Duis, M. (1995). Making time for authentic teaching and learning. *Kappa Delta Pi Record, 31*(3), 136–138.

Elster, C. A., & Moje, E. B. (1993). Literacy and diversity: Do we need dichotomies or not? In D. J. Leu and C. K. Kinzer (Eds.). *Examining central issues in literacy research, theory and practice.* 42nd Yearbook of the National Reading Conference.

Evertson, C. (1989). *Classroom management for elementary teachers.* Upper Saddle River, NJ: Prentice Hall.

Gilman, D., & Hassett, M. (1995). More than work folders: Using portfolios for educational assessment. *The Clearing House, 68*(5), 310–313.

Lemlech, J. K. (1994). *Curriculum and instructional methods for the elementary and middle school*. New York: Merrill/Macmillan.

Morrison, G. S. (1993). *Contemporary curriculum K–8*. Boston, MA: Allyn & Bacon.

North Carolina Department of Public Instruction. (1997). North Carolina Standard Course of Study. Raleigh, NC: NCDPI.

Rosenshine, B., & Meister, C. (1994). Reciprocal teaching: A review of the research. *Review of Educational Research, 64*(4), 479–531.

Santrock, J. W. (1995). Dubuque, IA: Wm. C. Brown.

Schmoker, M. (1996). The key to continuous school improvement. ERIC Document Reproduction Service No. ED395368.

Veenman, S. (1995). Cognitive and noncognitive effects of multigrade and multiage classes: A best evidence synthesis. *Review of Educational Research, 65*(4), 319–382.

Waterhouse, L. (1993). Student portfolios: Portfolio pioneers. *Kappa Delta Pi Record, 31*(1), 38.

Wong, H. (1991). *The first days of school*. Sunnyvale, CA: Harry K. Wong Publications.

Zahorik, J. (1996). Elementary and secondary teachers' reports of how they make learning interesting. *The Elementary School Journal, 96*(5), 551–565.

❖ ❖ ❖   SUGGESTED READINGS

Barth, P., & Mitchell, R. (1992). *Smart start: Elementary education for the 21st century*. Golden, CO: North American Press.

Carnegie Council on Adolescent Development. (1989). *Turning points: Preparing American youth for the twenty-first century*. New York: Carnegie Corporation.

Johnson, M. L. (1993). *Education on the wild side: Learning for the twenty-first century*. Norman, OK: University of Oklahoma Press.

Postman, N. (1995). *The end of education: Redefining the value of school*. New York: Alfred A. Knopf.

Schlechty, P. C. (1990). *Schools for the twenty-first century: Leadership imperatives for educational reform*. San Francisco: Jossey-Bass Publications.

U.S. Department of Education. (1997). *A call to action for American education in the twenty-first century*. Washington, DC: U.S. Government Printing Office.

❖ ❖ ❖

7

THE UPPER ELEMENTARY PROGRAM: GRADES 3 THROUGH 5

Chapter Objective and Focus:

To present content and processes that are taught in Grades 3, 4, and 5 in traditional and nongraded environments

In recent years, the concern for public education has been evidenced by the large number of reports criticizing the varying degrees of expectations found in public education. The large volume of educational legislative action by individual states also has reflected this problem. The reports have increasingly criticized public schools for high dropout rates, ill-prepared teachers, and the lack of skills students receive to sustain themselves in a modern society.

Initial criticism focused on the poor preparation of high school graduates. However, the impact of classroom performance throughout the grade school years was soon recognized; most notably, the foundation that was built in the early childhood grades and the strengthening of the basics through more specific content instruction in the later elementary grades. Today, most proponents of educational reform realize the need for a solid educational foundation in the elementary school years.

With this new emphasis on the importance of a sound basic education, the National Association for Elementary School Principals (NAESP), in co-sponsorship with the Carnegie Foundation, approached the reform of elementary education from several perspectives, including curriculum, accreditation, and research, with input from teachers, principals, parents, and community leaders (Salyers, 1990).

Elementary curriculum, like all aspects of American society, reflects the national diversity inherent in the American culture. Therefore, there is no single elementary program that can be considered effective for all schools and communities. Effectiveness is determined by the interaction of the defined curriculum with a variety of other factors that impact instruction and learning within a particular school setting.

THE HISTORY OF ELEMENTARY EDUCATION

Most of America's earliest settlers in the late 1600s and early 1700s were western and northern Europeans fleeing religious and ethnic persecution. Education for these groups often included religion as the fourth "R," with religion usually being the base upon which skills in reading, writing, and arithmetic were built. The children of more affluent individuals and groups returned to Europe for a more extensive education. Conflict between church and state in regard to education was nonexistent, because the state took no role in education. However, this resulted initially in limited to nonexistent educational opportunity for the poor and unchurched. Consequently, charity schools began to emerge, becoming so common that there were sometimes more charity schools than students to fill them.

Common schools, predominantly found in New England, are often considered the forerunner of public education. These were founded by the Puritans for the purpose of passing their religious doctrines on to the next generation. Common schools were local schools, with all curricula and instructional decisions made by committees of local citizens. It was expected that a child be literate before entering the common school at the age of seven.

The determining impetus for public education was initiated in Boston in 1818 when a committee found that 90 percent of the city's children attended school. Armed with this data, public school advocates decided to focus on the disadvantaged 10 percent of the populace who did not engage their children in educational pursuit. In spite of the facts that eight different charities provided primary education to the poor and that the committee recommended that public primary schools not be established, advocates advanced their campaign for public schools. Their efforts were fruitful and resulted in the first primary schools in Boston. In 1857, the National Education Association was founded and it immediately began its campaign to establish public education as a national norm (Blumenfeld, 1984).

Near the end of the nineteenth century, the primary curriculum of basic reading, writing, and arithmetic was expanded by an elementary curriculum. While the primary curriculum emphasized reading as oral expression, writing as spelling and handwriting, and arithmetic as counting and basic skills of computation, the elementary curriculum added the element of thinking through the study of these basics in their relationship to such content areas as science and social studies and the application of these basic skills and concepts in building a foundation for personal and social living (McNeil, 1999).

This beginning of public education in the early 1800s has now burgeoned into a huge federal bureaucracy. Issues of curriculum and program rights of control exist at all levels of government involvement.

Child-rearing needs in the twenty-first century are completely different from the needs and interests of students of previous generations, even as recently as the 1980s. To give justice to any topic concerning curriculum, educators must consider the current diversity and changing demands of a modern society. While the school systems of the sixties engaged in experimentation, such as open schools, the late seventies and eighties became a time of renewed "back to basics" curricula. The shift in the 1980s further focused on the exit skills of high school students with added demands of curriculum evaluations identified through testing and score reporting (Wiles & Bondi, 1997).

With over fifty percent of mothers now employed in the workforce, many children already come to school completely socialized to the school environment through experiences in day care centers and kindergartens. Schools, therefore, consider the variable of preschool experience when making curriculum decisions. Another potent force in curriculum development is the special needs of thousands of non-English speaking students currently entering the nation's schools.

School choice, the popular concept of the 1990s, has now been considered or enacted in the majority of states. Many parents like the feeling of choice because of its relation to the ideals of democracy and a democratic society. The only problem may concern the creation of a socially, economically, and racially polarized and divisive society.

DEVELOPMENTAL NEEDS AND INTERESTS

The upper elementary school child does not experience the bumps, starts, and spurts that are found in the developmental advance of younger children, exemplified by the method in which Aesop's rabbit ran his race with the turtle. Instead, this child has developmental patterns that appear to be more correctly aligned with the turtle, "slow and steady." This may be due to many of the significant changes that occur roughly between the ages of seven and eleven. While not particularly overt physically, these changes are taking place more covertly within the cognitive, moral, social, and emotional domains.

The upper elementary school child operates in Piaget's concrete operational stage. This period of cognitive development finds children engaged in several major intellectual accomplishments. While these developmental milestones are separate, they are related in their impact upon a child's intellectual maturation.

The first major milestone is the ability to consider more than one aspect of a problem. A familiar example of a younger child's inability to conserve quantity is seen in the child's considering if the amount of water in two glasses is the same when the water is poured from one glass to the other—from the short, wide one to the tall, narrow one. The preoperational child can consider only one element of difference between the two containers, usually height, and answers the question based upon his assumption that taller is more, even though the water just came from the other glass. The upper elementary child in concrete operations can consider multiple aspects of shape, examine the question relative to these multiple aspects of volume and, concurrently, will realize that, although the shape of the water is different, the volume is the same because it is the same water. The ability to consider multiple aspects of a problem or issue enables a child to recognize that other children are not "all good" or "all bad," and also allows children to examine their own behavior and actions from a less self-centered perspective. In curriculum development, the upper elementary school child is now ready for a purposeful integration of content and basic skills, allowing for more in-depth, critical, and creative examination of content.

The second major intellectual milestone concerns the development of mental operations, the ability to consider and examine problems symbolically. Instead of manipulating actual objects when engaging in concept practice and development, the child is now capable of using symbolic representations of the concrete and mentally manipulating information to solve problems. This does not mean that "hands-on" problem solving skills are no longer needed; it does mean that the relative abstractness of the "hands-on" experience can be greater. Developmentally critical examples of this milestone are adding and subtracting, ordering, and classifying.

A third major intellectual milestone of Piaget's concrete operational stage of development is the ability to control one's own behavior—to reflect upon what action or behavior is appropriate for a situation and then tell oneself to do it without the need for external regulation or direction. As a teacher, one may hear the parent of a third grader respond to comments regarding how well-behaved her child is in school with, "Well, I'm glad he knows how to act here. He certainly doesn't at home!" This incongruity may result from the child's realization that it is appropriate and expected that he will exercise self-control at school. He may have learned that the same expectations are not present at home, so he adapts his behavior to the situation.

Kohlberg examined the child's moral development, the level at which a child is able to reason about his or her own behavior and the behavior of others. The upper elementary school child normally operates in Kohlberg's third stage of moral reasoning in which concern is shown for the approval and feelings of others and for behaving appropriately. However, human development is fluid, and does not progress from one stage to the next in a smooth transition. A nine-year-old may behave in one situation as one who is functioning in Kohlberg's third stage by seeking the approval of others (well behaved in class). In another situation, this same child may function in Kohlberg's second stage by placing his or her own needs first ("Momma, I can't set the table right now. My favorite TV show is on!") or in Kohlberg's fourth stage in which a child considers laws and rules as absolutes which must be obeyed in all circumstances (The bathroom monitor writes up a child for talking in line when that child says thank you to the child in front of him in line for holding his lunchbox while he went into the restroom. "No talking in line means no talking in line.").

Socially and emotionally, most upper elementary school students are in the middle childhood stage of development. Changes in social and emotional behavior occur for a variety of reasons. During early childhood, the speed and direction of a child's development were established and now the child is in an overtly relatively stable holding pattern that can be compared to cross-country air travel. Take-off may be rough or smooth. The type of take-off a passenger experiences may impact his response to what occurs during the flight. A rough take-off may cause increased anxiety every time air turbulence is evident. A smooth take-off may enable the passenger to respond to common air turbulence with less visible anxiety. However, no matter how a passenger responds superficially to the events of the flight, the experience does get him from one place to another.

A child's social environment—shared with parents, siblings, peers, teachers, extended family, and other significant individuals—has a tremendous impact on the child's social development. This social environment determines limits, whether loose or firm, and behaviors within those limits. During middle childhood, a child in an emotionally healthy environment will experience an expansion of limits and increased freedom in choice of social behaviors within those limits as he begins to think and behave independently in a mature and intelligent manner.

During middle childhood, children prefer same-sex friendships and groups. Through their experiences with peers, children develop social cognition. They begin to recognize that what they do in social relationships impacts others and vice versa. Through their experiences with peers, the development of their self-concept continues to be molded. Their perception of their individual competence is influenced by the extent to which they fail or succeed in their experiences.

THE UPPER ELEMENTARY CURRICULUM

Perhaps the greatest need before establishing the purpose of any curriculum content is clarifying the essential prerequisites needed for program development and implementation. Purpose is first established because curriculum plans and content always reflect decisions of someone or most often some group or group's values (Wiles & Bondi, 1997). The organization of a quality school reflects not only the overall philosophy of the school, but also a list of comprehensible goals developed by school officials and parents alike. Whatever the given curriculum or philosophy upon which it is based, the curriculum must support the school's mission.

Curriculum development, therefore, is a logical process based upon a school's, district's, state's or nation's established mission, which begins with clear goals and proceeds as cause and effect relationships to desired student outcomes. Later, these decisions are fine-tuned as needed to maintain or enhance achievement of the desired outcomes. Other decisions for developmental needs are based on high academic expectations and standards, emphasis upon quality learning during classtime with minimal interruptions for administrative purposes, and a pleasant, safe, and professional school climate with strong community and parental support (Unger, 1991).

As presented in the previous chapter, curriculum, then by definition and in its simplest terms, is the course of study for any given content or subject. Curriculum is also defined as the plan for learning. In the majority of societies throughout the ancient and modern eras, curriculum has most essentially included grammar, reading, rhetoric, mathematics, and literature. Today, those same ideals of curriculum are expressed and most modern curriculum designs have also included the five major areas of content: English, mathematics, science, history, and foreign language.

NATIONAL CURRICULUM STANDARDS

Since the appearance of *A Nation at Risk* and the consequential *Goals 2000*, many educators have openly and aggressively rallied for a set of national curriculum standards. It is necessary for them to repudiate arguments against national standards, arguments that insist that (1) national standards will remove control from the local school systems, control they now enjoy (Allen & Brinton, 1996); (2) student performance is too varied and that teachers cannot teach to so many varied student performances; (3) high achievers will be held back (Nolan, 1996); (4) teachers would end up "teaching the test"; and (5) standards would put too much of an emotional strain on students (Stevenson, 1996).

Those educators in favor of national standards believe that standards will actually allow local school districts more control over what they require their students to learn. There is in existence today a hidden national curriculum developed by textbook publishers, standardized testing services, and college and university entrance requirements. Textbooks constitute a large part of the curriculum (Morrison, 1993). A local school district may get to choose textbooks for its students, but publishers maintain control in choosing the content of that book, thereby choosing a large part of that school district's curriculum. Textbook publishers select the content of textbooks based on achievement and aptitude tests and college entrance requirements, balanced with "what is palatable for various constituencies and interest groups . . . all the while honoring current fads and buzzwords." (Allen & Brinton, 1996, p. 3) So, once again, the local school systems are only choosing the textbook, not the curriculum content.

Content

The basis for any elementary educational program, whether national or local, private or public, is the quality of the two most basic subjects, reading and writing. Schools that fail to teach their students this knowledge will never recover from their failure. To teach reading and writing effectively, the elementary school curriculum must include imaginative, exciting and challenging literature. Teachers should be careful not to "kill and drill" students using "basal" readers, thereby turning students off to any reading at all (Unger, 1991).

Instead, reading should be self-motivating for each individual student. Obviously, students must learn the basics of reading, including phonics, but reading should also be fun and enriching. Unfortunately, slavish reliance and over-dependence on basal readers can destroy a student's desire to read.

Unlike those in middle and secondary schools, elementary school teachers are usually responsible for the entire core curriculum for their students, without any change in classes. While this method allows teachers flexibility in scheduling subjects and in-depth inquiry, it may be disadvantageous in that teachers may not be qualified to teach every subject.

The curriculum of the elementary school, like other areas of school, must be designed for a variety of learner needs and with proper allocation and sufficient time to accomplish the school's educational objectives. According to the National Association of Elementary School Principals, the elementary school student must be engaged in a minimum of five hours of instructional time, exclusive of recess and lunch periods (Salyers, 1990). This content must be maintained over the course of a minimum of 180 instructional days, with no interruptions for administrative or social purposes.

The National Association of Elementary Principals (NAESP) recommends that all elementary school staff members be qualified by preparation and experience for the positions to which they are assigned, and that the principal be the person responsible for determining the allocation of human resources within the school. Classroom teachers should be assigned a maximum of 15 pupils per class, with priority ratios given to younger children. Instructional specialists should be assigned based on student need and other support staff, including psychologists and counselors, should be employed to address student needs. Preservation of a quality school environment also requires a student body, at the elementary school level, to be less than 400 pupils, along with a minimum of 180 academic days containing a minimum of five hours of instructional time per day (Salyers, 1990). Instructional time, to ensure quality, must be free of interruptions. Teachers should have at least ten workdays beyond the days school is in session to prepare instructional materials and lessons. Promotion and retention policies should be clearly written out and understood by school personnel, parents, and students and involve factors such as age, social adjustments, parental support, and teacher recommendations.

Content of curriculum in the elementary school should be selected from the basic disciplines of language arts, mathematics, science, social studies, arts and health. Curriculum developers at the national, state and local levels develop and select content. Due to the lack of a national curriculum guideline or standard, each individual school system must look at the learning needs and expectations of the 13,000 school districts in this country. While many textbook selections and curriculum projects are designed to accomplish this task, the classroom teacher is the final decisionmaker in establishing content in the classroom. Content also must consistently be examined to reflect the changes in scientific knowledge, as well as the social and culture realities of the times (Morrison, 1993).

Appropriate elementary school curriculum content is today most often determined by the testing programs chosen to establish national scoring standards. Most teachers know this as "teaching for the test." Testing programs and accountability legislation has further increased the demands to teach more reading, writing and mathematics.

One of the most controversial topics facing elementary education today involves the teaching of reading. Hence, the continued controversy over phonics versus whole language. While this may be an emotional debate for many parents, it is also a political one, with many legislators demanding that certain skills be taught in their districts. Even though the school systems have no shortage of reading programs producing millions of children who can read with each program, millions of nonreaders still exist within the school systems. While reading has received the greatest amount of funding and classroom time than any other content area in the elementary agenda, it is still uncertain whether the reading debate has been settled.

Responding to the demands of colleges that students must become better writers, elementary and secondary schools as a result have devoted more time to teaching and honing students' writing skills.

Teaching mathematics has proven more effective when adapted to the special developmental characteristics of elementary aged students. The focus has shifted away from computational skills to a combination of computational skills and concrete manipulatives, along with reasoning ability. Because of the increase in computers in the elementary schools, students must now perceive and understand structure in mathematics between textbook and content taught. Researchers assessing mathematics classrooms found important differences between the curriculum of the textbook and the teachers' topic. Use of computers and interdisciplinary units have given elementary school teachers new instructional options for content and skills objectives.

Language arts includes the four modes of intercommunication skills of reading, writing, listening and speaking and are interrelated in the developmental sequence. Beginning with listening and speaking, and continuing with reading and writing, children start to comprehend and use language skills. Because of the reciprocal relationship between all four interrelated communication areas, all four skills must be taught in a holistic approach.

The reading needs of any language arts program must include the development skills of decoding and comprehension in order to produce individuals who can use functional and literary materials. Though many reading specialists disagree on the proper approach to learning reading, students failing to comprehend and use these skills will most likely face a life of underachievement (Wiles & Bondi, 1997).

Third grade is the last grade for students to master the "basics," such as reading, writing, and arithmetic. Children should at this point be able to read children's literature and the front page of the newspaper (Unger, 1991). The importance of a solid foundation cannot be emphasized enough, because without a basic core, students will be held to substandard performance levels. Described below are examples of what can be found in many state curricula.

As the following examples illustrate, the upper elementary school curricula contain a large volume of content. However, most fourth and fifth grade teachers do not have the educational background to teach the entire curriculum with the specificity it deserves. Grade level teams often divide content area teaching responsibilities to increase opportunity for individual teachers to have more planning time. Many educators feel that elementary schools that rely on one teacher to teach and know the entire school curriculum are no doubt "substandard" (Unger, 1991).

The Department of Education recommends the following standards related to fourth and fifth grade education:

English
- Introduction to critical reading, independent reading and book reports, advanced grammar skills, spelling and composition.

Social Studies
- Grade 4: U.S. History to Civil War
- Grade 5: U.S. History since 1865

Most national and state standards recommend specific content that allows for more direct instructional involvement by students.

Mathematics

- Intermediate arithmetic and geometry, number theory, negative numbers, percentages, the Pythagorean theorem, basic probability.

Science

- Grade 4: Earth science and related topics
- Grade 5: Life science and related topics

Foreign Language

- Introduction to foreign language, basic vocabulary, grammar, reading, writing and conversation.

Fine Arts

- Music and visual art will include knowledge of great composers, musical styles, elementary music theory, great painters, and creative projects.

Physical Education/Health

- Team and individual sports, first aid, drug prevention and appropriate sex education.

Following is the fourth grade curriculum as recommended by the Commission on Elementary Schools, specifically, in-depth listing of requirements.

English

Reading

- Two periods devoted to English.
- English selections will include classical children's literature.
- Critical reading skills, with examination of character, relationships and differences between fact and fiction.

Writing

- Requirement of at least one writing assignment daily.
- Review of grammar and writing skills.
- Grammar will include study of compound subjects, predicates, verb tenses, sentence structure and proper word usage.
- Expansion of creative writing and expository skills.

Rhetoric

- Poetry recitations, recitation of self-authored work, participation in dramatic scenes and oral book reports.

Library

- Daily use of library facilities to prepare written and oral reports.

Technology

- Introduction to keyboarding and word processing.

Mathematics

Calculation

- Comprehension of addition, subtraction, multiplication and division using two and three digits.
- Understanding of place values, ratios, rounding, and whole numbers.
- Introduction to algebra and mental arithmetic.

Geometry

- Symmetry and congruence, parallel and perpendicular lines, acute, right and obtuse angles.

Technology

- Continued use of calculators and computers.

Social Studies

History

- In-depth study of North American history and geography, from early settlements to the Civil War.
- Study of various colonial settlements and their founding countries, the Declaration of Independence, the Constitutional Convention, the Louisiana Purchase and westward expansion.
- Development of study and research skills.

Geography

- Tracing the 13 colonies, westward migration, and routes to the Pacific.

Civics

- Functions of the three branches of government, the evolution of the two-party system, and constitutional issues surrounding slavery.

Science

Scientific Method

- Explanation of the scientific method.

Earth Sciences

- Rock formation, glaciers, erosion, fossil fuel, weather and atmospheric conditions.

Biology

- Life cycle and behavior of insects. Basic knowledge of bones and muscles in human body.

Physics

- The use of heat as a form of energy and heat transfer.

Foreign Language

- Usually Spanish or French, with exception based on "Immersion" schools in Japanese or German.
- Basic and rudimentary elements of language and grammar structure.

Fine Arts

Music

- Students will have music class at least twice per week.
- Private instrument lessons, along with choral harmony.

Drama and dance

- Opportunity to participate at least once each semester in grade school productions.

Art

- Studio art twice per week, using pencil, charcoal, chalk, pen and ink, watercolor, clay and paper.
- Survey of art history including great artists.
- Includes field trips to museums and art exhibits.

The Fifth Grade Curriculum, as recommended by the Commission on Elementary Schools, follows:

English

Reading

- Two periods per day.
- Continuation of critical approach to interpreting literature, emphasizing more complex selections, biographies, novels, plays and essays.

Writing

- One assignment per day with emphasis on research skills, revision and editing.
- Work will display knowledge of grammar abilities, inverted word order, prepositions and conjunctions.

Rhetoric

- Recitation of poetry and original student works, performance of dramatic scenes.
- Preparation and delivery by each student.

Mathematics

Calculations

- Expansion of four basic computations to include negative numbers.
- Study of prime numbers, factors, multiples, the number line, infinity, percentages, and use of manipulatives, such as Cuisenaire rods.
- Conversion of decimals into fractions and the opposite function.
- Introduction to basic algebra, including variables, linear functions, and graphing.

Geometry

- Use of protractor to measure angles, drawing and measurement of triangles and quadrilaterals.

Technology

- Use of more complex computer software programs, along with geometric shapes.

Social Studies

History

- American history and geography, from Civil War to present.
- Events leading to Civil War, slavery, reconstruction, industrial revolution, immigration, World Wars I and II, the Great Depression, the Cold War and Vietnam.

Geography

- Memorization of the 50 states and their capitals. Identification of states on map.

Science

Life Sciences

- Reproduction of plants and flowers, photosynthesis, basic structures and functions of the human body, food groups and nutrition.
- Evolution, dinosaurs and prehistoric life.

Earth Sciences

- Geological eras, water movements, pollution problems and conservation.

Physics

- Complex machines and mathematical concepts related to machinery.

Research

- Study of cross-sections of plants.

Foreign Languages

- Introductory Spanish or French, unless otherwise stated.
- Continuation of language studies from fourth grade.
- Emphasis on vocabulary, customs, and geography of countries and respective language.

Fine Arts

Music

- Continuation of fourth grade programs.
- Once a week instrumental work, which may include band instruments.
- Students learn technical skills for performance of instruments.

Art

- Continuation of fourth grade program, in more depth and breadth.

Processes

After the curriculum is developed, the next step is to determine how the teacher should teach. The processes used are the hypotheses related to planning effective learning for students and determining how those students learn best. Each individual, it must be noted, has a particular learning style consistent with the approach used to try to learn things. Knowledge of the various categories used for students' individual learning provides the teacher with insight to create and promote the proper learning environment.

The best way for students to learn anything is to allow them to identify with it personally (Borman & Levin, 1997). This begins with some interest on the part of the student. The state of wanting to know is the perception phase. Next, the information is obtained and put to use, which is more commonly called thinking. The search for meaning is known as the conception phase. Once the information is understood, the ideation phase begins.

Some educators insist that a set of national curriculum standards would take control out of textbook publishers' hands and return it to the local school authorities. The standards would present the goals and schools would decide which specific content would satisfy those goals. Instead of relying on a publishing company to provide the content of the curriculum, the local schools would have the option to create their own content, choosing literature and supporting materials that matched what they want their children to learn, rather than accepting the content contained in a bland textbook and teaching around it.

STATE STANDARDS

The key figures that tend to reflect the quality of a state's public school system are spending per pupil, spending on education as a percentage of government revenue in the state, average annual teacher salaries, pupil-teacher ratio, graduation rates, percentage of teachers reporting student behavior problems, and the number of teachers involved in making educational decisions (Unger, 1991).

The average amount spent per pupil in each state for 1989 was $3,739. However, it is unlikely that any state or school district was able to provide a quality education for less than this amount in relation to the fact that the top-rated public and private schools spent an average of $8,000 to $10,000 per day, while many boarding schools averaged $20,000 per year (Unger, 1991). Granted, overspending does not guarantee a quality education, because there is no way to determine how much money is allocated to academics versus sports and extracurricular activities. A better figure to use in determining how much is spent on academics is teacher salaries.

The percentage of educational spending in relation to overall government spending shows how a particular state determines its educational priorities in relation to other needs and services. The states with the highest percentage of educational spending are Texas and Arkansas, with education funding comprising a total of 28% of all state and local spending; however, both states rank below the average per teacher salary expenditure which means spending is not related to teacher and academic expenditure.

The average annual teacher salary for 1990 was just over $28,000, with the beginning teacher salary under $20,000 per year. Low teacher pay results in high absenteeism and low morale. States that had below average annual teacher pay had schools and districts with teacher strikes, school closures, and educational turmoil—all of which produce low-quality education.

For the U.S. as a whole, the average pupil-teacher ratio is a respectable 17.4 to 1. Unfortunately, states or districts with 25 to 30 students per class are doing little more than babysitting. Rare is the teacher who can teach or maintain order in a classroom of that size. Roll call alone can take ten minutes of a teacher's time in these situations. The top-ranked schools in the nation correlate pupil-teacher ratios at a maximum of 10 to 15 students per class.

The graduation rate per state also identifies the dropout rate. Regrettably, the U.S. had only a 72.6% graduation rate in 1990, which reflects a 27.4% national dropout rate. High state dropout rates among secondary students can be a reflection of poor quality schools with low student and teacher morale and poor preparation in the basics in early grades.

Perhaps the most telling statistic is the percentage of teachers reporting behavior problems. This reflects the quality of the public school district and its response to drug, alcohol, and disruptive behavior problems. A word of caution is in order for teachers and others not to draw the erroneous conclusion that these problems do not exist in low incident-reporting districts. This may be a result of the opposite problem—teachers who don't report such problems for fear of retribution (Unger, 1991).

The most underrated statistic is the percentage of teachers involved in the academic curriculum choosing process. Unfortunately, too many of these decisions are the result of political battles between special interest groups and politicians, both academically unqualified and concerned with other agendas that interfere with their ability or desire to make quality educational decisions. The community must respect the academic personnel within a state or district and have confidence in their teaching ability.

Since the mid-1980s, most states have remained actively engaged in continuous assessment and revision of state curriculum standards. State legislators in the late 1990s pledged to raise the salaries of teachers and simplify the process of removing ineffective teachers from the classroom. Some states put accountability and bonus systems in place in the mid-1990s to increase school-site accountability as site-based decisionmaking was also encouraged through state legislation.

Some futurists have now expanded the basics to include problem solving, critical and creative thinking, decisionmaking, flexibility and adaptability, and working collaboratively in order to prepare students for a future that contains significantly more unknowns than knowns. What is known, however, is that students must be prepared for an information-driven society in which technology will make obsolete many of the current employment opportunities and telecommunication advances will bring technology increasingly into the interpersonal and social arenas.

Philosophically, a futurist perspective in curriculum development is based upon the goal of equipping students with the "new basics" which they will need to meet the demands, personally and as citizens, of a democratic society and interdependent world in the information age. These new basics include mastery of enabling skills such as reading, writing, and computing and those skills that allow individuals to work cooperatively with flexibility and adaptability as they engage in critical and creative thinking to solve problems (Myers & Myers, 1995).

State curricula for third through fifth grades, through on-going study and revision, reflects this futurist perspective. Literacy is defined much more broadly than reading and writing. It includes learning to communicate through reading, writing, speaking, listening, and viewing and espouses that these must be rewarding experiences. It promotes communication as using language in natural and purposeful ways and views literacy skills as interrelated processes by which the learner comprehends and conveys meaning not only in reading for pleasure, but in examining content and knowledge from other disciplines. It requires that students be engaged in a learning environment where they are encouraged to think critically and creatively about ideas, relate the content of the message to personal experience, and understand the content in relation to other content.

Language Arts for Grade Three

Third graders in most states read many types of texts—literary, informational, and practical. They distinguish between fact and opinion and note and chart details. These students interpret poetry and infer main ideas, lessons, or morals in a variety of prose. Students in this grade use a variety of reading strategies to construct meaning for text. Emphasis is placed upon reading silently for extended periods of time for pleasure and information.

Third graders typically write a variety of poetry and prose and can support their ideas with references to their reading. They use a variety of prewriting activities, revise their writing by adding detail, and recognize incorrect spelling.

Social Studies for Grade Three

The third grade program is designed to increase children's understandings about community life in a variety of contexts. In this study, children compare aspects of their own and other familiar communities with those of other cultures and times. Students are made aware of some of the relationships between ways of living, the physical environment, and human traditions. They are introduced to problems confronting communities, the groups interested in these problems, and the ways communities seek to solve their problems. They study basic relationships among communities—how they may be combined to form larger political units, and how they may be linked together by cultural heritage and geographic and economic ties.

Through studies concerned with communities in similar and different patterns of community living, children begin to gain understandings about citizenship in other cultures, the religious and cultural traditions of others, economic activities in differing societies, and the lives of families and children in a variety of settings. These settings should include Africa, Asia, Europe, and Latin America as well as the United States and North America. In each unit of instruction, at least one other culture should be examined for purposes of finding similarities and differences in institutions and ways of living.

The program at this level is also concerned with how and why communities change. Awareness of change enables children to perceive that while all societies change, they do not necessarily change at the same rate. Children learn as well that each society has certain institutions and traditions that bind it together and give it continuity. By examining community life in the past, children are made aware of the cultural, political, and economic factors that help bind communities together in time. Time periods considered for these purposes should include the colonial and pre-Civil War periods, the period around 1900 (approximately one hundred years ago), and the 1940s and 1950s (or the time when children's grandparents were children). In each unit of instruction, at least one other time period is examined for purposes of finding similarities and differences in institutions and ways of living.

As students learn about communities, they become increasingly adept at using information-gathering and processing skills. They become more skillful decisionmakers. As they enlarge their understanding of communities different from their own they become more accepting of diversity and develop constructive attitudes toward change and uncertainty. By engaging in appropriate and carefully structured classroom and school activities, they grow in their capacities as young citizens.

Language Arts for Grade Four

Fourth graders continue to read many types of text—literary, informational, and practical pieces. Through reading, they can make connections with situations beyond their own experience. In narrative writing, they recognize organizational patterns in text and motives of characters. They can make inferences, draw conclusions, and are learning to support their opinions about what they read. Fourth graders are becoming more skillful at following written directions and in reading for information in content area texts, reference materials, and periodicals.

Fourth graders write narratives, information articles, and practical "how to" pieces. They are learning to use more detail, sequence, and description in their narratives. As members of "reading/writing groups" they can give suggestions for revision to each other. They edit their written work for basic sentence formation, usage, mechanics, and spelling.

Social Studies for Grade Four

In fourth grade, students proceed from community studies to a study of the state. As students examine Arizona, for example, they learn about the characteristics of the people of that state. They explore geographic regions, learning about the landforms, climate, and resources of the state. Fourth graders are introduced to the concept of culture and learn about the state's social, economic, and political institutions. In studying Arizona, students begin to view the state in the broad context of other regions—the southwest, the nation, and the world at large.

As students learn about this state, they develop concepts and generalizations from history and the social sciences. These concepts and generalizations, developed in fourth grade, will be further refined in grades five through seven as students examine other world regions. Concepts for the study are drawn from history and the social sciences, but the primary discipline is geography, especially cultural geography.

As students acquire information about Arizona, they use maps as well as other resources. They use this information to make decisions or to form generalizations about problems and issues related to the state. They develop self-management and social skills from classroom activities that help them learn to consider the viewpoints and lives of others different from themselves. Finally, as they study about the political institutions of the state and participate in classroom and school activities, their skills of civic participation are sharpened.

For example, in their study of Arizona as a state, students will address competency goals that engage them in an investigation of these basic questions:

- Who are the people of Arizona and what are their values and beliefs?
- What is the environment in which people in Arizona live?
- How is Arizona society organized?
- How do the people of Arizona make a living?
- How has Arizona changed over time?

LOCAL STANDARDS

The same criteria used to evaluate statewide school districts is also necessary for selecting and evaluating local school districts. Most likely, if spending per pupil, teacher salaries, pupil-teacher ratios and graduation rates are below the national average, so is the quality of education. As in many larger cities, teacher salaries may be supplemented by the state.

At this point, adjustments may be made to goals, expectations, and techniques. Most often, the curriculum needs of the students are determined locally by school or district staffs. To determine those needs, many local officials use citizens groups or study teams from the school community. Also important in local curriculum decisions is understanding the local commerce and industry (and tax base) and producing citizens who can meet the demands of those industries. Also, student, school, and community needs must be assessed as to the current growth rate of the community with seasonal or short-term adjustments to population resulting from the presence of migrant workers and military personnel (Wiles & Bondi, 1997). As a result, each school district is unique.

Elementary education profiles of standards usually are more limited than secondary education, which relies on graduation, promotion and retention rates (Unger, 1991). Also, secondary schools use college entrance exams, such as the SAT, for national rankings. Local standards are determined by the school board and the superintendent and should reflect the conditions within a given society, including temporary or seasonal migrations, as well as local industrial needs.

NONGRADED CURRICULUM

Nongraded education goes by many different titles: mixed-age or multi-age grouping, heterogeneous grouping, open education, ungraded grouping, vertical grouping, and family grouping. All of these terms are slightly different in connotation, depending upon when and where they are used, but they all describe the basic practice of teaching children of different ages and abilities together, without dividing children on the basis of chronological age. Usually, the practice involves placing children ranging in age by three years or more in one class (Gaustad, 1995). The purpose is to allow students to move at their own individual pace. In this way, they are able to make continuous progress, rather than being promoted once a year (Gaustad, 1992).

The ungraded method focuses on the socialization of the mixed levels of children. Its goal is to maximize the benefits of interaction and cooperation among the various age levels of the students. Teachers encourage children to turn to each other for help with things like basic literacy and numeracy skills. Older children help younger children, and in so doing learn patience and acceptance of the younger children's skill levels. The opportunity will "give them some of the desirable early experiences of being nurturant that underlie parenting and helping others who are different from oneself" (Katz, 1992, p. 2). The younger children learn to model the older children in expectation of when they become the older members of the class. All the children turn to each other for social and intellectual support, thereby relieving the teacher of some responsibility. Through this departure of dependence on the teacher, all the students become much more independent at an earlier age.

The concept of a nongraded curriculum is far from new, being based on the one-room schoolhouse of America in years past. Only some schools, less than 1,000 by 1980 (Muse, Smith & Barker, 1987), are still required to teach by this method due to the paucity of students in their rural regions. Graded classrooms have become the norm in the remainder of the country, thereby forcing nongraded education to become looked upon as an experimental method of teaching.

The switch from multi-aged classrooms to the graded classroom as the normal venue for curriculum has occurred in the last hundred years, due mostly to the difference in instructional and organizational skills required to teach in those settings. A nongraded setting requires much more instructional and organizational planning time than a graded setting. Teachers need substantially more training in child development, integrated curriculum, and instructional strategies (Gaustad, 1992). Teachers in nongraded settings must be able to design open-ended, divergent learning experiences appropriate for students who function at different levels. This requires proficiency in the use of qualitative assessment methods such as the portfolio and anecdotal reports. They must be able to determine when to use homogeneous and heterogeneous grouping arrangements and cooperative groups. They must be able to facilitate positive group interaction and guide students in learning social skills and independent learning skills. Since multi-age education includes team teaching, teachers must know how to plan and work cooperatively with colleagues. Most importantly, they must be effective communicators of multi-age practices to parents and other community members in order to build understanding and support for their use.

These skills are required to deal with the child-centered philosophy of the nongraded education model. The curriculum is delivered in a much more hands-on fashion. For instance, portfolios are used to evaluate progress and mathematical relationships are learned by sorting, counting, and measuring real objects, instead of learning out of workbooks. Homogeneous and heterogeneous instructional groups need to be planned and blended to fit along with general whole-class instruction. In addition, the class must be stimulated to become more independent learners and to become less dependent on help from the teacher. All of this takes an extraordinary amount of time, and not every teacher has the ability to cope with such a format.

Ungraded education is especially recommended for the primary grades because of concern about the high proportion of students who are retained during those years. There is a growing awareness that repetition of a grade level does not necessarily help students meet those grade level objectives. This method is also good for the primary grades because it "attempts to implement developmentally appropriate teaching and curriculum practices" and it allows for an additional opportunity to expand intellectual and social development (Katz, 1992, p. 1).

Some disadvantages of nongraded education that a perspective practitioner should be aware of include:

- younger children may become burdens to older ones and may be overwhelmed by more competent classmates (Katz, 1992);

- older and more experienced children may not get the challenges they need (Katz, 1992);

- teacher burnout may be higher due to insufficient planning time (Gaustad, 1992);

- teachers will need a substantial amount of additional training, which is costly in terms of both time and money (Gaustad, 1992).

Nongraded education will return to elementary education. To illustrate, as a result of the Kentucky Education Reform Act and the Oregon Education Act, these two states have initiated experiments in nongraded education which are being closely monitored by other states (Gaustad, 1992).

INSTRUCTIONAL TECHNOLOGY

Since the goal of any classroom, district or curriculum is to promote and provide for learning, the educational technology available to students must keep pace with the technological improvements invented and utilized in society. Most often the term "multimedia" is used as a general reference to any technology used to aid instruction. Multimedia, thus, means a combinations of any media such as computer, video, images and hands-on materials. Technology, when used correctly, provides teachers with the opportunity to enhance delivery and enrich class curriculum. As a result, the "more vivid and varied the sensory input the greater the likelihood that memory, understanding, and creative thought, (learning) will occur" (Borman & Levin, 1997, p. 134).

Educators are pressed to keep pace with the demands and ever-changing instructional options that result from the technological advances of the 1990s. The technological instruments of personal computers and fax machines offer the possibilities of unlimited teaching alterations in the classroom. One particular factor in the increased change in technological improvements and upgrades is that schools are the single largest sales market in the U.S. for new technology.

While each decade has seen its own technological miracles, such as television in the 1950s, transistor radios in the 1960s, video cameras in the 1970s, and facsimile machines and CD-ROMS in the 1980s, none has impacted the learning process more than the 1990s' inclusion of the Internet. The Internet decade will bring the integration of the previously discovered tools, giving each student worldwide access to information and technology from home or the classroom (Wiles & Bondi, 1997).

Educators in the next decade must avoid the previous technological mistakes of the 1980s and early 1990s by creating technology that is meaningful to content and classroom learning. The 1980s and early 1990s saw little integration of computer hardware and software with traditional courses, while true visions of how the new technology could enhance learning were nonexistent.

The twenty-first century must have the goal of using technological reforms to maintain control of the programming function. Today's technology can be used to improve communication and knowledge. Education will be redefined by the technological advances and integration of technology in the future.

Technology available for classroom instructional use includes such hardware as computers, Laserdiscs, CD-ROM players, modems, LCD panels, scanners, digital cameras, VCRs, and cassette recorders. Software technology includes word processing, desktop publishing, multimedia, and computer-assisted instruction.

Computer literacy in grades 3 through 5 is most often determined by the students' attitudes toward computers and their programs. The students' attitude should be one of willingness and confidence to become involved with computers. Sadly, the prevalence of computers in the classroom has yet to spark a renewed learning design. Rough estimates suggest that no more than five percent of schools are truly using the power of computers (Morrison, 1993).

SUMMARY

Elementary curriculum, including Grades 3, 4, and 5, is in the midst of turbulent change. The change necessarily follows the beginning of the end of the industrial age and the start of the new, so-called information age. The traditional curriculum is being examined under the microscope of educators everywhere and changes are being proposed and experimented with. Vibrant changes already exist in schools: integrated language arts, or Whole Language. The realization of hands-on, real-life math and science instruction, as well as the integration of those mathematics and science skills, are being called for by both mathematics and science education experts. Social studies standards are seeking to integrate language arts, science, and corresponding math skills.

New teachers can be trained in the nuances of the future curriculum standards and instruction methods, but older teachers may not to be as flexible to the coming necessary changes. And not only teachers, but administrators, politicians and parents who remain in the industrial mindset will cause glitches in the smooth transformation of the curriculum.

The changes will come, but they will occur slowly, over time. The innovative styles of curriculum standards and processes will become integrated into the schools. Time, along with changes in the economy, will support the futurists of the next generation.

✣ ✣ ✣ DISCUSSION QUESTIONS

1. How do elementary children in grades three through five differ developmentally from children in grades K-2?

2. What does it mean to "teach to the test"? Is this an appropriate practice? Why or why not?

3. Discuss the strengths and weaknesses of a nongraded curriculum. Is this an effective curriculum? How so?

✣ ✣ ✣ CLASS ACTIVITIES

1. Outline the history of elementary education in a timeline format.

2. Make a chart that compares national, state, and local standards in two content areas.

✣ ✣ ✣ REFERENCES

Allen, D. W., & Brinton, R. C. (1996). Improving our unacknowledged national curriculum (National Standards: Pro and Con). *The Clearing House, 69,*(3), 140–143.

American Association for the Advancement of Science. (1989). *Science for all Americans.* ED 309 059. Washington, DC.

Biehler, R. F., & Snowman, J. (1986). *Psychology applied to teaching.* Boston: Houghton Mifflin.

Blumenfeld, S. (1984). *NEA: Trojan horse in education.* Boise, ID: The Paradigm Company.

Borman, S., & Levin, J. (1997). *A practical guide to elementary instruction, from plan to delivery.* Boston: Allyn & Bacon.

Elkind, D. (1976). *Child development and education.* New York: Oxford University Press.

Elkind, D. (1984). *Ego development: The core of a healthy personality.* [Video]. Davis, CA: Davidson Films.

Gaustad, J. (1992). Nongraded primary education. *ERIC Digest, 74.* ED347637. (http://www.ed.gov.database/ERIC_Digests/ed347637.html), 59–63.

Gaustad, J. (1995). Implementing the multiage classroom. *ERIC Digest, 97.* ED381869.

Gorman, R. M. (1972). *Discovering Piaget: A guide for teachers.* Columbus, OH: Charles E. Merrill.

Jacob, S. H. (1984). *Foundations for Piagetian education.* Lanham, MD: University Press of America, Inc.

Katz, L. G. (1992). Nongraded and mixed-age grouping in early childhood programs. *ERIC Digest, 74,* 47–52. ED351148. (http://www.ed.gov/databases/ERIC_Digests/ed351148.html)

McNeil, J. D. (1999). *Curriculum: The teacher's initiative* (2nd ed.). Upper Saddle River, NJ: Merrill/Prentice Hall.

McNergney, R. F., & Herbert, J. (1995) *Foundations of education.* Boston: Allyn & Bacon.

Morrison, G. S. (1993). *Contemporary curriculum K–8.* Boston: Allyn & Bacon.

Muse, I., Smith, R., & Barker, B. (1987). *The one-teacher school in the 1980s.* Las Cruces, NM: ERIC Clearinghouse on Rural Education and Small Schools.

Myers, C. B., & Myers, L. K. (1995). *The professional educator: A new introduction to teaching and school.* New York: Wadsworth.

National Academy of Sciences. (1995). *National Science Education Standards.* Washington, DC. (http://www.nap.edu/readingroom/books/nses/html/)

National Council of Teachers of Mathematics. (1989). *Curriculum and evaluation standards for school mathematics.* Reston, VA: National Council of Teachers of Mathematics, Inc.

Nolan, K. J. (1996, February). A standard divided is no standard at all. *Basic Education, 40*(6), 7–10. (http://www.c-b-e.org/articles/nolan.htm)

North Carolina Department of Public Instruction. (1985). *Teacher handbook.* Raleigh, NC: Author.

Salyers, G. D. (1990). *Standards for quality elementary and middle schools.* Alexandria, VA: National Association of Elementary School Principals.

Stevenson, H. (1996, October). Striving for standards. *Basic Education, 41*(2), 2–6. (http://www.c-b-e.org/articles/stevens.htm)

Unger, H. G. (1991). *What did you learn in school today: A parent's guide for evaluating your child's school.* New York: Facts On File.

U.S. Department of Education. (1995, Fall). *A teacher's guide to the U.S. Department of Education.* (http://www.ed.gov./pubs/TeachersGuide/pt4.htm.)

Wakefield, A. P. (1997). Thinking about math thinking. *Kappa Delta Pi Record, 33*(3), 103–105.

❖ ❖ ❖ SUGGESTED READINGS

Brown, F. (1992). *The reform of elementary school education*. Malabar, FL: Krieger.

Postman, N. (1995). *The end of education: Redefining the value of school*. New York: Alfred A. Knopf.

Schlechty, P. C. (1990). *Schools for the twenty-first century: Leadership imperatives for educational reform*. San Francisco: Jossey-Bass.

Tanner, D., & Tanner, L. (1995). *Curriculum development: Theory into practice* (3rd ed.). Upper Saddle River, NJ: Merrill/Prentice Hall.

Uchida, D. (1996). *Preparing students for the 21st century*. Arlington, VA: American Association of School Administrators.

✧ ✧ ✧

8

THE MIDDLE SCHOOL:
GRADES 6 THROUGH 8

Chapter Objective and Focus:

To present content and processes that are
taught in Grades 6, 7, and 8 in traditional
and nongraded environments

THE MIDDLE SCHOOL PURPOSE

A middle school is a separately organized and administered learning environment for early adolescent students. Operationally, the middle school plan is different from a traditional secondary school design, such as a junior high. For example, the middle school tends to organize students and teachers into "teams" that relate to each other within units smaller than the total school population. Middle school students usually range in age from ten to fourteen. The grade levels are usually from grade six to eight, although some middle schools begin at grade five. The developmental growth stages of middle school students range from late childhood to early adolescence.

In some cases, middle schools were originally established to alleviate overcrowded conditions in elementary and high schools. Since the 1980s, middle schools have become a distinct way of thinking about the education of pre-adolescent and early adolescent students (Ornstein & Behar, 1995). Therefore, the purpose of the middle school is to provide an educational setting for children in the preadolescent and early adolescent years. Concepts and focus for middle schools differ; however, the general philosophy is to provide an educational transition for children between elementary and high schools. Attempts to describe middle schools beyond the broad statement would compromise the diverse nature of the middle school level and the students it serves. Responding to the unique developmental needs of the middle level student is what makes a middle school program effective.

At the beginning of the twentieth century, G. Stanley Hall published the first significant text on adolescence in which he argued that adolescence is a distinct stage of life. He classified programs to provide a broader range of exploratory courses and activities to encourage student discovery and interest development (Alkin, 1992).

Sharon Harris (1992) defined middle school as "unique and transitional" in all elements of organization and design, containing some elements of the elementary setting while preparing students for the freedom, instructionally and socially, of the high school setting. Elementary students are usually in self-contained, teacher-directed classrooms within groupings that are chronologically based and in which emphasis is placed upon basic skills. Instructional support is facilitated by the parent-teacher relationship. High school staffing is departmentalized by subject with emphasis on in-depth study of content, and students are grouped for instruction based upon subject. They move independently from class to class at period change. Instruction is more student-centered and, concurrently, the student has a major impact on the effect that his relationship with staff has on his learning experience. In the middle school setting, students have a greater peer group with which they interact on a daily basis than is found in the elementary school through the establishment of teams; however, their movement and instructional performance are monitored on a personalized basis by team staff members. The team concept allows flexibility in scheduling and the implementation of developmentally appropriate grouping and instruction based upon the needs of the curriculum and the student. Each student is assigned an advisor, possibly the homeroom teacher, who monitors the student's progress over the period of the school year.

The Carnegie Report (1996) stated that the period of pre-adolescence and early adolescence is "a crucial turning point" in establishing life's direction for young people. The rapid pace of change in the twenty-first century that these young people will experience amplifies the need for appropriate intervention in fostering a positive attitude towards learning, alternatives to destructive behavior, and establishment of healthy practices.

THE EVOLUTION OF MIDDLE LEVEL EDUCATION IN THE UNITED STATES

Historically, the financing and establishment of organized schooling was not directed by the U.S. Constitution. Instead, each state assumed the responsibility for educating the next generation. As the population of the United States grew, local governments built secondary schools or high schools and extended the elementary or primary schools to eight years. The purpose of the primary school was to build a base of knowledge for all Americans to have the necessary skills of citizenship. The high schools were attended initially by the brightest students planning to attend college. Vocational schools for technical education or other specified job training also extended the primary school education for students.

The Establishment of the Junior High School

In 1918, a set of recommendations was delineated in the *Cardinal Principles of Secondary Education*, which called for a separate institution for early adolescents. The *Principles* advocated that elementary schools should include the first six years of education and that secondary education be divided into two designations: junior and senior periods. The *Principles* also supported the push for early college preparation when, in 1888, Charles Eliot, the president of Harvard College, explored the possibilities of shortening college programs if college prep courses were of a higher quality. Another group of strong proponents for a separate school for young adolescents came from new knowledge about human growth and development. Many studies published by Edward Thorndike and James M. Cattell quantified irregular ability levels in different areas and extreme differences among individuals. These studies revealed variances in physical rates of development as well as rates in social, emotional, and intellectual abilities (Messick & Reynolds, 1992).

The first junior high schools were created in Columbus, Ohio, and Berkeley, California, at the turn of the twentieth century in response to concepts originated in the late nineteenth century and the early twentieth century. The inception of the idea of separate schools for adolescents was prompted by an impetus to solve major problems existing in the 8/4 organization of schools. The Committee on Economy of Time in Education proposed reorganization of the traditional 8/4 plan to a new 6/3/3 plan (Alvermann & Muth, 1992). The 8/4 organization of eight years for elementary or primary education followed by four years of high school was not the initial target of reform. The number of high schools in 1920 increased at a rapid rate due to a population explosion after World War I. The great changes of lifestyle as a result of industry and the enormous increase in the number of elementary students continuing beyond basic elementary grades created a need for a more widely differentiated curriculum, for funding of various school programs, and for a definite function or goal of schooling in the United States (Briggs, 1920). Berkeley led the country in development of a 6/3/3 model. Many school systems throughout the country began to use this organizational plan.

Forces in the creation of the junior high school included the economy or management of time, the high drop-out rate, the wide variety of learners, and the unique needs of adolescent learners. The exploratory nature of junior high schools would allow students to make informed decisions about their future career and allow schools to educate students at a responsive intellectual level. The growth of the junior high brought about many educational advantages: a reduction in the drop-out rate, the introduction of the exploration concept and guidance services, an opportunity to schedule co-curricular activities, and an age-appropriate setting for the implementation of many innovative programs (Alvermann & Muth, 1992).

Junior high schools were first oriented to introduce subject matter by departments, they offered little choice of subjects and promoted students based on grades, and they implemented a social organization designed to develop personal responsibility and the best interests of the group. Although the junior high school of 1920 was intended to be more responsive to the preadolescent than the primary or secondary environment, most evolved into mini-high schools. Criticism of junior high education resulted because of its similarities to the senior high school program: emphasis on specialization by subject matter or by department, abstract and formal lectures, college preparatory orientation of class offerings, athletics, large music programs, and formal dances (McKay, 1995). Because a research base was not available to help create the unique nature of the junior high school, the gradual movement to a subject orientation like the high school was inevitable.

In the first half of the twentieth century, the United States was fast becoming a strong industrial leader and emerging as a world power. The development of junior high schools paralleled the nation's industrial and financial growth. Assembly lines, job specialization, and the efficiency of management transferred to the organization of school faculty and staff members as they labored to produce the product of effective education. At the end of the industrial age, during the late 1950s to early 1960s, the need to reexamine the schooling of early adolescents became paramount as declining academic achievement was identified as due to the mismatch between the developmental needs and the educational environment. At this time, following World War II, the critics of junior high schools became more numerous. Critics suggested that the junior high school was not serving the needs of the adolescent. The junior high concept omitted knowledge of young adolescents as a factor in its organization and program design. The practices of counting ninth grade course requirements toward college credit, engaging students in junior varsity sports and sophisticated social activities (proms), and involving students in competition for superlatives and other highly competitive awards caused adjustment difficulties for the students and led many educators to become concerned about the purpose, program, and organization of the junior high.

Others believed that a special school could respond to the unique physical and emotional needs of preadolescents and early adolescents. The conflicting views of those who saw the junior high school primarily as a training ground for the intellectual challenges of high school and those who saw it as an institution to serve the developmental needs of learners often generated heated debates. Using the work of developmental psychologists and physiologists as an intellectual rational, critics of junior high schools in the early 1960s proposed the establishment of a new kind of school to serve preadolescents and early adolescents. They proposed that the new school be called a middle school.

The Transition from Junior High Schools to Middle Schools

The middle school focuses on serving the needs of the students. It is a school that will support young adolescents in making the transition from elementary school to high school, while providing students a wider range of learning options without adopting the strict departmentalized high school structure. Through exploratory options, many middle schools aim to provide greater opportunity for pupil self-direction (Tanner & Tanner, 1995). Team teaching allows an opportunity to address the needs of students in grade level interdisciplinary teams. Elective courses are traditional as well as exploratory. Exploratory courses offer students the opportunity to dabble in many areas to develop and extend interests. Generally, the focus of the middle school is on the developmental needs of the early adolescent student (see Table 8.1).

When preadolescents begin their junior high or middle school years, they often have problems moving from a small, neighborhood school to a much larger and often impersonalized institution. Changing classes and teachers up to six or seven times a day creates barriers to the development of stable peer and adult relationships. The junior high traditional format of stop and start work is unsettling as it restricts creativity and concentration. The intended

TABLE 8.1
Junior High School/Middle School Comparison

	Junior High School	Middle School
Reason for Creation:	Formation of a school that is developmentally appropriate for the special learning and emotional needs of preadolescent students	
Origin:	1910–1920s	late 1950s–early 1960s
Characteristics:	Emphasis on high school level academics	Emphasis on developmentally appropriate activities and electives
	Departmentalized	Integrated teams of teachers
	Fixed-period schedules	Flexible block schedules
	High school orientation—no opportunity for counseling, individualization, or independent exploration	Individual orientation—celebration of diversity and emphasis on the needs of each student
	Variety of programs—fragments of various ideas	Holistic program
	Interschool athletics	Intramurals
	Teacher training—subject oriented	Teacher training—expanded training in human development

function of school is to teach students how to participate effectively in the work force, yet what job requires employees to collect all belongings and physically relocate to work on completely different tasks every fifty minutes? Awareness of these disparities and the unique needs of the preadolescent learner has grown exponentially since the establishment of junior high schools. The move to middle schools was necessitated by this awareness.

The middle school concept began to gain the attention of educators during the 1960s. At that time, supporters were concerned about three things: (1) the concern for academic excellence and specialization, (2) the belief that young people were maturing earlier, and (3) dissatisfactions with the typical junior high.

Early middle schools spanned three to five grades, always including grades 6 and 7. Age levels were considered more critical factors than grade levels, with approximate age range from 11 to 14 years of age.

Many early middle school educators and advocates were committed to the idea that high school preparation should not be the primary focus of middle school programs. They argued that certain psychological and physiological characteristics of students in the 11–to–14 age group required a special set of educational conditions.

Since middle schools first began to appear in the 1960s, the popularity of this concept has continued to increase. Middle schools have replaced junior high schools and become the dominant intermediate school type. The grade configuration of many districts that have middle schools is 5/3/4—five years in elementary school, three years in middle school, and four years in high school. This configuration was created by those who thought children matured earlier. The specific arrangement of schools between elementary school and senior high school varies from place to place. Some school systems have only middle schools. Others have only junior high schools. Others have both.

As originally conceived, middle schools are supposed to be heavily oriented toward serving students' special developmental needs. Many institutions called middle schools do reflect this kind of concern. On the other hand, many middle schools are designed very much along the lines of senior high schools, with a focus toward academic content that differs little from that of junior high school programs that initially prompted the establishment of middle schools.

Similarly, some junior high schools continue to see their role as primarily academic preparation institutions for senior high schools. However, other junior high schools have student-oriented programs that are every bit as responsive to learners' developmental needs as those in similarly oriented middle schools.

Patterns of design and philosophy of middle schools are rooted in different educational theories. The development of these patterns has a long history. One glaring conflict in school design lies beneath the definition of the school. Is it a middle school by title only, which functions as a junior high, or it is a middle school in title and function? Junior high schools are traditional. Similar to high school, courses are departmentalized. Elective courses are set up to provide students with thorough knowledge of subject matter. Emphasis is placed upon knowledge acquisition and to prepare students for high school.

It is simply not accurate to suggest that middle schools care about students, and junior high schools care about subjects. Conclusions about schools must be based upon an examination of individual school programs, not whether they are called middle schools or junior high schools.

The formation of middle school education in the United States has been unlike other contemporary education programs in that it is an adaptation of historic philosophies and organizations. However, the middle school is uniquely different from its predecessor, the junior high school, and other programs because of its strong association with research in human development, with special emphasis on the young adolescent.

The philosophical purpose of a middle level education program is to provide responsive education that fits the needs of the preadolescent learner. The transitory learning period joins the elementary school years to the high school years and is marked by a unique curricular program. Middle school teachers endeavor to help students reach academic curricular goals at prescribed performance standards by providing regular experiences of success. These experiences enhance the personal development of each preadolescent learner and are reinforced in an enriched middle level curriculum with age-appropriate choices and activities. In 1989, the Carnegie Council on Adolescent Development published their concerns for resolving the disparity between the special needs of the preadolescent student with the learning environment of junior high schools. That council's report, entitled *Turning Points: Preparing American Youth for the 21st Century*, pointed to the "volatile mismatch existing between the organization and curriculum of middle grade schools and the intellectual and emotional needs of young adults" (p. 8). The Council found that, as a result of this incongruity, many students experienced a decline in academic achievement and an increase in feelings of alienation and absenteeism, which resulted in a greater number of dropouts. The report called for middle grade reform in an effort to prevent a "divided society: one affluent and well-educated, the other poorer and ill-educated" (p. 9). To alter the disparate path of middle level education, the Council recommended specific actions that middle grade schools of the future should take.

In order to decrease alienation and foster success, the Carnegie Council recommended the creation of small learning communities through which students can develop fundamental relationship skills and be known individually by at least one adult in the school. Staff should be carefully selected and possess qualifications that include specific interest in and understanding of the preadolescent and training for middle grades. Parents should be engaged by including them in school program decisionmaking, regularly communicating to them about programs and their student's progress, and providing them with the opportunities and tools to reinforce the learning process at home. Community resources should be utilized through the development of partnerships and service opportunities.

Improved achievement and the development of healthy lifestyles should be emphasized by the establishment of a core academic program that enables students to communicate in a literate manner, think critically, make healthy life choices, behave ethically, and become responsible citizens. By providing a health care facilitator responsible for health care and counseling services for every middle grade school, emotional development and intellectual achievement would be enhanced. The instructional setting should include the use of cooperative learning and the flexible use of time (Carnegie Council on Adolescent Development, 1989).

Making the transition from the junior high concept reorients the subject matter–driven curriculum to a core curriculum involving interdisciplinary team teaching in flexible blocked classes and a choice of exploratory classes. The change to a middle school works best when the community, faculty, parents, and students are educated as to the unique needs of preadolescents. Visits to similar middle school programs and the establishment of a focused vision statement are two widely used strategies employed to ensure that the change leads to schools that meet the requirements relegated by the reform effort.

The metamorphosis of the most recent middle school design has restructured schools to achieve an organized structure, a planned curriculum, and a variety of methods of instruction. Students in middle schools are taught by teacher teams and individually monitored in teacher-student advisement periods or mentorships. Successful middle school programs have not fallen into implementing a single reform, but have utilized the benefits of several reform initiatives operating together in an integrated manner. The basic goal for reform is to create developmentally responsive schools to raise academic achievement of all students.

Achieving middle schools that are equally responsive to student needs is impossible if small steps are not taken. Talking about reform does not bring about action. "Speaking with One Voice: A Manifesto for Middle-Grades Reform," (Lipsitz, Mizell, Jackson, & Austin, 1997) proposes strategies to move from talk to action. These strategies require the commitment of educators, public officials, and the public throughout planning and implementation. Successful reform requires informing. As such, local, state, and national networks of professionals that provide peer support, community awareness, promote policy changes, establish continuity, and become professional communities supporting the reform ideas of change are critical to a successful transition.

School leadership must be informed and engaged at all levels of decision-making. At the school level, leadership will organize all plans, training, budgetary issues, and education of new administrative staff. At the local level, the superintendent will assure that district-wide support of the change is present. State leadership will result in policy changes that make adoption of middle school principles and practices obtainable. At all levels of leadership, data must drive decisions.

Practicing teachers will need professional development, integrated and ongoing, to maintain a focus on the elements of effective teaching. Teacher education programs must produce new teachers familiar with reform efforts and capable of evaluating their own teaching. Technical assistance is also essential for assessment of school program effectiveness and student progress.

The reality of change is inevitable. The challenge for educators is to meet established goals, predict the necessity for change, educate for awareness of the coming change, and assist in making a successful transition. The evolution from one philosophy to another, such as the transformation from a junior high school to a middle school philosophy, involves a process that resembles a journey rather than reaching a final destination. Change involves constant reform and development.

THE MIDDLE SCHOOL CURRICULUM FOR THE TWENTY-FIRST CENTURY

Research findings by Johnston and Markle (1986) on the effectiveness of middle school programs show mixed results. Middle schools have not significantly outperformed other schools; however, there have been increases in academic achievement and the perception of success. A strong middle level educational program is in place across the United States along with the awareness of the comprehensive need for reform efforts in teacher training, flexible organization, improved student achievement, various methods of instruction, and a modified curriculum.

Currently, middle school reform continues to solve complicated problems. Schools are challenged to refine effective cooperative grouping strategies and grouping of students based on achievement level. Homogeneous grouping has been proven generally ineffective, yet it does narrow the achievement range and therefore facilitates an effective and focused instructional environment. Middle school educators also struggle with the placement of ninth grade students. These students are placed in either 7–9 middle schools or 9–12 high schools. In the 7–9 school, the ninth grade students are placed in a program which is usually overly academic due to graduation requirements. In a 9–12 organization, ninth grade students move prematurely into high school. The ninth grade is a part of the preadolescent years of development because students are not prepared to handle the social, emotional, and intellectual requirements of high school. Where is the best place to put the ninth-grade student and, for that matter, the sixth grade student who also spans a transitional period from elementary to middle school?

Another problem facing middle level education continues to be the unsatisfactory degree of teacher preparedness and inadequate certification programs that produce teachers unable to meet the special needs of the preadolescent. Middle school teachers are prepared for high levels of academic content; however, they are not prepared for the varying levels of physical, intellectual, emotional and social behaviors of their students. Teachers also do not utilize teaching strategies appropriate for the middle level intellect. They are sometimes locked into a group of strategies and do not seek innovative approaches in implementing effective programs (Eichhorn, 1991).

A total analysis of the curriculum needs of middle level students has not been completed since the changes instituted in the late 1950s and early 1960s. *Sputnik* and the resultant space race promoted changes in the curriculum so that the United States could produce competitive scientists and educated citizens. Current curriculum reforms are being made to better fit the purpose of middle level education, education that is developmentally responsive to the preadolescent student.

ORGANIZATIONAL CHARACTERISTICS OF THE MIDDLE SCHOOL PROGRAM

Adolescence is a time of great physical, social, cognitive, personality, and moral change. The middle school, therefore, must be uniquely planned, staffed, and operated to provide a program that is truly focused on the rapidly moving and changing learners in transition from childhood to adolescence. It should be a school with facilities, organizations, curriculum plan, student services, instruction—indeed every aspect—developed and utilized to serve the developmental needs and characteristics of its unique membership (George and Alexander, 1993). In order to meet the developmental needs and interests of the early adolescent and effectively prepare these students for the transition to high school, the middle school must provide diversity, self-exploration, structure and physical activity. These goals can be accomplished through interdisciplinary units, block scheduling, exploratory programs, and advisory programs (Alvermann & Muth, 1992).

Interdisciplinary Teams

An integral pursuit of any organization is the development of its members into a functioning alliance of individuals who are committed to the same goals. School administrators have the dual duty to develop adults and children. Socialization factors concerning cooperation between adults are often overlooked when children seem to be the priority, as in education. However, adults, as well as children, benefit from adapting to new environments and finding solutions to challenging problems.

Teacher team building is critical in order to prepare teachers to work collectively and cooperatively to provide an instructional program for their shared groups of students that addresses their intellectual, social, psychological, and emotional needs. As a team, members share their individual strengths and provide feedback and support to each other (Harris, 1992). More than just a leader in the classroom, still more than an adult in society at large, teachers are role model images for children, teaching them to expand their minds, accept difficult situations, and be successful. Most parents will agree that the things children do best are the things that they see modeled. Regardless of the direct teachings, children more often imitate what they see rather than what they hear.

Team teaching offers the teacher the opportunity to watch as another adult interacts with a known group of children, to exchange ideas, and to develop strategies with another adult who has direct knowledge and understanding of the group of students involved. This enhances the teacher's performance and increases the value of the educational experience for students. Team teaching allows the teacher to provide instruction in the area of specialty. Therefore, the particular talents of the teacher can be employed to the fullest extent.

An open and accepting environment should be fostered by everyone in the school environment. In the selection of new staff, school administrators must be sensitive to the inherent possibility that new staff may present a professional threat to current staff. There are ways to prevent this. One way is to select staff members who are willing to work well with others. Another is to train teachers in working with others. Teaming does not just happen; it takes hard work from all school personnel. Clearly, hindsight offers a perspective for new staff development.

The keystone of the middle school is its interdisciplinary team organization. What teachers share with one another is the basis for how they are organized (George and Alexander, 1993). Interdisciplinary teams are small groups of teachers who teach the same group of students. The effect is that a number of small "schools," or communities, are created within a school (Alvermann & Muth, 1992, p. 5).

The interdisciplinary team organization of teachers and students serves to individualize instruction for students and groups of students. Organization of team teaching situations can vary according to the needs and resources of the school/school system. There are various forms of teams, ranging from small teams to large houses. The small interdisciplinary teams consist of one teacher from each of the core discipline areas and are usually grade specific (Alvermann & Muth, 1992). Multi-graded teams are made up of seventh and eighth grade teachers who keep the same group of students for two years. Multi-graded houses are created from two small sixth grade teams, two small seventh grade teams and one large eighth grade team. The students change teams as they progress, but they remain in the same house. The eighth grade teachers in these houses establish a relationship with sixth grade students long before they teach them in the eighth grade. A final type of teaming is the student/teacher progressive team. In the progressive teams, students and teachers move up grade levels together.

The purpose of teaming is to facilitate a smooth transition from the self-contained elementary classes to the departmentalization of high school classes. Together, teams plan interdisciplinary units, rules, grading practices, field trips, and special guidance issues for a single group of students. The team's benefit to teachers is in the professional development that accompanies its implementation and the increased likelihood of direct involvement of resource personnel with the instructional program. Teams also establish relationships with parents and can plan comprehensive measures to assist students in a family-like environment.

Hunt (1997) provides examples of some of the many things great teams do together, including, but not limited to: coordinating homework, tests, and quizzes; conducting joint parent conferences and full team meetings on a regular basis; establishing common grading practices; coordinating homework; implementing common rules and procedures; and meeting routinely and frequently to assure that open communication exists for student and program issues.

Team building and team teaching are evolutionary constructions. Once initiated, hard work is required to maintain current staff relationships, and orientation is required to integrate new members into existing teams.

Advisory Programs

Every student should have at least one adult with whom he can talk. This is accomplished through advisory programs in the middle school. Advisory programs allow teachers to build relationships with students and provide an opportunity for individual attention to be given to the student's educational, personal, social, and career development. Advisory programs allow every student to have a relationship with at least one adult in the school that is characterized by warmth, concern, oneness, and understanding (George and Alexander, 1992).

Block Scheduling

The school day in many middle schools has been reorganized to offer four blocked classes and an advisory period on an alternating day schedule. Students take eight classes over the course of the school year. The implementation of this type of blocked schedule or other form of modified block has many positive features. The extended classes provide opportunities for creativity in instruction and in-depth learning. Blocked planning periods allow for both interdisciplinary team planning and for individual teacher planning. Teachers and students have more one-on-one time in a relaxed classroom environment. The daily breaks between classes allow for a "cooling off" time if conflicts develop between students or teachers and students. Usually, the attendance rate improves for schools on a block schedule, the drop-out rate and discipline referral rate decline, and the school climate becomes markedly more positive (Queen & Gaskey, 1997). Blocked periods are not appropriate for all subjects. Modified versions may better accommodate the scheduling needs of courses that should meet every day or for shorter periods of time.

Exploratory Programs

The preadolescent's strong desire to be independent can be fostered in exploratory programs. The ability to weigh multiple options and make wise choices reinforces students' real-life decisionmaking processes. Students also benefit from the opportunity to learn more about their interests and talents (Alvermann & Muth, 1992).

DEVELOPMENTAL NEEDS AND INTERESTS

Characteristics of Middle Level Students

Middle school students have common physical, social, emotional, and intellectual characteristics. Physically, they cannot sit for extended periods of time and they experience great physical changes and metabolic fluctuations. These fluctuations and body changes cause many emotional problems such as feelings of alienation and insecurity. While preadolescents are often insecure and emotionally charged, they are also extremely social creatures. They explore the meanings of relationships and their ability to fit in as one of the accepted group. Paradoxically, these social behaviors are also met with the student's needs to express individualism and independence from the norm. Intellectually, the middle level student is concrete operational, highly inquisitive, and always searching for creative reasons to explain larger phenomena.

Middle-level instructional programs demonstrate the theory that the elementary or high school programs do not meet the adolescent's academic, social, and emotional needs. Researchers have repeatedly found that the brain grows in phases; therefore, preadolescents have different mental capabilities than elementary or high school students. Advanced placement classes are not the best answer for introducing high school challenges to middle school students (Toepfer, 1988). It may not be true that if students simply try harder, they can succeed. Learning involves readiness, and young adolescents need more concrete, hands-on experiences to maintain their interest and build for the processes of abstract reasoning.

Not only do middle school teachers have to differentiate for intelligence development and learning styles but also for the physiological changes of preadolescents. Bergmann (1986) explained the dichotomy of the middle grade student when she wrote of an average student as having a big toothy grin in December and braces in January; can be five feet tall in September and five feet six inches tall by the end of the school year in June; can appear to be running in place while seated in a desk; and can be extremely excited about a project, but never finish it. Middle school students are moving physically from a child's body into an adolescent's body, from concrete thinking to abstract, from a self-orientation to a more global view, from total belief of slogans to personal opinion, and from lower order reasoning to complex, higher order conceptualization (George & Lawrence, 1982).

Teachers must contend with the physical and intellectual changes their students are rapidly undergoing as well as the constant emotional fluctuations and social development needs. The dichotomy continues into the preadolescent's emotions and can be seen in erratic behaviors, regressions into childish behavior, the exaggeration of simple events, mood changes, sensitivity to criticism, a constant search for personal identity, and association with peers. Preadolescents push the limits of acceptable behavior, express a love of peers and a hatred of parents, want to know that they are loved and cared for by their parents or other authority figure, experience fears of alienation, and strive to establish relationships with members of the same and opposite sex (Schurr, 1996).

Cognitive Development

Middle schoolers' cognitive processes are unique. Cognitive processes refer to the ways in which one perceives, interprets, forms judgments about, and reacts to his environment. From the adolescent's reactions to the environment he develops the concept, generalization, and principles that aid him in making decisions, solving problems, and discovering and classifying new data. Several scientists have studied the cognitive development of early adolescents, including Jean Piaget and Erik Erikson.

Jean Piaget was a Swiss psychologist whose insightful descriptions of children's thinking changed the way educators understand cognitive development. Piaget classified middle school students in the concrete-operational stages. For educators, this means that students are able to solve concrete (hands-on) problems in a logical fashion, able to understand laws of conservation, and able to classify and separate things.

Erik Erikson proposed a theory of psychosocial development that described tasks to be accomplished at different stages of life. Erikson characterized middle school learners in the stage of Industry versus Inferiority, with Industry defined as the eagerness to engage in productive work. The school and the neighborhood offer a new set of challenges that must be balanced with those at home. Interaction with peers becomes important to pre-adolescents. The child's ability to move between these worlds and to cope with academics, group activities, and friends leads to a growing sense of competence. If a child has difficulty with these challenges, feelings of inferiority may result.

Cognitive theory is exemplified in the intellectual development of middle school students. Intellectually, middle school students tend to be curious and inquisitive; prefer active over passive learning activities; prefer interaction with peers during learning activities; want opportunities to express originality on an individual basis; and like to participate in practical problem-solving situations.

Physical, Social, and Emotional Development

The middle school student has several developmental needs and interests that range from the intellectual to the physical, social, and emotional. According to Tobin (1973), adolescents exhibit certain perceptions of physical development in relation to body development, appearance, and activity.

Adolescents' perceptions of their physical development as their bodies begin to exhibit overt physical signs of maturation include (1) an increased interest in their physical bodies, including functions and changes; (2) an awareness of the more advanced physical maturity of girls than of boys of the same age; (3) increased attention to personal appearance, including concern for skin blemishes, scars, obesity, and other irregularities; (4) a desire for conformity in dress and personal style; (5) extreme restlessness; and (6) talkativeness.

Although physical change and development are the most visible of the many changes that take place during a student's passage through the middle grades, the social and emotional changes adolescents experience are more dramatic (Williamson, 1996). Socially, adolescents are concerned with individuality, conformity, and the development of values. While they desire to be different and have a need to make personal choices, they demonstrate these traits within the overall limits of peer conformity. They have a strong need to feel part of a group, yet often experience frequent changes in their choice of close friends. They have a strong sense of right, wrong, and social justice.

Social adjustment and peer acceptance are extremely important to the proper development of the middle grade student.

Emotionally, the adolescent years are riddled with uncertainties and conflicts. Ambiguities are common in the emotional reactions of adolescents. They seek approval and acceptance by adults, yet are sensitive to criticism and easily offended. They want freedom, but fear the loss of security. They want independence, yet feel a need for direction and regulation. They want suggestions, which they will evaluate for their personal action. They need frequent experiences with success and want recognition for their efforts and achievements. One of their most exasperating traits is their impulsiveness, often evident in their wide range of overt behaviors and mood instability.

Being sensitive to a child's vast range of emotional and social expressions requires more than most parents want to handle. What then is required of the middle school teacher? He or she must be trained to present content material and equipped to address each student's unique level of cognitive change and emotional response. Students at this age require a variety of challenges to their interests and abilities. Middle schools have attempted to respond to this challenge by providing a time and place for social interaction. Educational innovations like exploratory courses, advisory groups, extracurricular activities, and intramural games are designed to complement the middle school curriculum by providing the necessary social activities, emotional needs, cognitive challenges, and physical demands.

NATIONAL CURRICULUM STANDARDS

When *A Nation at Risk* was published, a reform effort began that addressed the report that elementary, middle, and high school students were lacking in reading ability, problem-solving skills, and the ability to identify well-known figures and events from United States history. Various other task forces also compounded the crisis-like call for reform in the 1980s. Educational task forces such as the Carnegie Corporation and the Association for Supervision and Curriculum Development exerted pressures to address the deficiencies of the curriculum for the middle grades.

What the National Organizations Propose

Several national education-related organizations answered the presidential call to address education issues in light of the new millennium. Among those answering the call to national standards relative to middle school education were the National Middle School Association (NMSA), the National Council of Teachers of Mathematics (NCTM), the National Council for Social Studies (NCSS), and the American Association of School Librarians and School Counselors (AASLSC). Many organizations already had begun their work on disciplinary standards before the presidential encouragement.

The National Middle School Association (NMSA) defines, develops, and promotes middle level education. It supports a curriculum that responds to the unique needs of preadolescent learners by affecting the daily classroom environment and displaying a commitment to meet not only the intellectual needs, but also the interests and talents of students. The NMSA backs a curriculum composed of the key principles of understanding self and the world in a developmentally appropriate design with an emphasis on knowledge rather than information and concrete rather than real-world experiences. It encourages competent teachers to trust their instincts in addressing the developmental needs of the preadolescent student.

Additionally, the NMSA advocates a middle level curriculum that serves the adolescent's self-development. Social meaning thus grows out of questions young adolescents ask about themselves and the world around them as well as questions posed by the world around them of which they are unaware (NMSA, 1993).

The Association for Supervision and Curriculum Development and the National Association of Secondary School Principals agree that the middle school concept must be communicated to administrators, teachers, students, and parents with clarity and persuasiveness. These organizations further agree that the unique purpose of the middle school should be upheld with logic and intensity (George & Alexander, 1993).

The National Council of Teachers of Mathematics (NCTM) has paved the way for all national standards curriculum reform efforts. In its "Curriculum and Evaluation Standards for School Mathematics," the council endorses the view that mathematics includes investigation and reasoning, communication, and contextual examination of concepts—much more than a continuum of concepts and skills. Information literacy, as presented within the mathematics curriculum, involves problem solving, the use of estimation, thinking strategies for basic facts, formulating and investigating questions from problem situations, and the use of computers, calculators, and other technologies. Assessment of mathematics also fits within the larger picture of information literacy, because the focus of evaluation is on using information in meaningful ways to demonstrate understanding (Martin & Zawojewski, 1993).

The National Council for the Social Studies' (NCSS) revised standards reflect a belief that students will need practice in information literacy skills in order to understand and apply concepts included in the social studies curriculum. Students must be able to connect knowledge, skills, and values to action through social inquiry. Helping students acquire the skills to make good decisions is the basis of the new social studies standards, and information literacy must go hand in hand (NCSS, 1993).

The National Committee on Science Education Standards and Assessment (NCSESA) is in the process of producing its national science standards, "Science for All" (NRC, 1993). Like the NCSS's standards, these standards emphasize inquiry-based learning, including the abilities to design and perform an investigation, abilities associated with critical thinking that allow application of science information literacy using a hands-on approach.

School counselors also have an interest in the national goals. Counselors are often the only mental health professionals to whom the students have access. As such, they are the professionals who bridge the academic and personal dominions of students' lives. The American School Counselor Association (1992) has addressed the National Education Goals and developed strategic solutions in their Contributive Program Strategies.

The Comprehensive Guidance Program Model focuses on student behavior outcomes, coordinated guidance services, developmental guidance needs for all students, and program evaluation and accountability. Specific counselor interventions include (1) assisting individual students in establishing meaningful educational and career goals; (2) identifying and working with potential dropouts at an early stage; (3) acting as liaison between at-risk students, their families and their teachers to support maintenance of grade level performance; (4) providing support in the development of good work and study habits, including attendance; and (5) understanding the impact of learning style on study habits. In order to directly impact performance, counselors can provide individualized assessment to assist teachers in the identification of specific learning difficulties and work collaboratively with teachers in the development of alternative learning strategies to promote success (Bleuer & Walz, 1993).

The Middle School Curriculum

A school's curriculum is defined by the total learning experiences and activities provided by the school. When planning the middle level curriculum or what is taught, special issues and problems must be recognized and addressed. The basic problem is that the middle level program is essentially a common core of general education classes taught to a widely differing group of students. Individual differences between preadolescent students are greater than those between elementary or high school students. While efforts in the elementary school and high school to address differences have been successful, the even greater ability differences of preadolescents are not being met in those middle schools where students take essentially the same classes.

Will a curriculum ever be able to meet the needs of such a diverse group of learners? In fact, the actual learning by each individual student is quite varied. Many educators view that curriculum is made up of the learning that he or she selects and incorporates into a personal body of knowledge. A disparity exists between the common curriculum planned by the school system and what is actually taught in the middle school.

The common curriculum of middle schools came intact from the junior high school. For the most part, the middle school curriculum is composed of separate subjects presented by specialists during a day of equal periods. The limited change is somewhat surprising considering that the initial impetus for change from the junior high was a need to create middle level schools instead of identical versions of high schools.

The basic program in the middle school curriculum includes the academic classes of language arts/reading, social studies, science and math. The second component of the middle school curriculum is the exploratory program, which includes art, music, vocational courses and physical education. These courses are usually offered during the same period of the student's schedule on a rotating basis. Other exploratory courses include drama, computers, speech, sex education, and foreign language. In the eighth grade, students may elect to take an extended exploratory course. Physical education is considered a separate program provided for groups of same-age students. Middle grade educators recommend intramural sports rather than interschool athletic contests. Activities and clubs are also considered part of the middle school curriculum.

The organization of students by interdisciplinary teacher teams is one of the major distinguishing characteristics of middle schools. A team of teachers, most often comprised of one teacher from each of the four core areas, teaches a single group of students. They plan together to integrate student learning, provide feedback on individual student progress, and improve student learning. Interdisciplinary teams are used by many middle schools in the United States. If teams are not formally utilized, this may be a goal in a school's reform efforts.

The explicit curriculum is undergoing changes and close scrutiny, but attention must also be paid to the implicit curriculum. Organization, policy, and program designs may teach students lessons not intended by educators. Homogenous grouping may teach students that some groups of students are special and therefore deserve more attention. Students also learn from the long list of rules and regulations that adults do not trust students or consider them responsible for their own actions. However, students may also learn positive lessons from good role models as they watch teacher professionalism or learn about developing caring relationships with students and other teachers.

The future curriculum of middle schools may truly deal with curricular issues rather than organizational logistics. Beane (1990), in *A Middle School Curriculum: From Rhetoric to Reality*, proposed a unified general education curriculum built around students' personal concerns and social issues. Simply meeting the needs established by the traditional curriculum is no longer enough. Students in future middle schools will benefit from the initial struggle to separate preadolescent education and the subsequent changes in program to provide a curriculum based on the developmental needs of the individual learner (Lounsbury & Clark, 1991).

STATE AND LOCAL REQUIREMENT PROCESSES

The curriculum of a school is the result of planning by many groups outside and inside of the school itself. State committees, textbook committees, state departments of education, professional organizations, special interest groups, and the school district committees play roles in developing the curriculum (George & Alexander, 1993). The actual process of designing the curriculum varies, yet developmental patterns of creating exemplary schools exist when appropriate services for planning are provided:

1. A framework of goals that individual schools can use to develop school-specific programs.

2. Consultants or coordinating assistance in planning for all curriculum areas.

3. The organization of system-wide councils to coordinate the sharing and planning between schools of different levels.

The U.S. Department of Education made grants to 23 states to develop standards and curriculum frameworks in certain critical subjects (Federal Initiatives, 1994). Forty-two states had a state framework or curriculum-related document in mathematics and science education in place at the end of 1994. Concurrently, half of the states were developing a new framework or standards document in math or science.

Performance standards are developed to describe what a student should know and be able to do at each grade level. The performance standards delineate observable behaviors so that a school can measure to what extent it is meeting the goals of its total mission. The educational goals of a middle school usually include academic proficiency in the core classes, mastery of basic computing skills, and career exploration. All these goals contribute to the mission of helping students make decisions and become responsible members of society.

The reasons for establishing a core group of standards include raising performance expectations for all learners, promoting continuous improvement in teaching and learning, strengthening accountability and local control, and ensuring that conditions for learning provide appropriate opportunities for learning to occur.

Content and Process Focus

Most of the attention that has been focused on middle level education has centered on improving the climate and organization of the school. Curriculum appears to be less of a focus by supporters outside the educational arena and by administrators. The lack of clarity about the crucial relationship between content and process in curriculum development at the middle school level is symptomatic of the middle school's isolation from the mainstream. Content and process are simply question and answer. One of the major faults of schooling, and perhaps a reason why content tends to be denigrated, is that teachers are constantly giving students answers to questions that they have not asked. Such practice provides students with information rather than knowledge, and it breaks the fundamental unity of content and process. Content and process are inextricably bound. Knowing what is important and what is worth knowing allows teachers to help in students' applications of important principles to many endeavors (Arnold, 1991).

Another reason for the attack on content and process is the emphasis on grades rather than learning. Perhaps the most powerful force negatively influencing curriculum is educators' obsession with measurement. Educators must meet the mandates of the state by focusing on the grades rather than the student. However, students need a curriculum that is rich in meaning, not rich in grades.

A curriculum rich in meaning can be described in three ways. First, the curriculum deals with information that is important and worth knowing. Yet arguments abound over what is important and what is not. Dewey said that important ideas and experiences open doors to new learning. Educators learn from experiences that lead to future growth and development. Second, a meaningful curriculum deals with values. Values are constantly taught. Students should be encouraged to reflect upon their responses to critical issues. The process involves critical thinking, which allows for exploration. Third, both content and methodology must relate substantively to the needs and interests of young adolescents. Unfortunately, developmental responsiveness has become a cliché; the term is bandied about but seldom understood or applied to curriculum. Developmental responsiveness is a must.

Content and process involve students thinking for themselves and about themselves. Therefore, the curriculum should be relevant to the young adolescent. Content and process should be a view of something the students can do for themselves for intrinsic reasons. Middle school education needs a vision of curriculum that enables students to see that the world is full of exciting ideas and that education can make them more vital, interested, and interesting persons. Educators need to implement a curriculum rich in meaning (Arnold, 1991).

Exemplifying this focus, the Georgia Middle School strives to facilitate the planning, implementation, and continuous improvement of all phases of middle level education as it continues to promote its acceptance as a distinct entity uniquely different from either the elementary or high school program. In conjunction with this, it assists with the design and implementation of specific programs of middle level program evaluation for the state of Georgia and represents middle level education in professional and public discussions of policy and educational programs. It also acts upon its belief in the importance of maintaining a cooperative relationship with organizations, agencies, and groups that are committed to the positive development of early adolescents (Georgia Middle School Association, 1997).

INSTRUCTIONAL TECHNOLOGY

Educational technology is a term widely used in the field of education (and other areas), but its meaning is open to interpretation. The word technology is used by some to mean hardware, the devices that deliver information and serve as tools to accomplish a task; but those working in the field of technology use the term to refer to a systematic process of solving problems by scientific means. Hence, educational technology properly refers to a particular approach to achieving the ends of education. Instructional technology refers to the use of such technological processes specifically for teaching and learning.

The most recent definition of the field (which uses the term instructional technology) was published in 1994 by the Association for Educational Communications and Technology (AECT): Instructional Technology is the theory and practice of design, development, utilization, management, and evaluation of processes and resources for learning.

The field is essentially a twentieth-century movement with its major developments occurring during and immediately after World War II. While the movement began with an emphasis on audio-visual communications media, the field gradually became focused on the systematic development of teaching and learning procedures that were based in behavioral psychology. Currently, major contributing fields are cognitive psychology, social psychology, psychometrics, perception psychology, and management (Ely, 1995). Technology courses have historically been offered as electives because these were viewed as irrelevant. However, society is quickly becoming more technological. Therefore, technology courses must be provided, and the most important aspects of technology in the lives of the common man must be areas of emphasis (Johnston & Johnston, 1996, p. 28).

Technology has quickly become one of the most popular methods of instruction at all levels of education, especially the middle school. A vast array of technology is available for use in the classroom. Through technology, every learner can become active. It is the key to addressing individualized differences, especially in the middle school. Technology has four practical applications in the school: as a separate subject, a surrogate teacher, an instructional tool, and a catalyst for transforming the learning process.

As an instructional tool, technology enhances learning in the regular classroom. The Internet provides students with access to a variety of information from all over the world. Students are finding that video games, as well as educational programs (CD ROMs), are helpful in content learning. However, the computer with educational software and video games is not the only type of technological enhancement available to educators and students.

Video cameras are becoming exciting tools for schoolwork, used in book reports to family histories. The video camera could be known as learning by doing. As a technological tool that is easily operated, the video camera motivates students to create their own thoughts and makes learning transparent.

Technology transforms what is learned as well as how and where it is learned. It allows the classroom to becomes a workplace and engages students in meaningful, product-oriented activities that focus on authentic problems, issues, and opportunities (Johnston & Johnston, 1996).

The North Carolina Instructional Technology Plan (1994) was designed to improve student performance and enhance the teaching/learning process through the effective use of technology. Students must be empowered through the use of technology to think more critically, communicate more creatively, and solve problems more analytically. The U.S. Department of Labor's SCANS report in 1992 projected that the demand for technologically literate workers in North Carolina would increase threefold by the year 2000. In order to facilitate school/curricula improvements and provide students with the needed skills and competencies, a comprehensive, information technology infrastructure was essential. Within middle school classrooms across the state, North Carolina educators were directed to provide students with role models for using technology to become effective and efficient users of twenty-first century tools and resources. The North Carolina Standard Course of Study emphasizes word processing, database, spreadsheet, and telecommunication mastery at the middle school grades. These productivity tools are ideally suited to curriculum integration activities.

CLASSROOM MODELS AND STUDY

Just because a middle school says it is a middle school doesn't mean that it operates as a middle school. There are many middle schools still operating as junior high schools. However, more and more middle schools around the nation are seeing the benefits of the middle school concept and they are switching over. This section provides a cursory view of a variety of working classroom models used to actively engage students in regular and exceptional education programs and examines studies conducted to determine the effectiveness of block scheduling, flexible scheduling, and modified week programs.

Block scheduled classes for 7th grade students in two Texas middle schools did not show significant change in student achievement levels in either underachievers or high achievers (Schroth & Dixon, 1995). However, in the implementation of block scheduling for middle school for blind and deaf students, longer class periods on alternating days were found to have advantages for teachers. Interdisciplinary teams were facilitated by the longer planning periods (Rettig and Colbert, 1995). Parents of gifted students are more concerned than most about their children's growth in knowledge attainment. A flexible delivery model based in a Pennsylvania middle school program delivered rigorous curricular content through both group lecture and one-to-one instruction.

Each method of teaching depends upon the needs of the student. Timing, it has been said, is everything (Ruder, 1994). As a major factor in most aspects of life, time management is critical in education. Various time management models have been designed to maximize instructional effectiveness throughout the middle school arena. Two methods of school week modifications are cited as examples of the quest for effective use of time.

In Alberta, a junior high school developed a four-day school week. Each day was extended by 40 minutes. The longer day resulted in more classes taught in a shorter time (Litke, 1994).

Center Middle School is located in Kansas City, Missouri. For years, this school has implemented many of the components of the middle school: team teaching, interdisciplinary instruction, elimination of tracking, homeroom advisory periods, common planning time for teachers and, most recently, block scheduling. The school adopted the middle school concept in 1990 and immediately noted a marked improvement in building climate and student attitudes toward learning (Hackmann, 1995).

Northridge Middle School is located in Charlotte, North Carolina. It opened to students in the fall of 1996. This exemplary middle school has implemented middle school components from the beginning. Block scheduling, interdisciplinary units, team teaching, advisory programs, exploratory programs, common planning times, elimination of tracking, and more can be observed in this school. All of these things have contributed to the positive attitudes of students, staff, and teachers in this school.

Bloomfield Hills Middle School is located in Michigan. It is a middle school that is dedicated to providing a curriculum that meets individual academic, creative, emotional, physical, and social needs in a supportive, enjoyable environment that fosters care, trust, and respect for all students. Bloomfield Hills Middle School has focused its curriculum on technology, language arts, math, and science.

NONGRADED MODELS FOR THE MIDDLE SCHOOL

Nongraded, ungraded, multiage grouping or continuous learning schools have no grade designation or grade level standards. Students are reclassified frequently according to individual progress. Aspects of subject matter taught are designed for the various abilities of the child. Frequently, provision is made for independent study and research by students (Blair, 1993). Implied in the definition of this type of school is the task of redefining the curriculum. The school must be held accountable for teaching specified objectives, yet it cannot be grade-specific as there are no distinct grade categories.

Nongraded, multiage grouping addresses the needs of middle school students by addressing their diverse learning interests and styles. Children of the same age level can learn at different rates. For years, teachers have grouped students by ability groups within one classroom and had to manage all levels of performance simultaneously. The nongraded, multiage model allows students to be grouped by ability and interests in a flexible and fluid manner. However, ability grouping is not the focus of the program; it is merely a byproduct. Completion of a prescribed set of objectives allows students to pursue new topics and progress through them with confidence and success.

The philosophical constructs of non-graded primary schools are easily lent to middle school environments. Students have the opportunity to join groups studying advanced topics to preview without being evaluated for their participation. This construct gives students opportunities to pursue advanced topics for the sheer enjoyment of learning without fear of failure. Students tend to learn those things in which they have an interest faster than subjects that do not affect their interests.

Scope and Sequence

Nearly all children begin school wanting to learn and believing that they are capable of learning. Yet within a few years this eagerness seems to disappear (Anderson & Pavan, 1993). Nongraded schools are what some suggest is the answer to keeping the eagerness to learn. They are schools that have been criticized and under much scrutiny because of the methods of evaluation: there are no grades. However, a nongraded school is much more than a school in which no grades are applied.

A nongraded school is a school in which individual differences in the pupil population are accepted and respected and which provides extensive variability in instructional approaches in order to respond to varying student needs. Learning is intended to be challenging as well as pleasurable and rewarding. Development in cognitive, physical, aesthetic, social, and emotional spheres is nurtured. The administrative framework is flexible and provides opportunities for each child to interact with children and adults of varying personalities, backgrounds, abilities, interests, and ages. Students are enabled through flexible arrangements to progress at their own pace. Curricular areas are both integrated and separate. The expected standards of performance in the core areas of the curriculum are clearly defined, so that the points to be reached by the end of a designated period are well known. Specific content learning is generally subordinate to the understanding of major concepts and methods of inquiry and the development of the skills of learning. Student assessment is holistic, to correspond with the holistic view of learning. Evaluation of the learner is continuous, comprehensive, and diagnostic. These characteristics promote a system that is highly teacher-managed and controlled (Anderson & Pavan, 1993, p. 64).

Advantages and Disadvantages

The author believes that, as with any program, there are advantages and disadvantages to nongraded schooling. Some of the advantages and disadvantages are listed below.

Advantages of nongraded schools

- maximizes individual potential
- positive learning environments
- teacher as facilitator of learning
- variety of learning materials
- students working at an appropriate level

Disadvantages of nongraded schools

- change of child's placement at any time
- goals set by student with teacher
- no predetermined sequence
- individual curriculum (Anderson & Pavan, 1993, p. 69)

Systems wanting to incorporate the nongraded model should incorporate research within the decision to implement. The advantages and disadvantages should be weighed very heavily. School officials should realize that each school situation is inevitably so unique that some of the ideas of nongraded schooling may not seem workable or appropriate. Schools should create awareness through examination of research and models of schools that have already implemented the model and promote the school-home partnership to promote strong parental involvement and community support.

IMPLICATIONS FOR FUTURE TEACHERS

In the immediate future, the average person will change careers more than five times during a lifetime. Teachers must change and adapt with the quickly shifting society to educate students who will be able to deal with the flexible nature of the future. Students must have a positive self-image, a competent knowledge of technology, and an ability to think critically.

There may not be one specific way to improve schools in the future (Raspberry, 1991). Parents in the future will demand more choice in schools, which may lead to more open enrollment and teaming choices in the middle schools. Within one district, students may be able to choose to attend a technology school, a center for at-risk students, a magnet arts school, a language immersion school, or a math and science school.

Schools and teachers will become more globally engaged through the use of the Internet. Resources gained through national and global networking will help students learn to understand, appreciate, and communicate with individuals of all cultures and nationalities.

Colleges and universities should be at the forefront of educational innovation. The focus of higher education must change. Teacher training must not perpetuate the status quo or reemphasize the problems of the past. Teachers must be prepared to meet the demands of the classroom by completing an education containing practical preparation, good teaching models, and relevant human development research. College instructors and professors in colleges of education should demonstrate effective teaching to promote positive experiences for college students. College students are the future teachers of the United States. If they endure a negative experience, they may convey this negativity in the way they treat their own students and view the career of teaching. Perpetuating lifelong learning should be paramount for teacher education and middle level education.

Middle level schools and practicing teachers must accept the challenge of addressing students' achievement needs (Williamson, 1995). Teachers will find it imperative to continually educate themselves in order to educate students. Part of this process includes being "user friendly," that is, knowledgeable of the middle school learner cognitively, physically, socially, and emotionally. Middle level educators should be sensitive to the maturation process of young adolescents because this is when the shaping of the adult personality occurs. Teachers must care and create a warm, inviting climate for students.

Educators are faced with the words of Herbert Spencer, "What knowledge is of most worth?" (Tanner & Tanner, 1995). As we enter the new millennium, educators must predict with foresight the needs, values, and concerns of a personally and socially relevant education. The middle school segment of the educational system offers educators a dependable benchmark; however, adolescent students will always have developmental and social needs as well as content requirements. This provides educators a decisive advantage for preparation. Amidst all other concerns, creative and constructive thinking skills should be encouraged and developed. As we know from the past, change is inevitable. It will remain part of the future.

SUMMARY

The push to realign junior high school into the 6–8 middle school came from research on the development of the preadolescent and the realization that the onset of puberty is occurring earlier than ever before. Making this transition from a junior high school to a middle school, reforming the current middle school curriculum, and maintaining competency in a rapidly expanding technological world must be viewed as an on-going journey. While other levels of education offer unique situations, the middle school has special combinations of naivete, the need for growth, and sheer excitement. All of these characteristics embodied in thirty students in a classroom can be alarming to some people. Educators of middle level students must take steps toward improving education with a unique understanding of preadolescents and a realization that reform is organic and must constantly change to fit the needs of an ever-changing society.

Paving the road for middle school students to make a smooth transition to high school is a challenging task for educators and reformers. Successful middle school programs provide appropriately high expectations, experience with success, and individual choice. Yet instead of forcing preadolescents into higher level thinking, whether they are ready or not, schools should educate each student at the rate and pace that his or her capabilities and developmental readiness will allow. Middle level educators must deliver students to the high school who have a real chance for success.

Along with the differentiation of instruction and age appropriate intellectual activities, the social, emotional, and physical needs of the preadolescent learner must be addressed. Interdisciplinary teaming, advisory programs, exploratory programs, and flexible scheduling promote the education of the whole middle level student body.

The outlook for middle level education holds much promise as well as a great challenge for future educators. Middle school students need a learning environment that is different from that found in elementary or high school. The challenge is to continue the journey toward reform and prepare students for survival in the twenty-first century. The Carnegie Council on Adolescent Development (1989) recommends that continuing evolution of the middle school can be achieved by creating small communities for learning, strengthening the core subjects that are taught to all students, ensuring success for all students, and improving academic performance by fostering good health and fitness. Middle school teachers and administrators need to have primary responsibility for making decisions about the experiences of their students, families must be reengaged, and the communities must become involved.

If educators connect these characteristics to curriculum and instruction, student success will be assured in the middle school. The middle school will then become the turning point for each student's last best chance for an education that is rich in meaningful curriculum.

✤ ✤ ✤   DISCUSSION QUESTIONS

1. Discuss two opposing educational philosophies and determine which would be the better philosophy for the future of middle level education.
2. Should new teachers be required to begin professional development courses immediately after beginning a new position? Justify your response.
3. Why must the middle school provide diversity, self-exploration, structure, and physical activity in its curriculum?
4. Identify the five most important competencies needed by a middle school teacher.
5. List and describe four characteristics of the middle school.
6. What would you propose to your national organization as an area of need to address within curriculum frameworks?
7. What are the student's responsibilities for meeting expected objectives in a nongraded school setting?

✤ ✤ ✤   CLASS ACTIVITIES

1. What are some major principles of a curriculum as suggested by the National Middle School Association?
2. Trace the history of the junior high school and identify the factors that led to the establishment of the middle school.
3. Describe the ways technology can be used for instruction. Design a Power-point presentation that can be used in schools for inservice.

✤ ✤ ✤   REFERENCES

Alexander, W. M., & McEwin, K. C. (1989). *Schools in the middle: Status and progress.* Columbus, OH: National Middle School Association.

Alkin, M. C. (Ed). (1992). *Encyclopedia of educational research. 6*(3). New York: Macmillan.

Alvermann, D. E., & Muth, D. K. (1992). *Teaching and learning in the middle grades.* Boston, MA: Allyn & Bacon.

Anderson, R. H., & Pavan, B. N. (1993). *Nongradedness: Helping it to happen.* Philadelphia, PA: Pennsylvania Technomic Publications.

Arnold, J. (1991, November). Towards a middle level curriculum rich in meaning. *Middle School Journal*, pp. 8–12.

Beane, J. A. (1990). *A middle school curriculum: From rhetoric to reality.* Columbus, OH: National Middle School Association.

Bergmann, S. (1986, August/September). Action sheets for counselors and advisors. *Middle Grade Network News.* Tampa, FL: National Resource for Middle Grades Education.

Blair, B. G. (1993). What does chaos theory have to offer educational administration? *Journal of School Leadership, 3*(5), 579–596.

Bleuer, J. C., & Walz, G. R. (1993). *Striving for excellence: Counselor strategies for contributing to the national education goals.* (Report No. ED357317). Ann Arbor, MI: ERIC Clearinghouse on Counseling and Personnel Services.

Briggs, T. H. (1920). *The junior high school.* Boston, MA: Houghton Mifflin.

Buffie, E. G., & Jenkins, J. M. (Eds.). (1971). *Curriculum development in nongraded schools.* Bloomington, IN: Indiana Press.

Carnegie Council on Adolescent Development. (1989). *Turning points: Preparing American youth for the 21st century.* Washington, DC: Carnegie Corporation.

Cotton, K. (1993). *Implementing a nongraded elementary program: Konnoack elementary school, Winston-Salem, North Carolina.* School Improvement Research Series (SIRS). (Snapshot #29. http://www.nwrel.org/scpd/sirs/8/s029.html)

Dickinson, T. (Ed.). (1993). *Readings in middle school curriculum: A continuing conversation.* Columbus, OH: National Middle School Association.

Eichhorn, D. H. (1991). Why middle schools? *Middle Level Education: Programs, Policies and Practices.* National Association of Secondary School Principals.

Ely, D. P. (1995, September). ERIC Digest, ERIC Document Reproduction Service. No. ED387117

Finks, H. *Middle school handbook.* Boston, MA: National Association of Independent Schools.

George, P., & Alexander, W. (1993). *The exemplary middle school* (2nd ed.). Orlando, FL: Harcourt Brace College.

George, P., & Lawrence, G. (1982). *Handbook for middle school teaching.* Glenview, IL: Scott, Foresman & Company.

Georgia Middle School Association. (1997). (http://www.newlink.net/education/org/ga/GMSA/purpose.html)

Hansen, J. C. (1995). *Interest assessment.* (Report ED389961). Greensboro, NC: ERIC Clearinghouse on Counseling and Student Service.

Harris, S. (1991, Fall). The principal's role in helping middle level students at risk. *Schools in the Middle,* 3–5.

Johnston, H., & Johnston, L. L. (1996, February/March). Technology: Ring our present and future into the classroom. *Schools in the Middle,* 26–30.

Johnston, J. H., & Markle, G. C. (1986). *What research says to the middle level practitioner.* Columbus, OH: National Middle School Association.

Lipsitz, J., Mizell, M. H., Jackson, A. W., & Austin, L. M. (1997, March). Speaking with one voice: A manifesto for middle-grades reform. *Phi Delta Kappan, 78*(7), 533–540.

Litke, C. D. (1994). Implementing the modified four-day school week. *Alberta Journal of Educational Research, 40*(3), 271–281.

Lounsbury, J. H., & Clark, D. C. (1991). *Inside grade eight: From apathy to excitement.* Reston, VA: The National Association of Secondary School Principals.

Martin, H. M., & Zawojewski, J. S. (1993). Dealing with data and chance: An illustration from the Middle School Addendum to the Standards. *Arithmetic Teacher, 41*(4), 220–223.

McKay, J. A. (1995). Schools in the middle: Developing a middle-level orientation. The practicing administrator's leadership series. ERIC Document Reproduction Service No. ED383094.

Messick, R. G., & Reynolds, K. E. (1992). Middle level curriculum in action. ERIC Document Reproduction Service No. ED338624.

Ornstein, A. C., & Behar, L. S. (Eds.). (1995). *Contemporary issues in curriculum.* Boston, MA: Allyn & Bacon.

Queen, J. A., & Gaskey, K. A. (1997). Steps for improving block scheduling. *Phi Delta Kappan, 79*(2), 158–161.

Raspberry, W. (1991, July 28). Program lets schools take risks. *Eugene Register-Guard.*

Rettig, M. D., & Colbert, C. K. (1995). Redesigning the school day: A user-friendly schedule. *Perspectives in Education and Deafness, 13*(4), 2–3, 9.

Ruder, R. (1994). A three-pronged approach to talent development. *Middle School Journal, 26*(2), 61–63.

Schroth, G., & Dixon, J. (1995). The effects of block scheduling on seventh grade math students. ERIC Document Reproduction Service No. ED387887.

Schurr, S. (1996). Balancing act: Student-centered and subject-centered instruction. *Schools in the Middle, 6*(1), 11–15.

Tanner, D., & Tanner, L. (1995). *Curriculum development: Theory into practice* (3rd ed.). Upper Saddle River, NJ: Merrill/Prentice Hall.

Toepfer, C. F. (1988). What to know about young adolescents. *Social Education, 52*(2), 110–112.

Williamson, R. D. (1995). Leadership: A focus on leadership for student achievement. *Schools in the Middle, 5*(2), 17–22.

Williamson, R. D. (1996). Modifying structure: A resource for improved student achievement at the middle level. *NASSP Bulletin, 80*(578), 17–23.

❖ ❖ ❖ SUGGESTED READINGS

Anderson, R. H., & Pavan, B. N. The nongraded school. [Video]. Bloomington, IN: Phi Delta Kappa.

Berryman, S. E. (1992). *Integrating academic and vocational education: An equitable way to prepare middle level students for the future.* New York: ERIC Clearinghouse on Urban Education.

Brown, B. F. (1963). *The nongraded high school.* Upper Saddle River, NJ: Prentice Hall.

Eisner, E. W. (1994). *The educational imagination: On the design and evaluation of school programs* (3rd ed.). Upper Saddle River, NJ: Merrill/Prentice Hall.

Hackmann, D. A. (1995, November/December). Improving school climate: Alternating block scheduling. *Schools in the Middle,* 28–32.

Howard, E. R., & Bardwell, R. W. (1966). *How to organize a non-graded school.* Upper Saddle River, NJ: Prentice Hall.

Hunt, K. (1996, March). Teaming: The guts of the middle school. Presentation at NCMSA state conference, Greensboro, NC.

Lewis, A. C. (1992). Middle schools come of age. *Education Digest, 58*(2), 4–7.

Lounsbury, J. H. (1991). The middle school curriculum—Or is it curricula? *Middle Level Education: Programs, Policies & Practices.* Columbus, OH: National Association of Secondary School Principals.

Lounsbury, J. H. (Ed.). (1992). *Connecting the curriculum through interdisciplinary instruction.* Columbus, OH: National Middle School Association.

Morrison, G. S. (1993). *Contemporary curriculum K–8.* Boston, MA: Allyn & Bacon.

National Middle School Association. (1995). *This we believe: Developmentally responsive middle level schools.* Columbus, OH: National Middle School Association.

Pennsylvania Department of Education. (1994). *Mathematics curriculum framework.* Harrisburg, PA: Author. (http://www.enc.org/reform/fworks/ ENC1795/1795.htm)).

Rollins, S. P. (1968). *Developing nongraded schools.* Itasca, IL: F. E. Peacock Publishers, Inc.

Schlechty, P. C. (1990). *Schools for the twenty-first century: Leadership imperatives for educational reform.* San Francisco, CA: Jossey-Bass Inc.

Thornburg, H. (1901). Early adolescents: Their developmental characteristics. *The High School Journal, 63*(6), 215–221.

IV

PATHWAYS TO INSTRUCTION

❖ ❖ ❖

9

THE INSTRUCTIONAL UNIT

Chapter Objective and Focus:

To describe the elements of an integrated
unit of instruction and provide examples
of exemplary unit designs

In Part Three, the process of integrating the instructional program within and across grade levels was presented. In this chapter, the focus is on designing an integrated unit using a step-by-step approach. After every step is completed, the unit will be ready for use in the classroom. Different formats for integration are provided for comparison and evaluation. Once the lesson design is completed, the concept of master unit will be taught using a similar format. Exemplary master lessons are provided for analysis and further study.

Educational systems in the past placed emphasis on teaching the academic disciplines as unique, separate entities. However, it has become a challenge in the 1990s to begin looking at education with a greater holistic approach. Teachers of today and tomorrow are challenged to integrate each subject with many other disciplines, thus creating a much wider knowledge base for each student. Many teachers are eager to learn exactly what integrated units involve and how to implement these into their own classrooms.

One hundred years ago, John Dewey suggested that if teachers applied ideas from one area of the curriculum to others, learning would be more relevant and interesting to students. He believed that students would be much more likely to internalize the importance of connecting ideas. If teachers teach the disciplines separately, students are likely to see them as unconnected and discontinuous. However, with teachers working together and exchanging ideas and observations, students may be able to see the relevance and importance of the theme they are studying in its entirety, as well as its separate disciplines. If students are to truly learn and see the material they are studying as authentic, it must be relevant to their lives. An integrated unit is one that promises students will be personally engaged in their learning. This type of learning style helps to bring a much greater motivational appeal to the students as well as the teachers.

Integrated units are more likely thought to be taught in the classrooms of early childhood educators. Preschool and Kindergarten teachers routinely plan their instructional patterns around central themes. However, integrated units are now becoming a vital part of elementary and middle school programs. For example, the New York State Education Department currently requires teachers in grades three through eight to develop at least one integrated project with students in their classes each year. It is believed that with integrated units implemented into classrooms, four possible goals may be mastered:

1. Students will grow more confident.
2. Students will work together cooperatively.
3. Students will develop social and ethical consciousness.
4. Students will learn to think on their own. (Post, p. 5)

Because these goals are often mastered by using integrated units, students are allowed opportunities to learn through a variety of teaching methods. Each student learns differently. This "theory gives educators a way of thinking about individual gifts of students, and how to accommodate teaching these gifts" (Brondt, 1988, p. 34).

MAJOR TERMS

Theme

When an integrated unit is taught, it is usually organized around a central theme. Students investigate that theme using as many of the differing disciplines as they can in order to assist them in their inquiry. Themes can vary greatly and tend to be very broad. It is the teacher's responsibility to listen to the needs and interests of his or her students in order to choose a central theme that will be relevant and interesting to that particular age group. Possible themes include: space, family, change, environment, flying, dinosaurs, relationships, etc. Examples of more comprehensive themes to be examined by older students are the Mediterranean Lands, the Middle East, biomes, the revolutionary war, etc. In thematic studies, students have the opportunity to observe connections and relationships among the various disciplines that teachers have chosen to integrate into each particular unit.

After both the students and the teacher have selected a theme, the teacher can then guide the planning process with the students' comments in mind to incorporate many different disciplines into the unit. The teacher points out the relationship of the different subjects to show students how all the subjects work together to accomplish a specific objective.

Rationale

Every integrated unit should have a rationale for implementation. Both teachers and students need to know the reason and importance of the unit they will be studying. Students need to understand how the theme they are studying relates to the whole picture. The rationale can answer questions such as: Why is this topic important? What difference will it make if I understand this topic? How will I use this information? It is important that the topic being taught is relevant to the students, and that the students see and understand this relevance.

Major Expectations and Main Objectives

The unit objective is an important component in planning for a successful integrated unit. Unit objectives can be broken down into two categories. First, there are the large focus areas to be accomplished, which the author calls the major expectations. These can also be referred to as the overall unit goals. They focus the purpose of the entire unit of work. These objectives state the major expectations the teacher has for students upon completion of the unit.

A second type of objective is content or process, also known as a main objective. Main objectives are the short-term objectives included in a single lesson. These objectives provide a measure by which the teacher can assess the effectiveness of instruction. This type of objective usually follows a behavioral format and answers one of the following questions: Whom? What? Under what conditions? How well? This objective explains what the student is to learn from each particular lesson. This objective also states what is to be mastered through the main activities in the unit.

Establishing objectives and making the students aware of these objectives are important in planning a successful integrated unit. Objectives allow the teacher and the students to remain focused during the unit. Objectives tell the students what they will be held responsible for and what they will be evaluated on. They are important in allowing the activities and lessons to further understanding in specific, established areas. The teacher must make sure that the objectives are stated clearly and are thoroughly understood by all students before beginning the unit.

Unit and Lesson Plan Designs

One model of a unit plan was described by Chris Stevenson as a "description of ideas and lessons related to a central theme to be studied by a group of children" (Stevenson, p. 33). The unit plan is constantly changing and continuously developing in order to better meet the initial objectives and the students' needs. In the initial unit design, only one, fully developed lesson plan is necessary. This lesson plan will be the one used to introduce the unit. It should be planned with something in mind to orient the students to the theme and allow them to become excited and enthusiastic about the material they will be studying. This initial lesson will help students to begin responding to the unit theme. The teacher then is able to determine and develop the other lessons according to the students' responses. (Note: The author recommends that an entire unit be completed prior to implementation of the unit.)

When developing each lesson, the teacher should include statements of the skills and/or knowledge to be emphasized, how this learning is relevant to students, and what students will know or be able to do as a result of participation in the lesson. Complete lesson plans can be prepared from these descriptions. In writing a unit plan design, it is important that the teacher have specific objectives allowing different cognitive levels to be reached. Sometimes a teacher can design an integrated unit plan by using a web that suggests some possible lessons relating to a particular theme the students will study.

Coding Procedures and Task Analysis

Coding procedures are used in order to organize the main objectives with the enabling activities. These coding procedures are determined by the teacher or group of teachers according to what works best for them. Use of coding procedures saves the teacher time, and keeps planning organized and consistent. Task analysis is used to show the individual tasks that students will be performing throughout the units. Tasks can be organized in the form of a web map or another preferred form. Examples of both coding procedures and task analysis are given in the integrated unit on biomes that appears later in this chapter.

Enabling Activities

The enabling activities are the actual experiences students complete to learn the content, which has been determined by the main objectives. This includes the specific content and the methods used (discussion, inquiry, cooperative learning, discovery, and so on).

Unit Evaluation

At the end of the unit, students and teacher should evaluate the entire unit. This helps the teachers know what was and what was not successful in the unit. The successful activities can be used again. Those that were not as successful should be modified or discarded. The teacher can learn a lot from the comments of the students. Sometimes the theme of the unit is not relative to students and, therefore, students are unable to relate to the topic. Other times, the problem is in the way a particular lesson is presented. Whatever the comments, it is important for the teacher to be aware of the pros and cons for using this unit again.

STEPS IN DESIGNING AN INTEGRATED UNIT

❖ ❖ ❖

Fifth Grade: *Jenny of the Tetons*

For this unit, a popular children's book is used to integrate several content areas for students who are performing well at the fifth grade level. The first step is to determine the major theme for the unit. As will be seen later, once certain elements are defined, the teacher has an opportunity to choose selections from the book based upon the specific curriculum standards he or she plans to develop.

Theme

The theme of a unit is the generalized term or statement that embraces the focus of the major content to be taught.

> **Example:** The focus of this unit is *racism*. This is an age-appropriate topic and an issue that students will continue to face in the future. In this model of an integrated unit, the teacher selects a novel or other appropriate literature before looking at the specific content that needs to be taught from several areas to be implemented. In this case, *Jenny of the Tetons* by Kristiana Gregory was selected.

Main Expectation

The next step is to determine the major ideas that are to be taught about racism by establishing the major expectation, which is the cumulative outcome desired for the students.

Example: At the completion of this unit, the student will be able to identify, apply, and extend techniques for overcoming stereotypes in our society.

Rationale

The rationale gives us the reason or need to teach this particular topic. The rationale should be an integral part of the curriculum.

Example: *Jenny of the Tetons* explores topics such as racism, life styles, culture, and environmental awareness. This integrated theme unit is designed to introduce fifth grade students to the concepts of stereotypes and racism. Students will construct their own ideas about the white settler stereotypes and prejudice and explore how these prejudices affected their interaction with the Native Americans.

Task Analysis

In the task analysis, it is important for the teacher to divide the main elements of the major expectation into several of its supportive components.

Example: Upon completion of this unit, students will be able to identify and compare the life styles, religions, cultures, and forms of communication of Native Americans and our present society. Students will also be able to identify cultural transmissions between the two groups. Students will transfer this knowledge of stereotypes by identifying, applying, and extending techniques of overcoming stereotypes and prejudice.

In the process of task analysis, it is helpful to create a web or diagram of the major content from the objective (Figure 9.1) and compare that with the focus content of the novel. At this point, the teacher will be able to see several content areas that begin to surface. In this case and in this curriculum, the teacher has determined that several concepts, facts, or generalizations are to be taught throughout the year. The teacher can now select from these and integrate many into the unit instead of teaching these in an isolated format. Once the objectives from the curriculum or specific program are selected, the teacher places them into what is known as main objectives.

Main Objectives

Main objectives are supportive in nature in that the summation of these should allow the learner to maximize his or her opportunity to master the major expectation in an integrated framework. Main objectives are listed by subject or process and numbered, as shown in the following examples.

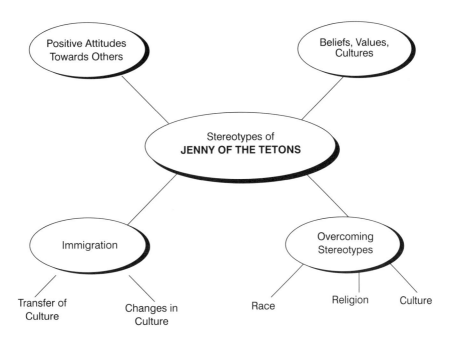

FIGURE 9.1
Web Diagram for Using *Jenny of the Tetons* to Examine Racial Stereotypes and Prejudices

Citizenship (C)

C-1   The student will be aware of the effects of alcohol use.

C-2   The student will be aware that people consume alcohol for a variety of social, psychological, and physical reasons for which, in
most cases, there exist safer and more acceptable alternatives.

C-3   The student will develop the ability to relate positively to others.

C-4   The student will be able to identify stereotypes.

C-5   The student will be able to describe techniques for overcoming
stereotypes.

Communications Skills (CS)

CS-1   The student will prepare to read by setting purpose(s) for reading.

CS-2   The student will identify story elements in various types of literature to aid in comprehension.

CS-3   The student will evaluate his or her own writing and that of peers.

CS-4   The student will develop positive attitudes about himself/herself,
others, and art.

CS-5   The student will develop individual responsibility while participating in creative drama activities.

Problem Solving (PS)

PS-1   The student will understand the nature and relationship of science to human endeavor.

PS-2   The student will understand the nature and conservation of those resources that make up our environment.

PS-3   The student will demonstrate an understanding and use of properties and relationships of geometry.

PS-4   The student will understand and use standard units of metric and customary measure.

PS-5   The student will exhibit an understanding of the calculation of numbers.

Social Studies (SS)

SS-1   The student will assess the influence of major religions, ethical beliefs, and aesthetic values on life in the United States.

SS-2   The student will assess the significance of the physical and cultural characteristics of regions within the Western Hemisphere.

SS-3   The student will evaluate ways the people of the Western Hemisphere use, modify, and adapt to the physical environment.

SS-4   The student will evaluate the significance of the movement of people, goods, and ideas from place to place.

SS-5   The student will analyze changes in ways of living and investigate why and how these changes occurred.

Coding Procedures

By coding the main objectives, the teacher is able to avoid rewriting the objective in the lesson plan, be guided in the selection of which main objectives are to be chosen, and to easily record these in an abbreviated form. For example, PS-1, SS-2, etc.

Lesson

Lessons historically have been divided into predetermined periods such as 30 minutes or 55 minutes. As stated in the previous chapters for each grade division, the futurist designs lessons that permit the teacher to implement a lesson for three periods, two days or whatever time is practically needed. This is determined by the time needed for implementing the enabling activities.

The time needed for implementing the lesson is determined by the assessed projection of the type and amount of activities that must be developed to teach the concepts from more than two or three subject or process areas.

Lesson 1: "Confronting Stereotypes"

Main Objectives

C-4, C-5, CS-5

Presentation

The teacher will lead the class in a discussion of stereotypes. A stereotype is a false conception about another person based on some characteristic that he or she possesses.

Enabling Activity

Students will gain a deeper understanding of the stereotypes that they possess by playing a game called "What Am I Like?" In this game, each student will have a nationality or characteristic placed on his or her back. The students will have to walk among their peers and allow their peers to tell them about their ethnic group or nationality. The students will have to guess what the tag on their back says, based on the stereotypes that their peers give them.

After students have guessed their nationality or characteristic, they will assemble into groups according to their tags. They will discuss and record what their classmates said about their particular characteristic. Questions to guide their discussion are: How do you feel about what your classmates were saying about you? Why do you think we have those stereotypes? How can we avoid having those stereotypes?

Closure

After the small groups have had time to discuss how others stereotyped the characteristic they displayed, the class will discuss how stereotypes and prejudice affect themselves and others. The teacher will begin the discussion by reading the foreword in the book, *Prejudice: An Invisible Wall:*

> Prejudice, someone has said, is being down on something you're not up on. It is hating a person not because of what he is but because of the group he belongs to—black, white, Catholic, Jew, Italian, Mexican, rich, poor, old, young, or something else.
>
> Prejudice leads to children crying in hurt, human beings trapped in a ghetto, people bleeding and dying. . . .
>
> Does it matter if you are prejudiced? Is everybody prejudiced—or just other people? How can you recognize prejudice in other people—and in yourself? Are you born with prejudice—or do you learn it? What harm does prejudice do to its victims? What is the best way to defend yourself against prejudice? How are those who are

prejudiced justified by their views? What can you do to fight prejudice? Should you stand up for the rights of others—as well as your own? How far are we from achieving the American ideal of freedom and equality for all?

Student Assessment

Student assessment is the process of determining through formal and informal means the success or achievement of an individual's mastery of the main objectives. Detailed descriptions of student assessment procedures are given in Chapter 10.

> **Example:** The students will write a journal entry to describe prejudice and how they felt about being stereotyped.

Materials

A tag with a characteristic for stereotypes for each student.

Lesson 2: "Journal of Reactions to Reading"

Main Objectives

C-1, C-2, C-4, C-5, CS-1, CS-2, CS-3, CS-4, PS-1, PS-2, SS-1, SS-2, SS-3, SS-4, SS-5

Presentation

Each night, the students will read a section of *Jenny of the Tetons* and record their reactions to the story. As a class, discussion will be conducted of issues that arise as a result of the reading.

Enabling Activity

The students will be given a list of questions to consider when reading the book. They will use these questions to guide their writing in the journal.

Pages 1–15	How do you think it would feel to wake up and realize that your family had all been killed or had died from disease?
Pages 16–31	Why do you think Jenny shared the story about the death of her family with Carrie?

Pages 32–44	What stereotype do you have about people who drink a lot of alcohol?
Pages 45–56	Why does Jenny have blue eyes? What stereotypes do you have about people whose families integrate different ethnic groups?
Pages 57–77	How did Neal Benton exhibit his prejudice? How do you express your prejudices? Do you think you hurt other people?
Pages 81–90	How does Carrie overcome her prejudiced feelings toward Jenny? Describe a way that you can overcome one of your prejudices.
Pages 91–104	Do you have any stereotypes about women who hunt? Why was it necessary for Jenny and Carrie to be able to protect themselves?
Pages 105–114	Are marriage and styles of homes cultural traits? How do you stereotype others when their home or family structure differs from yours?
Pages 115–125	Was Jenny doing the right thing by helping her neighbors when they had the smallpox? Was it right to put her family at risk for contracting the disease? Do you avoid people who have diseases such as cancer, AIDS, hepatitis, mono? Why do you avoid contact with people who have certain diseases?
Pages 126–135	How do you react to people who have lost their families? Could you be happy if your family died from disease?

Closure

Every day, we will discuss the issues that the students addressed in their journals.

Student Assessment

The students will bind their journals and submit them for a grade. They will be graded on their thoughtful responses to the reading and discussions throughout the unit.

Materials

A copy of *Jenny of the Tetons* for each student.

A journal for each student.

Lesson 3: "Disease and Vaccinations"

Main Objectives

C-4, PS-1, PS-2, PS-5, SS-4, SS-5

Presentation

Explain to the students that, today, vaccines are available to protect children against seven diseases: diphtheria, measles, German measles (rubella), mumps, polio, tetanus, and whooping cough. Tell students that if a child is not immunized, he or she still runs the risk of contracting one of these diseases.

Enabling Activity

To help students understand how smallpox spread so quickly and extensively throughout the American Indian population, engage them in the following "doubling game."

Have students form a large circle. Stand in the center of the circle, holding a large piece of red paper. Tell students to begin walking clockwise around the circle. In about five seconds, instruct them to halt and face the inside of the circle. Give one student half of the piece of red paper. Tell the students that this is the first day of the smallpox epidemic and one person has just been infected. Have them walk clockwise as before, and when you have them halt, the "infected" student gives half of her piece of red paper to another student. Continue the game by simulating six days; each time the students halt, every person with a section of red paper gives half of it to another student who has not yet been infected. All of the students should be infected when the activity is finished.

Closure

Ask students to return to their chairs. Explain that because smallpox spread very easily, the epidemic infected thousands of people in a short time through their regular, daily contact. Emphasize that had the students lived in the 1800s, their whole class could have been infected in less than a week if each student had infected just one other student each day. Illustrate on the chalkboard the mathematical doubling of the spread.

Day	Persons Infected
1	1
2	2
3	4
4	8
5	16
6	32

Tell students that during the early smallpox epidemics in the Americas, as many as 70 percent of the infected people died from the disease. Ask students to calculate how many students in their class would be left if all were infected and 70 percent died.

Discuss the reactions that the students have toward people who have diseases. How do individuals stereotype these people? Discuss stereotypes such as: AIDS is a gay disease. Cancer is the punishment of God. People have mental disorders because they are bad.

Student Assessment

The students should be able to calculate how many people in the class constitute 70 percent. Students will describe how they stereotype people with health problems.

Materials

A sheet of red paper

Lesson 4: "Weather and Housing"

Main Objectives

CS-3, PS-1, PS-4, PS-5, SS-3, SS-5

Presentation

Discuss as a class how Beaver Dick's family migrated as the seasons changed. Tell the students how seasons are formed and how weather is affected by the seasons. The term "weather" refers to the condition of the air or the atmosphere at a given time and in a given place. The driving force behind weather is the sun. The sun's heat is responsible for the movement of the air; it creates convection currents, which cause sinking cold air to replace rising hot air. The sun's heat is also responsible for the water cycle of evaporation, condensation, and precipitation.

These processes—the sun's radiant energy (which provides heat and, thereby implicating, cold), moving air (wind), and precipitation (rain and snow)—constitute weather. Weather is also greatly affected by such factors as

Earth's rotation and its surface features, which influence how and where air and clouds will move.

Enabling Activity

Read the poem "All Kinds of Weather" and ask students for examples of how animals and humans are affected by weather. Discuss how Beaver Dick's family was affected by weather.

Explain to the students that they will keep a weather log for one week. They will hunt for evidences of weather and record them. They will also record ways that weather affected humans and animals. The students will work in groups to create a graph of the changes in weather.

The students then will examine how weather affects the style of house that a person may live in. They will discuss reasons that Beaver Dick's family migrated. The students will determine how the shape of a house affects the area of the house. They will construct a tipi and measure the base of the tipi to determine the area of the tipi. The students will calculate the area of their bedrooms and the area of their houses. The students will compare the areas of the three mentioned things.

Closure

After the students finish discussing the effects that shape has on area, they will construct a graph to visually represent the average areas of their bedrooms, houses, and the tipi.

Student Assessment

Each student will be responsible for a weather record. The students will work in groups to create graphs of the weather and areas of living space.

Materials

A weather log for each student

Materials to create a tipi

Graphing paper

Lesson 5: "Waste Not, Want Not"

Main Objectives

C-4, C-5, PS-1, PS-2, PS-4, SS-1, SS-2, SS-3, SS-4, SS-5

Presentation

"Take what you need, leave the rest to roam, and it'll be there to help you the next time." The Native Americans' way of life may best be described as waste not, want not. They realized that the resources of the earth were not limitless and that they must be used with care.

In *Jenny of the Tetons*, Jenny is careful to remove any traces that she could leave behind. She always used every resource available to her, but she used them wisely.

How did the white settlers' use of natural resources differ from that of the Native Americans? How did this cause prejudice between the two groups?

Enabling Activity

To further the students' understanding of the role they play in recycling and the use of natural resources, the students will keep a log of all the items they throw away for a week.

To illustrate the speed of decomposition, the class will bury a couple of items from each of the mentioned categories. Every student will hypothesize about which items will decompose the quickest and the slowest. The class will dig up the remains after a week and compare how quickly or slowly each decomposed.

Closure

At the end of the week, the class will construct a graph that compares how much paper, plastic, and food was discarded in their homes. Also, the class will construct a graph of the speed of decomposition of the various items buried.

Student Assessment

Each student should be able to describe the effects of differing philosophies about resources of the Native Americans and white settlers. Each student should have a record of the waste they discarded in one week, hypothesis of decomposition rates, and a copy of the graphs of discarded waste and decomposition rates.

Materials

Items to represent paper, plastic, and food to bury

Lesson 6: "How Does Prejudice Affect People?"

Main Objectives

C-3, C-4, C-5, CS-3, CS-5, SS-1, SS-2

Presentation

Tell the students that they have been discussing the causes of prejudice and reflecting upon any personal stereotypes that they might have. Tell them they are going to explore the different ways that prejudice affects people.

Enabling Activity

The students will work in groups to discuss the different scenarios presented in the following stories.

After reading "The Greenies" and acting out "My Father Says . . ," the students will discuss how people become prejudiced and how they form stereotypes.

After reading "The Boy in the Mirror" and acting out "Express Stop from Lenox," the students will identify ways that victims of prejudice and stereotypes feel.

Students will identify and extend ways that they defend themselves from prejudice and stereotypes by acting out the different scenarios presented.

Student Assessment

Students will be expected to participate in each of the activities.

Materials

Prejudice: The Invisible Wall from Scholastic

✜ ✜ ✜

Unit Evaluation

Unit evaluation is the process of determining if the activities were appropriate and/or effective in the delivery of instruction.

Example: When the students complete this unit, they should be able to identify stereotypes and prejudices that they possess. They should also be able to create techniques to help them overcome these stereotypes. Throughout this unit, the students will be exposed to concepts such as recycling, weather, cultural transmission, beliefs, and values. The students will be able to explain the effects that each of these has on the creation of stereotypes.

Bibliography for Unit

Caduto, M. J., and Bruchac, J. (1989) *Keepers of the earth: Native American stories and environmental activities for children*. Fulcrum, Inc.

Frank, A. (1952). *Anne Frank: The diary of a young girl*. Doubleday and Co.

Gregory, K. (1989). *Jenny of the Tetons*. Harcourt Brace Jovanovich.

Hawke, S. D., and Davis, J. E. (1992). *Seeds of change: The story of cultural exchange after 1492*. Addison-Wesley Publishing Co.

Hoven, L. (1990). *Native Americans thematic unit*. Teacher Created Materials, Inc.

Peturson, R. and McAllister, N. (1992). *Innovations in science*. The Wright Group.

Scholastic. (1979). *Prejudice: The invisible wall*. Scholastic Book Services.

✛ ✛ ✛

MODELS FOR GUIDANCE AND PRACTICE

Fourth Grade: The Atmosphere

Major Expectation

Upon completion of this unit, the student will be able to identify, predict, apply, and extend those characteristics that will enable them to make proper judgments relevant to the atmosphere and the environment around them.

Unit Rationale

Upon completion of this unit, the student will be able to identify what an atmosphere is and the importance of it. Students will also be able to describe and interpret changes in atmospheric conditions and will be able to identify ways to protect their environment.

Task Analysis: Atmosphere and Weather

    I.   Water in the Air
   II.   A Cloud in the Making
  III.   The Atmosphere
  IV. Cloud Formations
   V.   From Clouds to Rain
  VI. The Weather Ahead
 VII. Weather and the Moving Air
VIII. Putting Rain and Snow to Use

Main Objectives

Arts (A)

A-1   The student will be able to demonstrate creative drawing and expression.

A-2   The student will be able to demonstrate use of several types of artistic media.

Advanced Technology (AT)

AT-1   The student will be able to utilize, read, or view media/technology and analyze content and concepts accurately.

AT-2   The student will be able to classify different types of television programs: news, situation comedy, science fiction, drama, and documentary.

AT-3   The student will be able to identify value and limitations of technological devices used in society.

Language Arts (LA)

LA-1   The student will be able to summarize, analyze and evaluate a variety of types of literature, both fiction and nonfiction.

LA-2   The student will be able to produce written products in a variety of modes using appropriate phases of a writing process that includes prewriting, drafting, revising, editing, and publishing and demonstrate the correct use of standard English in written products.

LA-3   The student will be able to express ideas clearly and effectively in a variety of oral contexts and apply active listening skills in the analysis and evaluation of spoken ideas.

LA-4   The student will be able to demonstrate research and study skills.

LA-5   The student will be able to identify and describe characteristics associated with poems.

Life Skills (LS)

LS-1   The student will be able to identify and describe factors that endanger health and protective behaviors that will avoid or minimize these risks.

LS-2   The student will be able to develop attitudes and skills needed to form and maintain healthy relationships.

LS-3   The student will be able to describe how the body develops and functions in order to adopt skills that minimize risks and promote healthy growth and development.

Mathematics (M)

M-1   The student will be able to identify relationships between numerical figures.

M-2   The student will be able to use numbers to quantify and to identify locations and specific objects in a collection.

M-3   The student will be able to develop a number sense for fractions and decisions.

M-4   The student will be able to make, estimate, and use measurements.

M-5   The student will be able to collect, organize, describe, use, and evaluate data.

M-6   The student will be able to use variables and open sentences to express relationships.

Science (S)

S-1   The student will be able to develop an understanding of the nature of science through experiential settings.

S-2   The student will be able to develop and use science process skills.

S-3   The student will be able to use scientific investigation to learn science concepts.

S-4   The student will be able to use media and technology to show that scientific knowledge about protection of the atmosphere and weather is shared and critiqued by scientists and the public.

S-5   The student will be able to identify characteristics, such as curiosity, persistence, and inventiveness that scientists exhibit while experimenting.

S-6   The student will compare and contrast variations in climate.

S-7   The student will identify how weather affects growing seasons.

Social Studies (SS)

SS-1   The student will be able to gather and interpret information to solve problems, make decisions, and plan solutions.

SS-2   The student will be able to identify and exhibit the skills of a good citizen in democracy.

SS-3   The student will be able to identify basic tenets of citizenship and government.

SS-4   The student will be able to define and apply basic geographic concepts.

SS-5   The student will be able to explain how society uses its resources to meet the needs of its people.

SS-6   The student will be able to recognize and appreciate cultural diversity in order to participate successfully in social groups.

(Note: At some point early in unit study, have students in groups weigh a slice of apple and record the weight. Then label each apple slice so that it can later be identified and place the slices in a warm, dry place to dry. The dried apple slices will be used in Lesson 8.)

Lesson 1: "Water in the Air"

Main Objectives

LA-1, LA-3, LS-1, M-1, M-4, M-5, S-1, S-3, S-5

Presentation

At the beginning of the lesson, tell students that they will be studying how water enters the air. To begin the lesson, display a drop of water in a dish to represent a drop of rain. Ask the students, How can we put this drop of rain back into the sky? (Accept responses without comment.) Then do enabling activity. Graph results. Explain why.

Next, explain how liquids can change to gases. Review the three forms of matter. Ask each student for examples of each. Ask, Where does water go when it evaporates? Why can't you see the evaporated water? Then place the smallest possible chalk dot on the board. Ask students if they can see it. Add more dots close to the first one. Ask again if they can see it. Ask, Why are you able to see the dot now? What other things are hard to see when there are just one or two of them? Now demonstrate condensation by holding a cool glass tumbler near the spout of a kettle of boiling water. Students can observe the droplets of water form on the glass.

Next, discuss the cycles that living and nonliving things go through daily. Have students name some others that they know of. Now introduce the water cycle. Ask, What changes does water go through again and again in a cycle? Encourage students to tell of their cooling experiences on a hot day. Ask, Why do you feel cooler in a wet bathing suit than a dry one? Why do you feel cooler when you sprinkle water on your face? For water to evaporate from rivers and oceans, what is needed? *(energy)* Where does the energy come from? *(the sun)*

Next, have students breathe out onto individual mirrors to see evidence of water vapor changing to liquid water. (Note: For hygienic purposes, students should not breathe on the same mirror.) Ask, What appears on the mirror? Where did the water come from? Now have them breathe into their palms. Ask, How did this feel? *(warm)* Why is the air you breathe out cooled when it touches the cool mirror? Show a demonstration (two tin cans, one with hot water, the other with cold water). Ask, Where does the water on the side come from? What could we do to the water in the can to find out whether it leaks through the walls of the can? *(use food coloring)* Is there any water on the side of the can containing hot water? *(no)* Why does only the cold can seem to draw water out of the air? Encourage students to speculate why. Ask, What happens to the air around the cold can? What happens to the water vapor in this cooled air? Why doesn't water vapor settle on the side of the warm can? Explain why this happens and discuss dew. Ask, Where does the water come from to form dew in the morning?

End the lesson by writing the word *humidity* on the board. Encourage students to speculate why humidity makes a difference in how one feels on certain days. Ask, On a hot, uncomfortable day, why do people sometimes say, "It's not the heat. It's the humidity"? Do you perspire more on a hot day or a cold day? *(hot day)* Do you perspire more when you exercise or when you sit still? *(exercise)* Can your body cool off as readily on a humid day? Why or why not?

For enrichment, discuss how an air conditioner cools a room. Have each student read the short handout, "How an Air Conditioner Works."

Enabling Activity

The cooling effect: Students can get evidence that evaporation requires heat. To do so, they first record the readings of two thermometers at room temperature. Then they wrap dry tissue around the bulb of one thermometer and the same size piece of wet tissue paper around the bulb of the other. Record the temperatures of each thermometer every minute. Graph the results. Write an explanation statement. *(The temperature of the dry thermometer remains constant while that of the wet one goes down as water evaporates from the tissue.)*

Closure

After all students have completed the activities, each student will write a short paragraph explaining how water is present and used in their daily lives. In their discussion, students will tell how they think they would feel in the different seasons.

Student Assessment

Students will share their paragraphs with the class. The teacher will then collect the students' paragraphs and scan for correct use of grammar and content.

Materials

Small amount of water	Two thermometers
1 tin can with hot water	Paper towels
1 tin can with cold water	Small mirror for each
Handout, "How an Air Conditioner Works"	

Lesson 2: "A Cloud in the Making"

Main Objectives

LA-1, LA-2, LA-5, LS-2, M-4, M-5, S-1, S-6

Presentation

Remind the students that by breathing on a mirror, they can make a little "cloud" on the mirror. Ask how this happens. Have them recall that the mirror cools their warm breath. Then water vapor in that cooled air turns to liquid water. The tiny droplets make the mirror cloudy. Ask, Does this give you a clue as to how a cloud in the sky is made? Encourage speculation before going on.

Put a balloon over the top of an empty jar. Then heat the jar by putting it into hot water. Ask, What do you think will happen to the balloon in a little while? Encourage speculation. After observable effects are evident, ask, Is this what you expected? What do you think caused the balloon to become slightly inflated? As students respond, provide specific feedback and additional questions to encourage more detail to explanations. Put the jar into cold water. Ask, What will happen if you then cool the jar and the air outside it? After observable effects are evident, ask, Why did the balloon expand in one experiment and contract in the other? What happens to the air inside the balloon when it is cooled?

Next, explain what happens when warm air meets cold air. Ask, What happens to air when it is heated? Is it light or heavy then? Where would you expect the air in this classroom to be warmer—near the ceiling or near the floor? Why? Show a diagram of a beach shore. Ask, What do the arrows in the diagram show? What pushes the warm air up? This moving air is wind; so, what is wind? Encourage discussion.

Ask the students to read the rhyming riddle "What Am I?" by Jean Conder Soule. Encourage students to write their own riddles, with or without rhyme, about aspects of the weather such as wind, rain, or clouds.

Next, explain how tiny droplets of water are in a cloud. On a sheet of paper, have students draw a line 2.5 cm long. Then direct them to use a sharp pencil to draw as many tiny dots as they can along the line and record and share results. Explain that rain droplets are much smaller than anything that can be drawn and that over 3000 cloud droplets can fit into the short line.

Enabling Activity

Pass out materials. Darken the room as much as possible. As students work with partners or in small groups, have them fill a jar one-quarter full of very hot water. Then, after quickly placing the lid tightly on the jar, have them turn the jar upside-down and place wrapped ice cubes on the bottom of the inverted jar. Shine the flashlight through the jar and observe. Ask, What do you observe in the jar? How do the tiny clouds form? What is the difference between the way model clouds form and the way real clouds form?

Enrichment: Read aloud the poem "Fog" by Carl Sandburg. Ask, A fog is near the ground; a cloud is up in the sky, far from the ground. How are they alike? Encourage student reaction to the poem.

Closure

After the lesson, read the following scenario:

> You are in a room that is very warm. You want to bring cool air in as fast as possible. Should you open the window at the bottom or at the top? Should you open it at both the top and bottom? Why or why not? How can you find out which is the best thing to do?

Have students write a short paragraph explaining why that they can share with the class.

Student Assessment

Have students research in the library for poems on weather and clouds. Each student will describe and explain how this form of weather occurs. They will also describe what a selected poem means to them in a short paragraph.

Materials

Jar with cover   Very hot tap water
Ice cubes in plastic bag   Flashlight

Lesson 3: "The Atmosphere"

Main Objectives

A-1, LA-1, LA-3, LS-2, S-5, S-6

Presentation

Tell students that today they will learn about how the earth's atmosphere is heated. Begin by asking students how they knew what to put on before coming to school this morning. Present several pictures showing children dressed in different amounts and types of clothing. Ask, What can you tell about the weather where these children live by the clothing they are wearing? What heats the earth?

Next, introduce the terms *atmosphere* and *radiation*. Display a picture of the earth showing how radiation is absorbed and reflected by the earth's surface. Ask students to discuss with a partner the causes of the uneven heating of the atmosphere. Accept all student hypotheses. Ask, How does the angle of the sun affect the temperature during the four seasons? Explain how land and water absorb radiation.

Enabling Activity

Provide the following instructions to students: Use two beakers. Put a thermometer into each beaker. Put each beaker into a plastic bag. Change one set of materials by closing the bag. Leave the other bag open. Place the beakers in sunlight. Record the temperature in each beaker every five minutes. Compare the temperatures of the two beakers and record for another fifteen minutes. Graph the results.

Ask, How does covering a beaker affect the air temperature in the beaker? Why is it important to put the bag over both beakers even though you closed only one of them? Does covering a beaker with dark plastic have the same effect on temperature as covering it with clear plastic? Discuss. Direct students to write a description of the experiment, results, and their interpretation of the results.

Closure

After the discussion, review all new terms and ask several more inquiry questions.

Student Assessment

Students will work individually to answer the following questions: How is the earth's surface heated? What is the main reason for the uneven heating of the atmosphere? How does the speed at which different materials absorb radiation affect air temperature?

Collect students' work and discuss questions.

Materials

Two small glass beakers   Two thermometers

Two plastic bags   Two dark-colored plastic bags

Picture of the earth's surface

Lesson 4: "Cloud Formations"

Main Objectives

A-1, AT-1, LA-3, LA-4, LS-2, S-1, S-4

Presentation

Tell students that today they will study the different types of clouds. They will begin by going outside to observe the clouds in the sky. Ask, Have you ever watched clouds? Do you know what the different shapes and forms of clouds are called? Write the following list on the board: long wisps of hair, marestails, feathers, curls, ringlets. Point out that all these words have been said to describe the shape of cirrus clouds. Ask students to study the photographs of cirrus clouds carefully. Ask, Which do you think is the best description of these clouds? What better description can you think of? Encourage students to offer their own descriptions of each type of cloud as they study it. Have students read a short story on clouds and their types. As a class, make a rhyming statement that will make remembering the cloud names easier.

Enabling Activity

Give students three pictures of cloud types. Have each student write down what cloud type they think each picture illustrates. Then direct them to trade pictures with classmates and name what type of cloud it is and what type of weather with which it is associated.

Closure

After the lesson, review all the types of clouds and have students describe what type of weather is associated with each type of cloud. The students will also complete a program on the computer that reinforces the different types of cloud formations.

Student Assessment

Ask students to predict what today's weather will be like by observing the clouds. Direct them to write what types of clouds they see and illustrate them.

Materials

Pictures of all types of cloud formations

Paper and pencils, crayons

Computer program on cloud formation and types

Lesson 5: "From Clouds to Rain"

Main Objectives

A-2, AT-1, LA-3, LS-1, S-1, S-3, S-5

Presentation

Tell students that today they will learn how rain comes from clouds. Ask, Does water in the clouds ever come back to earth? What would make it fall as rain? How do clouds stay up in the sky? Review the types of clouds and how they are formed. Discuss how droplets form and grow. Set up several class demonstrations that show how drops of rain are formed. Ask, What made the water from the bottom of the jar, i.e., the earth's surface, evaporate? *(heat)* What happens in the top of the jar, i.e., upper atmosphere, because it is cooler there? *(water vapor condenses back into droplets)*

Describe and explain the other types of precipitation (rain, sleet, hail, and snow). Illustrate on the board how frozen rain is formed. Ask, What is the difference between sleet and hail? *(Sleet consists of much smaller bits of ice. Hail is formed of many layers of ice.)* Write the following on the chalkboard: "Hot weather's ice; baseballs of ice." Ask students whether they think the descriptions apply to hail, sleet, or snow and justify their responses. *(Both apply to hail.)*

Review safety procedures for protection from different types of weather: To keep safe from rain, use an umbrella. To keep safe from hail and sleet, use an umbrella or keep your head and face covered. To keep safe from snow, wear thick warm clothing and protect face and extremities from cold.

Enabling Activity

Direct each student to make a shadow box that shows rain, sleet, hail, or snow. Guide students to explain what causes the kind of weather their shadow box illustrates. (Snowflakes may be paper cutouts. Hailstones may be layers of white paper glued together, onion style, around a marble. Sleet may be tiny clay pellets painted white. Raindrops may be drawn or made of paper cutouts.)

Closure

Have students display and explain their shadow boxes to the class. Display the boxes on the bulletin board. End with a review of the types of precipitation. Students will also complete a computer program on weather/precipitation and complete a worksheet that goes along with the program.

Student Assessment

Upon completion of the lesson, ask students to write a report that responds to the following:

> Right after a rain, look around the playground or the block near your home. Where does the rain go? Are any places lower than others? Where does the rain sink into the ground? Where does it pile up in puddles? How do you explain the differences between the different places? How does the ground get dry again? Tell what you see happening to the water. Also, tell what you think happened, even if you cannot see it happening.

Materials

One shoe box per student	Scissors
Construction paper	Crayons/markers
Computer program on precipitation with related worksheet	

For demonstration:

Two heatproof glass jars	Tape
Water	Cooking pan
Hand lenses	Safety glasses
Hot plate	

Lesson 6: "The Weather Ahead"

Main Objectives

A-2, AT-1, AT-3, LA-3, LS-1, S-4, S-6, SS-1, SS-4

Presentation

Write the following weather saying on the board: "Red sky at night, sailor's delight. Red sky at morning, sailors take warning." Ask, What weather does this saying predict? Point out that weather sayings were widely used before scientific weather forecasting and that some, like this one, were based on accurate observations. Continue by sharing that most weather changes come from the west: a red sunset accompanies dry, fair weather from the west; a red sunrise accompanies wet weather from the west.

Ask students to suggest occupations that depend on weather forecasts for planning or work preparation. *(bus drivers, farmers, mailmen, etc.)* Continue by asking, What other people must know what the weather will be like in order to plan appropriately for their activities? *(sailors, swimmers, picnickers, etc.)* What plans did you have to change because of the weather? Have you ever looked at the sky and decided it was going to rain? What made you think so? Were you right? Have students reflect on weather changes over the period of the last week and discuss the usefulness of weather reports in newspapers and on television. Stress that the reports depend on huge amounts of work by others.

Write the term "meteorologist" on the board. Ask students to read and discover what a meteorologist does. *(studies weather)* Point out that meteor means high in the air. Explain how a similar term came to be used for meteorologists who study the atmosphere and may, therefore, be thought of as studying conditions "high in the sky."

Show a video of several television weather forecasts. Ask, What kinds of information do meteorologists collect to predict the weather? As the students answer, write the following list on the board: temperature of the air, air pressure, humidity (amount of water vapor in the air), amount of rain and snow, wind speed, wind direction. Lead students to add "kind and amount of clouds."

Show pictures and describe instruments that have been used for years to measure weather conditions at the surface of the earth. Encourage students to make their own weather measurement instruments. Explain that weather vanes and some other instruments only measure weather conditions close to earth. However, to forecast the weather, forecasters have to find out what is happening in the upper air, too. Have students turn to other texts to learn how this is done. Have students discuss how a weather satellite can measure conditions and take photographs high above the earth. Explain how computers assist in weather forecasting and ask students to suggest other technological devices that are being used today.

Tell students that temperatures can be different at different geographical locations. Have them record daily high and low temperatures for ten different cities on a map of the United States and suggest why locations in different geographical areas had similar or different temperature forecasts. Promote discussion of major weather conditions that are currently making headlines in the news.

Enabling Activity

Direct students to work in pairs to write a weather forecast and act out that forecast for the class. Each demonstration must include pictures showing weather conditions and discussion of the types of weather-predicting instruments that might be used to make those predictions. Students will identify a geographical area and use actual data from a city in that area. If students have access to the Internet or a weather channel on cable television, suggest that they monitor weather over a period of several days to assess the accuracy of their forecast. For the specific day that they forecast, have students record temperatures and humidity at several intervals throughout the day.

Closure

Students will name several types of weather instruments that were discussed in the lesson. Direct them to state what a meteorologist is and what one does. They must also explain why weather forecasts are necessary for everyday living.

Student Assessment

Assess each student's participation in the demonstration of a weather forecast.

Materials

Video of weather forecasts   Television

Poster board   Thermometer for each student

Markers   Newspapers

Map of the United States for each student

Lesson 7: "Weather and the Moving Air"

Main Objectives

A-1, AT-1, LA-3, S-4, SS-1, SS-4

Presentation

Call on students to describe today's weather. After you get consensus, ask, Will the weather change? If so, why will it change? Why do weather stations collect information about conditions far away? *(Since air and water move, conditions elsewhere yesterday may be conditions at our location today or tomorrow.)* Have students read "The Restless Air Masses" handout. Ask, What do you think the air is like above each land? Introduce the term "air mass." Students should recognize that an air mass is simply a continuous portion of the air that has the same general characteristics—for example, hot and moist, cold and dry.

Ask students to study a handout of a map with weather conditions charted on it. Ask, What would an air mass from a northern ocean be like? *(cold and wct)* What would an air mass that comes from a tropical ocean be like? *(warm and wet)* Why do air masses from tropical oceans hold more water vapor than those from northern oceans? *(The warmth makes more water evaporate. Also, the warmer air holds water vapor, which in colder air would condense and form clouds.)*

Ask students to read the paragraph on "a mountain of cold air." Ask, Why does warm air moving in from the Pacific Ocean contain a lot of water vapor? Why do clouds form on the west side of the Sierra Nevadas? Give each student a map of the western United States showing physical geography. Explain what fronts are and when they occur. Give students the opportunity to experiment and label weather fronts on the computer program "Weather Forecasting."

Enabling Activity

Weather Movie Booklet: Make a cardboard pattern of an outline of the United States. Have students trace the pattern on ten pieces of paper. On each map, let students show cold fronts moving from west to southeast and warm fronts moving from south to northeast. Bind the book at the left edge so that the pages can be flipped at the right edge. Students can see their own movie of weather movement and change.

Closure

Have students share their movie booklets with others in the class. Do a short review of the vocabulary and terms presented in the lesson. Review past weather terms to develop a continuum of knowledge and understanding throughout the unit.

Student Assessment

Assess movie booklets on creativity and how well they reflect understanding of the movement of air masses.

Materials

>   Weather maps
>   Handout "Restless Air Masses"
>   Computer program "Weather Forecasting"

Lesson 8: "Putting Rain and Snow to Use"

Main Objectives

A-2, LA-3, M-4, S-3, SS-1, SS-4

Presentation

Begin the lesson by telling students that they are going to learn how to put rain and snow to use. Display some grapes and raisins. Inform students that raisins are grapes dried in the sun; that the water in them has evaporated. Explain that one fourth of the weight of a grape is water. Ask, How did all that water get into the grape? (Accept all answers for now.)

Ask, Why do communities need rain and snow? How can it be put to use? Other than grapes/raisins, what other dried fruits have you seen that are much smaller than the fresh fruit? *(dried apricots, apples, bananas, pineapple)* Give groups of students a scale. Have each group weigh a freshly cut slice of apple and record the weight. Next, weigh a slice of dried apple and record the weight. Ask, Which slice was the lightest? the heaviest? How much water have the apple pieces lost? Where did the lost water go? *(evaporated)* What other foods have a great deal of water in them? *(cucumbers and other vegetables, fruit juices, soups, milk, etc.)* Display an empty milk carton and a package of powdered milk. Point out that the powdered milk consists of the milk that was in the carton but with the water removed.

Ask, What evidence is there that much of the human body is composed of water? *(blood, urine, and perspiration)* Explain to students that they lose the equivalent of eight glasses of water a day. Ask, What do you do to get that water back?

Discuss the importance of clean water. Ask them to discuss the hazards of drinking from just any pond or lake. Ask, What might make the water unclean? Discuss water pollution and sources of pollution in the area in which you live.

Promote student discussion of the need for pure drinking water. Demonstrate simple filtering of water. Explain how water is cleaned and how particles settle from the water. Ask, What kind of material did the settling of water remove? *(large particles)* What kind of materials did the filter remove? *(small particles)* How does the filter work? *(It clarifies the water.)* What might be left in the water after it is filtered? *(germs, bacteria)*

Explain what acid rain is and how it is formed. Ask, How is acid rain harmful to plants, animals, and other objects? How might acid rain harm the food chain of humans?

Enabling Activity

Have students find out from the local water department the source of their drinking water and how it reaches them. They can develop simple symbols for and map the locations of watersheds, dams, reservoirs, purifying plants, and aqueducts.

Closure

At the end of the lesson, have the students review the terms learned. Have students show and explain how water is supplied to them in their homes and schools.

Student Assessment

Have students define *conservation* (the act of protecting from waste, loss, or injury) and discuss ways to conserve water.

Materials

Raisins, grapes, apples	Quart jar
Empty milk carton	Dirt
Powdered milk	Filter
County/area map	Water

❖ ❖ ❖

Unit Review: The Atmosphere

- When water is heated, its molecules gain energy and move faster. They go into the air as a gas, water vapor.
- Humidity is the amount of water vapor in the air.
- In cooled air, molecules of water vapor lose energy. They slow down and form liquid water.
- Clouds, fog, or dew may form when water vapor in cooled air condenses.
- When cloud droplets become large enough, rain falls.
- Snow is frozen water vapor. Sleet and hail are frozen raindrops.
- Weather forecasting depends on information about humidity, temperature, air pressure, and other conditions of the atmosphere.
- Changes in weather take place along the front where different air masses meet.
- Our water supply depends on rain and snow.
- Evaporation and condensation of the earth's waters—the water cycle—depends on heating and cooling of water molecules.
- Our understanding of the water cycle leads us to a concept of energy: If molecules gain energy or lose energy, their motion changes.

Crossword Puzzle: The Atmosphere

Use the following words to complete the statements. Then fill in the crossword puzzle.

expands	lighting	weather	reservoir	fog
sleet	radar	table	condenses	data
purifying	humidity	front	satellites	vapor
evaporates	meteorologists			

Across

1. When a liquid becomes a gas, it _____. *(evaporates)*
4. Water in the form of invisible gas is called water _____. *(vapor)*
6. When water vapor becomes liquid water, it _____. *(condenses)*
9. When impure water is made useable, the process is called _____. *(purifying)*
11. A huge electric spark that jumps from one part of a cloud to another part of the cloud or to the ground is called _____. *(lightning)*
12. Weather scientists are called _____. *(meteorologists)*

15. The condition of the atmosphere from day to day is the _____. *(weather)*

16. The place where two different air masses meet is a _____. *(front)*

Down

1. This word means "becomes larger." _____ *(expands)*

2. The use of radio waves to tell the direction, distance, and speed of a plane or a hurricane is _____. *(radar)*

3. The water _____ is the level of the water in the ground. *(table)*

5. A cloud close to the ground is called _____. *(fog)*

7. This word means information. _____. *(data)*

8. The amount of water vapor in the air is called _____. *(humidity)*

10. Instruments in space that orbit Earth and make weather observations are called weather _____. *(satellites)*

13. The area behind a dam where water is stored is a _____. *(reservoir)*

14. Frozen rain is called hail or _____. *(sleet)*

FIGURE 9.2
Solution to Crossword Puzzle

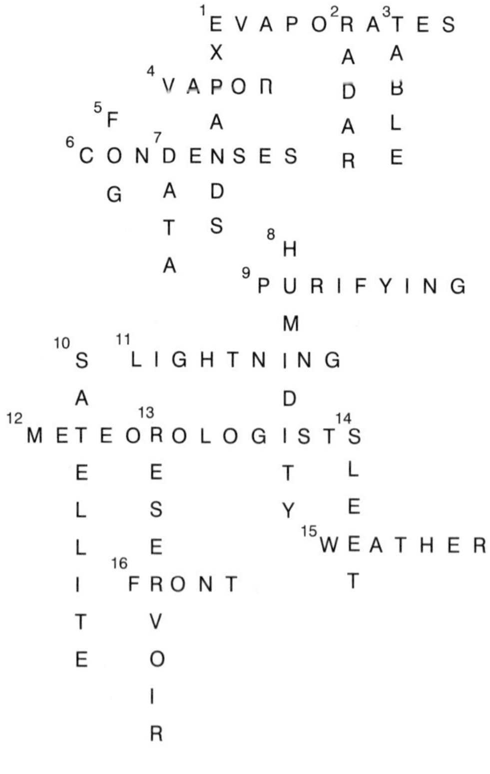

Unit Test: The Atmosphere

For each of the following, select and circle the letter of the answer that makes the statement correct.

1. When water evaporates, the molecules of water
   a. escape into the air.
   b. become liquid water.
   c. get closer.
   d. change into other molecules.

2. Heat can make molecules
   a. freeze.
   b. stop moving.
   c. a liquid.
   d. move faster.

3. When water vapor cools, it changes from an invisible gas to
   a. another invisible gas.
   b. a gas you can see.
   c. a liquid.
   d. a solid.

4. When the sun heats the surface of the ocean,
   a. water molecules escape into the air.
   b. water molecules slow down and disappear.
   c. the ocean cools.
   d. air molecules escape into the water.

5. When you breathe on a cool mirror, the damp spot that appears is made of
   a. condensed water vapor.
   b. molecules of cold air.
   c. oxygen gas that has become a liquid.
   d. pure oxygen.

6. When water vapor in air near the ground condenses on a cool surface, it is called
   a. cold water
   b. cold air
   c. dew
   d. sleet

7. To make liquid water evaporate,
   a. heat energy must be taken away from it.
   b. heat energy must be added to it.
   c. molecules in the water must not change.
   d. molecules in the air must be cooled.

8. To make water vapor turn into liquid water,
   a. no energy must be added to the water vapor.
   b. heat energy must be taken away from the water vapor.
   c. heat energy must be added to the water vapor.
   d. the molecules must move faster.

9. The "H" on a weather map shows
   a. hot weather.
   b. a high pressure area.
   c. heavy rain.
   d. a hurricane.

10. Cool air
    a. contracts.
    b. has no molecules.
    c. expands.
    d. weighs less than warm air.

11. When the air near the ground is below freezing in winter, raindrops may turn into
    a. lightning.
    b. hail.
    c. sleet.
    d. air.

12. When rain water goes through smoky air, it may form
    a. a watershed.
    b. a reservoir.
    c. acid rain.
    d. a filter.

13. When two air masses meet, the weather usually
    a. changes.
    b. gets hotter.
    c. stays the same.
    d. gets clear and cold.

14. Sweat helps to cool you because
    a. over half of your weight is water.
    b. you breathe out water vapor.
    c. it evaporates, taking heat from your skin.
    d. it is a body waste.

15. Acid rain is harmful because it
    a. tastes sour.
    b. can destroy the environment of living things.
    c. always contains poisonous gases.
    d. goes through smoky air.

❖ ❖ ❖

Fifth Grade: Biomes

Major Expectation

By the end of the unit, 5th grade students will be able to use science process skills, manipulative skills, computer/keyboarding skills, art skills, speech and communication skills, history skills, geography skills, nutrition and cooking skills, math skills, and language arts skills to research and describe a specific biome.

Unit Rationale

This unit concentrates on the study of biomes. It is an integrated unit designed for 5th grade students. The unit is designed to incorporate computer skills, art skills, language arts skills, speech and communication skills, history skills, geography skills, nutrition and cooking skills, as well as the science information necessary to develop a unit on biomes. The enabling activities will also allow students to develop their social skills as they work together to research and present their designated biomes. Students will also begin to develop an appreciation for differing environments in the world. The purpose of this unit goes beyond learning the mere characteristics of biomes. It is designed to create a wider knowledge base, and an appreciation of specific geographical areas.

Enabling Activities

The teacher will

1. review relevant concepts and terms: climate, temperature, rainfall, and organisms.
2. assign people to groups: four people per group.
3. assign each group a different aspect of the biomes.
4. instruct a representative of each group on how to use Microsoft Power-Point to develop a presentation.

Each group will

1. research their particular topic.
2. take notes on their particular topic.
3. make a bibliography from the books they used (APA format).
4. design a presentation computer instruction on PowerPoint.
   a. design seven slides (minimum)
   b. add graphics (clip arts)

    c. add notes

    d. add transitions, timing

    e. add graphs, map chart, with necessary data

5. make a costume for their presentation topic and come dressed for presentation in their costume.

6. make a map of the world, indicating where their team's biome is located.

7. write a final paper (three to five pages) not including the bibliography page (correct spelling and grammar; type final paper on a word processor; present final presentation as a group—must be five to seven minutes long). Students will need to show their group's PowerPoint presentation, describe their biome, dress in their costumes, add props if necessary. By the end of their presentation, all students should be able to pass a test on the different aspects of biomes.

An essay test will be given at the end of the unit.

Student Assessment

- Language Arts: Group grade (assessed by other students)
- Language Arts: Presentation grade (speaking)
- Language Arts: Research paper grade
- Arts: Props and costume grade
- Computer: Graphics and slides grade
- Science: Essay test grade.

Main Objectives

Arts (A)

A-1   Students will make a costume and/or props to add to their presentation. All members of the group must make a costume to represent their biome; for example, a cactus living in the desert.

A-2   Students will draw a map showing where the biomes of the world are located.

Affective/Social (AS)

AS-1   Students will exhibit a positive attitude toward scientific inquiry as a way of thinking and problem solving.

AS-2   Students will show curiosity, inventiveness, and critical thinking.

AS-3   Students will develop an appreciation for the struggles of early settlers in adapting to the biome they are studying.

AS-4   Students will be able to work in groups, each contributing a par-
          ticular task to communicate the information they obtained.
          (Example: Group secretary will type out the final paper for the
          group.)

Computer/Keyboarding (C)

C-1   Students will be able to work in PowerPoint in order to create a
          minimum of seven slides showing the different characteristics of
          their biomes.

C-2   Students will type the final copies of their papers on a word
          processor.

Cooking and Health (CH)

CH-1   Students will be able to try recipes with ingredients from their
          particular biome. This will be incorporated into their presenta-
          tion.

Geography (G)

G-1   Students will be able to identify, on a map of the world, where
          their particular biome is located.

G-2   Students will be able to identify the effects of the physical envi-
          ronment on their biome.

Language Arts (LA)

LA-1   Students will be able to demonstrate the ability to communicate
          through the writing of journals.

LA-2   Students will be able to use the media center and computer lab
          to research their designated biome.

LA-3   Students will write a three- to five-page paper using description
          to show the reader their biome.

LA-4   Students will write a bibliography to show at least five of the
          resources they used to gather their information. (Students will
          use APA style.)

LA-5   Students will be able to use speaking skills they previously
          learned when speaking in front of groups.

Math (M)

M-1   Students will be able to interpret given data from a graph.

M-2   Students will be able to construct a graph from data given to
          them, showing the number of specific populations of plants and
          animals that live in the area they are researching.

Science (S)

S-1   Students will be able to gain insights about the effect of climate and weather on plant and animal life in differing biomes around the world.

S-2   Students will demonstrate the ability to "list" plants and animals in a particular area.

S-3   Students will be able to list specific biomes of the earth, and give at least three characteristics of each biome.

S-4   Students will demonstrate the ability to describe observations and data through spoken and written words, graphs, drawings, diagrams, maps, and or mathematical equations.

S-5   Students will exhibit a positive attitude toward scientific inquiry as a way of thinking and problem solving.

S-6   Students will be able to compare and contrast different characteristics of different biomes.

Speech and Communications (SC)

SC-1.   Students will be able to use speaking skills to develop a five-minute presentation on their particular biomes.

Week 1: Monday–Friday

Main Objectives

AS-1, AS-2, AS-3, AS-4, C-3, G-1, LA-2, LA-4, S-1, S-2, S-3, S-5

Presentation

Students will be asked if they have ever been to a different area of the world, such as a desert or a rainforest. Those that have will be asked to describe what they saw. If nobody volunteers, or no one has ever been, the teacher will ask students to imagine what it would be like. The teacher will write the words they use on the board. The teacher will then explain to the students that they will be learning about different biomes. The teacher will give definitions of biomes, and review the meanings of words they have previously studied: climate, temperature, rainfall, plant and animal life, environment, and physical properties. The teacher will explain that all of these help to describe biomes. Students will take notes in their notebooks already specified for the unit on biomes.

Enabling Activity

The teacher will divide the class into groups of four, by having them draw cards from a deck. Once the groups have formed, the teacher will assign each group a different biome. Each member will be given a specific task, and the group, as a whole, will choose a team name that describes their biome. (For example, the Cereus Cacti Team is named for a cactus that grows in the desert). Once they have a designated name for their team, the competition between teams begins. They can make logos and banners for their team; whatever they choose to help excite their team. The class will then go to the Media Center to research their particular biome. They will use books, encyclopedias, magazines, computers, and atlases. The resources they will choose from will be lengthy. The teacher will also have a list of books on reserve for the students to use. Each group will need to take notes on note cards.

Closure

After the class has completed the research on their biomes and has taken all the notes they need, each group will type a bibliography, using APA format. The bibliography must contain a minimum of five sources. One must be a magazine article. One must be a book. One must be from the Internet. The other two can be from sources that they choose. The groups will turn in their bibliography and note cards on Friday.

Student Assessment

- Each group will turn in a bibliography.
- Each group will turn in note cards, organized, and titled.
- Each group will turn in a logo/banner with their team name and mission statement.
- Each team will be monitored throughout by the teacher and other members of their group.
- There will be a chart for each group, with members' names, showing the objectives of each member checked off when completed. A space for comments will also be beside each child's name.

Materials

Posterboard	Encyclopedias
Pens and crayons	Index cards
Materials on reserve in media center	Rulers

Week 2: Monday–Friday

Main Objectives

AS-1, AS-2, AS-4, C-1, LA-1, LA-2, M-1, M-2, S-2, S-3, S-4

Presentation

Each member of each team will begin by writing in their journal. They will write all that they can remember about the biome they researched. They will not be allowed to talk to other members of their group when they do this. The teacher will then explain that they will be going to the computer lab to learn about PowerPoint. The teacher will explain that, by the end of the unit, each group will develop and present a five-minute presentation to their class. She will explain that PowerPoint allows them to make slides and that these slides will be used to make up the bulk of their presentation. Once the groups are in the computer lab, the teacher will walk through and explain PowerPoint to the students. She will explain how to make slides, how to use transitions, how to add graphics, how to add graphs and charts, how to add clip art, how to change colors, and how to make a slide show.

Enabling Activity

After the teacher has thoroughly explained this information, students will be given time to explore PowerPoint on their own. Then, each group will type in the information they got from their research. They will incorporate clip art showing their biomes, make transitions, and add color. Each group will have a minimum of seven slides to use in their presentation.

Closure

At the end of the week, PowerPoint will be reviewed, and grammar and spelling will be checked on slides.

Student Assessment

- Students will be continuously monitored as they work on the computer.
- Students will turn in their disk twice—once on Wednesday and for a final time on Thursday.
- Group teams will again check off objectives when they are done and make comments on all group members of their team.
- Journals will be checked to see if they are completed.

Materials

Research cards students have completed   Disk

Computers with Microsoft PowerPoint   Journals

Week 3: Monday–Friday

Main Objectives

A-1, A-2, AS-1, AS-2, AS-4, C-2, CH-1, G-1, LA-1, LA-3, S-1, S-4

Presentation

The teacher will begin again by having each student write in their journal to comment on how they felt about using PowerPoint to make slides and show their information. Once journals are completed, the teacher will explain that this week they are going to continue to work towards their presentation. The teacher will explain that each group will turn in a three- to five-page paper typed and completed by the end of the week. This paper should be written from the research they obtained and the insight they have gained on their biome. The teacher will explain that this week will also be used to implement other disciplines to enhance their presentations.

Enabling Activities

Each student will be able to design their own costumes to represent something from their biome. The costume may be that of a plant or animal living in their biome. They are to decorate these costumes using any of the art supplies available. They are to wear their costumes to their presentations. Students will also be drawing a map of the world and highlighting where their particular biome is located. Finally, students may choose between using some ingredients that are found in their biome (for example, spices found in the rainforest) to cook something to share in their presentation, or find some music to play during their presentation that represents sounds from their biome (for example, sounds of raindrops falling).

Closure

At the end of the week, students should have their presentations ready to present. A three- to five-page paper should be written and typed on a word processor.

Student Assessment

- Groups will be continuously monitored.
- Journals will be checked and read.
- Group teams will check objectives and write comments, as will the teacher.
- A 3- to 5-page paper will be checked for content, grammar, spelling, and length.

Materials

Art supplies: glitter, glue, scissors, tape, markers
Audio tapes and player
Cooking supplies
Computer/word processor

Week 4: Monday–Friday

Main Objectives

AS-1, AS-2, AS-4, C-1, CH-1, G-1, G-2, LA-1, LA-5, M-1, S-1, S-2, S-3, S-4, S-5

Presentation

Students will begin the week by commenting in their journals how they have liked working in groups, the theme, the activities, and the art work done last week. After journals have been completed, the class will begin its biome kick-off. Each team will hang their banner or poster. There will be a little party with food from each biome. Students will have a 30-minute pep rally before their presentations. Students will be dressed in their costumes. The best costume will be voted on, and the winner will receive a prize.

Enabling Activity

The teacher will have the room set up with a computer and a big screen to show students' PowerPoint presentations. Each group will present their five-minute presentation and will show their slides and explain their costumes and props.

Closure

The teacher will have each group review the highlights of all their biomes and will have students take notes in their biome notebooks. If information is missing, the teacher will add it in conversation so students will have it in their note-books. The class will take a final test on the information covered by the students and teachers in the biome unit.

Student Assessment

- Students will receive a team grade on their presentation as well as an individual grade.
- Students will have a test on the information covered during the unit.

Materials

Students' disks   Computers with Microsoft PowerPoint

Students' props   Big screen to show slides

✛ ✛ ✛

Unit Evaluation

Art

- costume design—creativity and detail
- map of the world with correct location of biome

Computer/Keyboarding

- PowerPoint clip art, transition, color, 7 slides, graph
- final paper typed on word processor

Language Arts

- group grade on paper—grammar, spelling, content
- individual contribution—comments by teacher and students
- bibliography—5 sources, APA format
- journals

Math

- chart or graph showing population of plants and animals

Science/Geography/History

- evaluated by unit test

Speech/Communication

- speaking techniques, posture, confidence

✤ ✤ ✤

Second Grade Social Studies: Economics

Main Objectives

Social Studies

Citizenship/Government (CG)

CG-1 The student will explain ways local government collects and distributes money to fund services to citizens in the neighborhood.

CG-2 The student will identify specific local services provided to neighborhoods by the local government.

Economic Development (ED)

ED-1 The student will define and apply to his neighborhood and others the basic economic aspects of wants, needs, income, savings, producers, goods, and services.

ED-2 The student will describe sources of earning income in a neighborhood.

Geography Concepts (GC)

GC-1 The student will identify mountains on a map or a globe.

GC-2 The student will describe and compare the physical environment and its impact on life in the neighborhood.

GC-3 The student will describe various forms of individual and mass transportation found in neighborhoods in and around their locality.

Global Perspective (GP)

GP-1 The student will compare traits found in families and neighborhoods from another time or place with that of the students.

GP-2 The student will identify different roles performed by adults in the neighborhood and community.

Information Acquisition Skills (IA)

IA-1 The student will use information obtained through observation to identify problems, suggest solutions, and make decisions.

IA-2 The student will analyze information obtained through nonprint materials.

Communications Arts (CA)

CA-1   The student will make inferences and draw conclusions about a story.

CA-2   The student will identify the setting of a story on a map or globe.

CA-3   The student will function in a group by contributing ideas, taking turns, following correct sequence or procedure, and reporting group decisions.

CA-4   The student will respond to literature using oral discussion.

CA-5   The student will analyze rhymes.

Mathematics (M)

M-1   The student will solve application problems involving money.

M-2   The student will demonstrate addition and subtraction.

Psychomotor (P)

P-1   The student will communicate through art.

P-2   The student will communicate through music.

Science (S)

S-1   The student will identify basic concepts of weather.

Lesson 1: "Needs and Wants"—Camping Trip Activity

Main Objectives

CA-3, ED-1, IA-1, IA-2

Enabling Lessons

Tell the students that you are planning a camping trip by yourself to a mountain top where there is no electricity. Explain that you will have to carry all of your supplies and gear in one knapsack. Have examples of the items you feel that you "must" take with you. Show the students your list of supplies (TV, encyclopedias, prom dress, pork and beans, flashlight, jeans, sleeping bag, etc.). Give a reason why you "must" take each item. Items that are really "wants" should be described in a somewhat humorous manner. For example, "I need a TV so I can watch my favorite program." After you have gone through your list of items, tell the students you have a problem. "What am I going to do? I can't fit everything in my knapsack." Guide the discussion to a division of items into needs and wants. Ask, What is a need? *(Things that we must have to live, such as food, clothing, shelter, love and care.)* Ask, What is a want? *(Things we would like to have but can live without.)* Have chart paper prepared with needs on one side and wants on the other. Ask the students for help. Divide the class into five groups. Give each group paper with NEEDS printed on one side and WANTS on the other. Ask each group to write three items that you will need on the NEEDS side and three items you will want on the WANTS side. Tell them to choose a spokesperson for each group to report their findings. Tell them they will have five minutes to decide and write their choices. Bring class to large group and ask a student to repeat what a want is and what a need is. Have groups share their lists. Decide as a class whether the group lists are correct. If not, why not?

Student Assessment

- Students in groups will have developed lists, assigning items to categories of needs and wants.
- Students in groups will have contributed ideas, taken turns, followed correct sequence of procedures, and reported group decisions.

Materials

Camping trip supplies: canned goods, sleeping bag, jeans, dress, etc.

TV and encyclopedias from the classroom

Chart paper, markers, paper, and pencils

Lesson 2: "Needs and Wants"

Main Objectives

CA-1, CA-2, CA-4, ED-1, GC-1, GC-2, S-1

Enabling Lessons

Review needs and wants by showing pictures. Take a quick class vote to decide whether a picture is a need or a want.

Tell the students you are going to read a story set in Appalachia. This is a region of the Appalachian mountains located in West Virginia and Virginia. Show the students Appalachia. Tell the students that the people living in this area have long been among the poorest in the U.S. This story is set in the past, approximately ninety years ago.

Tell the students that Minna, a little girl in the story, has several needs that you will want them to remember as you read the story.

Read the story, stopping at appropriate places for discussion of the following questions: How are things alike or different compared to our neighborhood or family? What kind of weather is occurring? How does the weather affect life in the neighborhood? What time of year is it? How do you know? How do you know this story occurred at a different time than now?

After reading the story, ask students what Minna's needs are *(coat—clothing, people—love and care)*. Guide the students to see that she also needs an education.

Repeat the picture activity. This time, include the education (diploma) picture.

Student Assessment

- The students will have correctly voted on the pictures and identified wants and needs.
- The students will have correctly identified the setting of the story on the map/globe.

Materials

Pictures of pets, toys, clothing, food, and housing

Picture of high school diploma

The Rag Coat by Lauren Mills

Lesson 3: "Earn, Spend, and Save"— Alexander's Money Activity

Main Objectives

CA-3, ED-1, ED-2, GP-2, IA-1, M-1, M-2

Enabling Lessons

Tell the students you are going to read a book about a boy who spends $1.00. As you read the story, each student will calculate on a calculation sheet how much Alexander spends. Show the students an example of how to chart Alexander's spending. Discuss vocabulary words such as lox, earn, fine, token, and save as these appear in the story. Divide the students into five groups. Each group will discuss and compare their calculations and complete a chart using play money stickers. After completion of the chart, the groups will total the amount of money spent.

Using the chart, the students will review the economic concepts of earn, spend, and save.

Student Assessment

- The students will have completed the money chart.
- Students will have applied to their neighborhood certain basic economic concepts.
- Students will have solved application problems involving money, demonstrating addition and subtraction skills.
- The students will have functioned in a group by contributing ideas, taking turns, following correct sequence of procedure.

Materials

Alexander, Who Used to Be Rich Last Sunday by J. Viorst

Pencils, calculation sheets, play money stickers, and group charts

---

Lesson 4: "Earn, Spend, and Save"

Main Objectives

CA-1, ED-1, ED-2, GC-2, IA-1

Enabling Lessons

Students return to groups from previous lesson. Pass out the group charts. Ask students, How much money did Alexander spend? What are some of the things he spent money for? What are some ways in which Alexander could earn money? What are some examples of how people earn money in your neighborhood? Does the change of season affect how Alexander earns money? How? What are some jobs that can be done in the summer, in winter? Ask students to refer to their group chart. Ask, Did Alexander save any of his money? What are some things Alexander bought that he did need? Tell students, "Sometimes we spend money on things we want, like bubble gum. Sometimes we save money. Where do people save their money?" Have students name some things they would like to save their money for. Remind the students what Alexander was saving his money for *(a walkie-talkie)*. List the things the students say on the board under NEED or WANT. Tell the students, "We have discussed ways people earn money, spend and save money. You may want to remember what happened to Alexander's money when you are saving for something special."

Student Assessment

- The students will have made inferences and drawn conclusions about a story.
- The students will have described the impact of the physical environment on life in the neighborhood.
- The students will have described sources of earning income in a neighborhood.
- The students will have applied to their neighborhoods basic economic concepts.

Materials

Charts from Lesson 3
Alexander, Who Used to Be Rich Last Sunday by J. Viorst

Lesson 5: "Getting Goods"

Main Objectives

CA-4, ED-1, GP-1

Enabling Lessons

Read *The Ox-Cart Man*, discuss the difference between goods that are made and goods that are grown. Discuss the similarities and differences of gathering goods now versus the past. Discuss different methods of gathering and producing goods. Show pictures of different goods. Determine if the product was made or grown. Identify the method of gathering the product. Compare similarities and differences of gathering this product in different times.

Student Assessment

- The students will have applied to their neighborhoods basic economic concepts.
- The students will have compared traits found in neighborhoods from another time or place.
- The students will have responded to literature orally.

Materials

The Ox-Cart Man by Donald Hall
Pictures of made and grown goods
Examples of made and grown goods

Lesson 6: "Getting Goods"

Main Objectives

CA-3, GC-2, IA-1, S-1

Enabling Lessons

Discuss circumstances that prevent the production and distribution of goods. Show pictures of good and bad weather. Discuss the effects of weather on production or goods. Provide several weather reports. Determine if the conditions are suitable for production and distribution of goods. Recall what goods are. In pairs, list goods used in a day. Divide list into goods that are grown and those that are produced. Share lists with the rest of the class and review the production and distribution of goods.

Student Assessment

- The students will have listed goods as grown or produced.
- The students will have applied the concept of weather to production and distribution of goods.
- The students will have made decisions based on information obtained.
- The students will have described the impact of the physical environment on life in the neighborhood.
- The students will have functioned in a group by contributing ideas.

Materials

Pictures of weather, weather reports, weather forecasts
Chart of goods grown and produced
Pencils

Lesson 7: "From Factory to You"

Main Objectives

CA-1, CA-4, ED-1, GP-2, P-2

Enabling Lessons

Define factory *(a building in which things are made)*. Show pictures. Tell the students that in a factory people must work together to get a job done. People in a factory do different jobs to complete production of a product. Read *The Little Red Hen*. Ask questions such as, "Why did it take the little red hen so long to make her bread?" Ask students to suggest ways they are helpers and write the answers on the board. Teach the students the song "We All Work Together." Ask students, "How are products transported?" Have students suggest ways they learn about products. Discuss product advertisement.

Review factory, jobs, working together, production, transportation, and product advertisement.

Student Assessment

- The students will have suggested ways they are helpers.
- The students will have identified different roles performed by adults in the neighborhood.
- The students will have communicated through music.

Materials

The Little Red Hen   Magazines
"We All Work Together" (song)

Lesson 8: "From Factory to You"—Factory Production Activity

Main Objectives

CA-3, ED-1, GP-2

Enabling Lessons

Review the definition of factory. Demonstrate the car assembly process. Divide the class into five groups. Each group will be a factory producing cars. Assign jobs: wheel attachment, window attachment, and headlight attachment. Assemble the cars. Ask students, How many different jobs were there? What would happen if one worker did not do his job? Sing the song "We All Work Together."

Using the completed cars, review factory production and working together.

Student Assessment

- The students will have completed a car by functioning as a group.

Materials

Car parts   Glue

Lesson 9: "Getting Services"

Main Objectives

CA-5, CG-2, ED-1, GC-3, GP-2, P-1

Enabling Lessons

Read the poems. Identify services as jobs that workers do for others. Use the big book, pages 21–23, and cling sheet number 3 and ask students to identify services in the community. Ask what service each worker provides to the community. Ask what would happen to the neighborhood without these services. Identify ways service workers are paid.

Using the diagram sheet, discuss the flow of income. The students will use arrow stickers to indicate the income flow direction on the chart.

Identify volunteers as important service workers. Discuss jobs and services that students within the classroom perform.

Review using the completed diagram exercise, service workers, services and income.

Student Assessment

- The students will have diagrammed income from individuals to service workers.
- The students will have identified problems found in a neighborhood and procedures for dealing with them.

- The students will have applied basic economic concepts to their neighborhood.
- The students will have identified specific local services.
- The students will have analyzed the rhymes.

Materials

Roll Along: Poems on Wheels

Social Studies for a Changing World: Neighborhoods and Communities, big book and cling sheet #3

Diagram chart and arrow stickers

Lesson 10: "Getting Services"—Phone Book Activity

Main Objectives

CG-2, ED-1, P-1

Enabling Lessons

Review local services provided to the neighborhood. Using local services and phone numbers of the services, the students will make a phone book. Pass out prepared pages. The students will choose the correct color and shape for each phone number. Assemble booklet. Students can design their own cover for the phone book. Remind the students of the importance of all people in a community. Explain that each member plays an important role.

Using the chart with the outline, review how the neighborhood uses its resources to meet the needs of its people. Ask and answer questions to clarify each topic.

Student Assessment

- The students will have communicated through art in completing their phone book.
- The students will have applied basic economic concepts to their neighborhoods.
- The students will have identified the specific local service provided to neighborhoods.

Materials

Chart with unit outline
Prepared book pages and cutouts
Glue, pencils, crayons, stapler

✛ ✛ ✛

MASTER LESSON DESIGN

The Judicial System

Some teachers find that it is easier to develop mini-units, which are often referred to as master lessons.

Grade Levels

Mixed 4th (12), 5th (6), 6th (7)

Class Description

The lesson was conducted at Newell Elementary School After School Enrichment Program. The oldest group (Group V) is a mixed group of students in the 4th, 5th, and 6th grades. The socio-economic status is predominantly middle class with some lower middle class. The group is racially mixed with 18 white students and 7 African American students.

Unit Structure

The focus was on the judicial system and due process.

Main Objectives

Due to the nature of the mixed group, objectives were taken from several different grade levels.

Social Studies

- Upon completion of this unit, the student will be able to identify examples of responsible citizenship and make inferences about consequences of irresponsible actions. (4th grade)

- Upon completion of this unit, the student will be able to describe rights of citizens (e.g., justice). (4th grade)
- Upon completion of this unit, the student will be able to gather information from several sources and analyze social situations that involve ethical and moral dilemmas. (5th grade)

Communication Skills

- Upon completion of this unit, the student will be able to recognize and recall the main idea and supporting details in a reading selection. (4th)
- Upon completion of this unit, the student will be able to summarize information. (4th grade)
- Upon completion of this unit, the student will be able to determine the sequence of events and ideas. (5th grade)

Instructional Strategy

Class discussion and simulation

Procedure/Materials

The lesson will begin with a class discussion on the judicial system and due process. The teacher will pose questions to the class to ascertain the level of knowledge. Additional information will be provided as needed by the teacher. The class will be divided into groups representing the prosecution team, the defense team, the jury, and witnesses. The book *The True Story of the Three Pigs by A. Wolf* (written by Jon Scieszka) will be read to the class. The trial will be loosely based on this story. The jury will be sequestered in another room while the story is read. The teams will be given one class period to develop arguments and a witness base. Finally, the entire class will participate in the trial of A. Wolf for the murder of the three pigs.

Time Management/On Task Engagement

The classroom will be arranged to accommodate areas for the different groups (prosecution, defense, witnesses, and jury) and the various groups will be separated within the room to develop their legal arguments. Prosecution and defense teams will be provided with copies of the book *The True Story of the Three Pigs by A. Wolf* for reference. They will also be provided with paper and pencil and access to other materials they may want to use to create evidence. The teacher will circulate around the room to monitor student progress and ensure that all students are on task. The jury will be provided with quiet games and activities to do while the others are building their cases. The jury will also be given verbal instructions on their duties as jurors.

Instructional Technology

None used in this lesson.

Review and/or Focus

The class discussion will begin by the teacher asking the class if it is legal for the police to arrest someone and put them in jail for an extended period of time. This will lead to a discussion on due process covering topics such as arrest, trial by jury, individual rights, burden of proof, evidence, and legal procedures.

Statement of Intended Outcomes

We are going to use the concepts of due process and legal procedures to conduct a simulated trail of A. Wolf for the alleged murder of the three pigs.

Instructional Presentation

After the review of due process and general legal procedures, the teacher will give guidelines for accepted courtroom procedures regarding evidence, questioning of witnesses, and responsibilities of the judge.

Guided/Assisted Instruction

The students will then be divided into groups (prosecution, defense, witnesses, and jury) to develop their cases. The teacher will circulate around the room in order to listen to the groups and ask questions as needed to ensure that the guidelines are being followed. Additional instructions will be given to the small groups if needed. The groups must work together to develop a strategy for defense or prosecution. The jury will be instructed at this time about their responsibility to be fair and impartial, to base their decision solely on the evidence presented, and about the difference between the terms "shadow of a doubt" and "reasonable doubt." The judge will also be instructed about general court procedures such as sustaining or overruling an objection. The students will be brought together in the courtroom setting to conduct the trial. Each team will present its arguments to the jury. The jury will be sequestered in another room and given time to deliberate its verdict.

Closure

The entire class will be brought together to discuss the main points of the case and the resulting verdict, as they pertain to the judicial system, due process and legal procedures. The teacher will lead the class discussion and select individuals to answer questions or make comments to ensure all students have a chance to participate in the discussion. The teacher will monitor students' comments for accuracy and correctness.

Instructional Monitoring Procedures

Circulate throughout the room, being careful to stand in a position where the entire class can be seen. Closely monitor the behavior of certain individuals who may present behavior problems. Select groups carefully to avoid serious personality conflicts. Move from one group to another often enough so that no one group becomes frustrated due to waiting a long period of time to ask questions. Monitor the progress of each group carefully so that the amount of time given for each phase can be altered if needed.

Student Assessment/Instructional Feedback

Student assessment will be conducted throughout the course of the trial. Progress will be monitored to ensure that the basic concepts of due process and legal procedures are being used to develop the legal arguments and in presentation of the arguments to the jury. The class discussion at the end of the trial will also determine if the intended concepts were learned. Feedback will be given to the students throughout the lesson with special emphasis during the case preparation phase and monitoring of the jury trial.

AUTHENTIC ASSESSMENT AND EVALUATION OF STUDENT WORK

Authentic assessment is crucial in any integrated unit. Assessment should be done periodically throughout the unit by both the teacher and the students. Evaluation of the students during the unit allows the teacher to modify the unit according to the comments and interests of the students. Assessment of the students, by the teacher throughout the unit, allows the teacher to know which parts of the unit the students are mastering, and which parts need to be reviewed and taught again. This should be done by assessing the main objectives after each activity and lesson. It is counterproductive to continue investigating the theme on a deeper cognitive level if the previously taught objective has not been mastered. Students may become confused and frustrated, thus losing enthusiasm and interest in the theme.

Evaluation is essential; however, few teachers agree on the best way to assess students. The traditional assessment was done through examinations and tests, a more formal form of assessment. This type of assessment filters the students' knowledge through a list of test questions. The student plays a passive role, and the responsibility lies more heavily on the teacher. Authentic assessment, however, asks that both informal and formal evaluations are implemented into the evaluation process. Authentic assessment provides actual examples of students' work and also permits students' expression of feelings about the material. Examples of informal, authentic assessment proven to be extremely successful are portfolios, checklists, videotapes, and reporting.

Portfolios involve both the teacher and the students. They provide a vehicle for reflection and interaction between the student and teacher. They also provide a good indication of what students are truly learning as they go along. Portfolios allow students to demonstrate growth in areas not easily measured by examinations. Examples of documents and materials that can be included in student portfolios are notes and memos by the teacher and students, examples of students' work, journals, students' observations, analysis of what has been gained, teachers' direct observations, audio and video presentations, photographs, and any other types of documentation that illustrate the student's interaction with unit content.

Choosing the right kind of assessment is important in order to make sure that the unit has been evaluated correctly. The assessment should directly assess the students' ability to master the objectives already clearly designated for each main objective and each major expectation. The teacher should also try to assess how the students reacted to the theme that was chosen and the enabling activities for each lesson. This can be done through questionnaires completed by the student, focused discussions, and/or journals.

SUMMARY

Integrated units are becoming more and more appealing to teachers in the education profession today. There are many advantages to using this type of unit, and teachers are becoming increasingly aware of them. For example, integrated units promote the development of multiple intelligences. Replacing isolated, subject-centered, disciplinary instruction with integrated units helps to facilitate the development of concepts and skills for more students. It helps to provide for individual development in the different intelligence areas (musical, interpersonal, kinesthetic, spatial, logical-mathematical, and verbal intelligence). Integrated units also allow social interaction among teachers and peers. As the students interact with each other, differing cultural values, beliefs, and opinions are brought into the learning process. Integrated units also provide a way to investigate real life situations by using more than one discipline at a time. The use of integrated instruction has encouraged students to use skills associated with as many disciplines as can be applied logically in their investigations of a theme (Wood & Jones, 1994).

There are many pros and cons to consider when deciding if an integrated unit is the most effective method to use to achieve student understanding of the material at hand. Some positive aspects of the integrated unit are:

- The integrated unit uses inquiry process.
- The content to be studied is meaningful.
- There is a good deal of group interaction.
- Students are directly involved in the learning procedure.
- The atmosphere for learning is nonthreatening to students.
- The material taught is of high interest to the students.
- It provides for different levels of learning.
- It involves a greater area of learning styles.
- It makes learning fun for the students.
- Finally, it helps to clarify connections between the disciplines.

On the other hand, some problems to consider when using an integrated unit are:

- Integrated units require flexibility of time.
- Extra planning is required initially.
- Constant assessment is required throughout implementation to allow for changes if needed.
- Integrated units often require more than one try in order to be successful.
- The noise level is often higher than in a lecture-oriented classroom.
- Finally, the material in integrated units is not always commercially available in the format needed to be taught.

Whether integrated units will be an asset or a hindrance to teaching becomes the decision of the individual teacher and the team of teachers who are choosing to participate. It is not a simple decision, but requires a great deal of commitment, time, thought, patience, and sacrifice. However, interdisciplinary methods enable the teacher to develop units that focus both on topics of immediate interest to children and on the elements that help them understand that knowledge is not bounded by the traditional curriculum divisions. The successful students of tomorrow are not the ones who can memorize all the facts in each separate discipline, but the ones who can cope with new and unfamiliar situations and learn the material in a creative manner.

Future teachers need extended practice in several types of unit and lesson design. The futurist must remember that reality is always integrated. Why should instruction be any different?

❖ ❖ ❖ DISCUSSION QUESTIONS

1. What do integrated units and master lesson plans have in common?
2. How does the coding process work to decrease paperwork and increase teacher time?
3. How does the integrated unit compare to the more simple subject or traditional unit?

❖ ❖ ❖ CLASS ACTIVITIES

1. Compare the strengths and weaknesses of the integrated unit. Highlight any components you would modify.
2. As a class or in groups, examine the component of the master lesson design and compare these with the units from above. Which design does your group prefer? Keep in mind that when doing integrated lessons, these can be from within grade as well as across grade levels.

❖ ❖ ❖ REFERENCES

Wood, K. D., & Jones, J. P. (1994). Integrating collaborative learning across the curriculum. *Middle School Journal, 25*(3), 19–23.

10

CURRICULUM AND INSTRUCTIONAL EVALUATION

Chapter Objective and Focus:

An examination of the issues that impact curricular and instructional evaluation and methods of evaluation

---

In the United States, evaluation began in the common school. In 1838, Horace Mann, the father of the common school and the first State Secretary of Education, persuaded the Massachusetts legislature to pass an education act that required that a "register" be kept with specific information on each student. Originally, students were evaluated by oral exams, but educators switched to written exams to increase efficiency and specificity of what was being tested. Essay exams became a popular way to evaluate students' knowledge.

Essay tests encouraged standard administration, but did not guarantee invariable and standard interpretation. Edward Thorndike and others began to develop scales for consistency in evaluating students and allowed comparison between different schools for spelling, mathematics, penmanship, English composition, and history.

In the 1920s, the use of educational and psychological testing grew. These tests included true-false, multiple choice, fill in the blank, and matching items. The tests were created to fix some of the problems associated with essay tests. Educators who believed that essay tests were the only true test of knowledge opposed these objective tests. Additional criticisms were that the tests measured only memory recall and recognition of facts and did not measure the students' process of knowledge of the subject. Various types of evaluation (assessment) will be discussed in this chapter.

CURRICULUM EVALUATION

Webster's New World Dictionary (1997) defines evaluation as "to judge or determine the worth or quality of; appraise." Curriculum evaluation is the process of collecting and processing data for decisionmaking about the merit of an educational program. This data may include (1) objective descriptions of goals, environments, personnel, methods, content, and results; and (2) recorded personal judgments of the quality and appropriateness of goals, input, and outcomes (Shafritz, Koeppe, & Soper, 1988). Educators today have a greater concern about curriculum than has previously been expressed in the history of curriculum evaluation. Curriculum is the guide and "if you do not know where you are going, you may end up in the wrong place" (Payne, 1992).

Curriculum evaluation is a continuous process. In the short term, it is that which is more readily observed at the school and district level. In the long term, it is society's judgment. Many districts evaluate in cycles. There are two particular forms of curriculum evaluation—*formative* (used to help improve a curriculum) and *summative* (used to assess the value of the curriculum).

Formative evaluation is used during the planning stages of the program to improve it. This form of evaluation provides immediate feedback. One example is formation of a sample class to "test out" a new math curriculum's content. With the information gained from this sample, immediate changes can be made. Formative evaluation points out potential problems. Overall, its purpose is to discover deficiencies.

Summative evaluation occurs after a curriculum or program has been approved for use. It provides information about the program's worth. Classroom teachers are involved in this level of evaluation because they deal with the curriculum daily. It is used to decide whether to continue or discontinue the curriculum. Summative evaluation is much more common than formative evaluation. All curriculums should be evaluated on a continuous basis. Suggested guidelines to assist in establishment of a program of evaluation and/or to help improve a current one consist of a series of decisions: (1) when to evaluate, (2) what, specifically, to evaluate, (3) whom it is to serve, (4) who should guide evaluation, (5) what questions to address, and (6) how to report findings.

In 1893, the *Committee of Fifteen*, a committee on elementary studies, was appointed by the NEA which set the direction for elementary school education and curricula that has been maintained to the present. The committee supported the concept of an eight-year elementary education that primarily emphasized grammar (hence the designation "grammar school") and secondarily emphasized literature, arithmetic, geography, and history (Shafritz, Koeppe, & Soper, 1988).

Curriculum evaluation has continued for years with little evidence of change. Overall, curriculum evaluation is difficult and expensive, but necessary for the success and future of the students. In the long run, it is difficult to determine if the current curriculum is successful because educators cannot easily follow students after graduation to see how they apply their learning in their lives. Short-term assessment of curriculum success is achievable because of the educational community's ability to follow students from one grade to another and to graduation.

The American National Standards Institute suggests the following basic attributes for evaluation of educational programs: utility, feasibility, propriety, and accuracy. Utility is defined as those standards that are intended to insure that an evaluation will serve the information needs of the intended users. Utility includes the following:

- *Stakeholder Identification:* Persons involved in or affected by the evaluation should be identified, so that their needs can be addressed.

- *Evaluator Credibility:* The persons conducting the evaluation should be competent and trustworthy to perform the evaluation, so that the evaluation standards achieve maximum credibility and acceptance.

- *Information Scope and Selection:* Information collected should be broadly selected to address pertinent questions about the program and be responsive to the needs and interests of the clients and other specified stakeholders.

- *Values Identification:* Perspectives procedures and rationale used to interpret the findings should be carefully described, so that the basis for value judgments is clear.

- *Report Clarity:* Evaluation reports should clearly describe the program being evaluated, including its context and the purposes, procedures, and findings of the evaluation, so that essential information is provided and easily understood.

- *Report Timeliness and Dissemination:* Significant interim findings and evaluation reports should be disseminated to intended users, so that these can be used in a timely fashion.

- *Evaluation Impact:* Evaluation should be planned, conducted, and reported in ways that encourage follow-through by stakeholders, to increase the likelihood that the evaluation will be used.

The second basic attribute suggested by the American National Standards Institute is feasibility. Feasibility is defined as those standards that are intended to ensure that an evaluation will be realistic, prudent, diplomatic, and frugal.

- *Practical Procedures:* The evaluation procedures should be practical, to keep disruption to a minimum while needed information is obtained.
- *Political Viability:* The evaluation should be planned and conducted with anticipation of the different positions of various interest groups, so that the cooperation of these groups may be obtained, and so that possible attempts by any of these groups to curtail evaluation operations to bias or misapply the results can be averted or counteracted.
- *Cost Effectiveness:* The evaluation should be efficient and produce information of sufficient value, so that the resources expended can be justified.

The ANSI (American National Standards Institute) defines propriety, the third basic attribute, as those standards that are intended to ensure that an evaluation will be conducted legally, ethically, and with due regard for the welfare of those involved in the evaluation, as well as those affected by its results.

- *Rights of Human Subjects:* Evaluations should be designed and conducted to respect and protect the rights and welfare of human subjects.
- *Human Interactions:* Evaluators should respect human dignity and worth in their interactions with other persons associated with an evaluation, so that participants are not threatened or harmed.
- *Complete and Fair Assessment:* The evaluation should be complete and fair in its examination and recording of strengths and weaknesses of the program being evaluated so that strengths can be built upon and problem areas addressed.
- *Disclosure of Findings:* The formal parties to an evaluation should ensure that the full set of evaluation findings along with pertinent limitations are made accessible to the persons affected by the evaluation, and any others with expressed legal rights to receive the results.
- *Conflict of Interest:* Conflict of interest should be dealt with openly and honestly, so that it does not compromise the evaluation process and results.
- *Fiscal Responsibility:* The evaluator's allocation and expenditure of resources should reflect sound accountability procedures and otherwise be prudent and ethically responsible, so that expenditures are accounted for and appropriate.

The final basic attribute listed by the ANSI is accuracy. Accuracy is defined as those standards intended to ensure that evaluation will reveal and convey technically adequate information about the features that determine worth or merit of the program being evaluated.

- *Program Documentation:* The program being evaluated should be described and documented clearly and accurately, so that the program is clearly identified.
- *Context Analysis:* The context in which the program exists should be examined in enough detail to ensure that its likely influences on the program can be identified.
- *Described Purposes and Procedures:* The purposes and procedures of the evaluation should be monitored and described in enough detail to ensure that these can be identified and assessed.
- *Defensible Information Sources:* The sources of information used in a program evaluation should be described in sufficient detail to allow the adequacy of the information to be assessed.
- *Valid Information:* The information gathering procedures should be chosen or developed and then implemented to assure that the resulting interpretation is valid for intended use.
- *Reliable Information:* The information gathering procedures should be chosen or developed and then implemented in a manner that ensures that the information obtained is sufficiently reliable for intended use.
- *Systematic Information:* The information collected, processed, and reported in an evaluation should be systematically reviewed, and any errors found should be corrected.
- *Impartial Reporting:* Reporting procedures should guard against distortion caused by personal feelings and biases of any party to the evaluation, so that evaluation reports fairly reflect the evaluation findings.

Methods of Curriculum Evaluation

Long-Term Analysis

Along with the ANSI recommendations for the basic elements of program or curriculum evaluation, there are two types of curriculum evaluation: long-term and short-term analysis. Long-term analysis techniques are used to conduct evaluations over extended periods of time. This type of analysis can be achieved by several methods. One example is the case study. According to Lynn Davey (1991), case study methodology involves an in-depth, longitudinal examination of a single instance or event. It is a systematic way of looking at what is happening, collecting data, analyzing information, and reporting the results. The product is a sharpened understanding of why the instance happened as it did and what might be important to look at more extensively in future research.

Several types of case studies can be used in long-term analysis: illustrative, exploratory, critical instance, program implementation, program effects, and cumulative. *Illustrative case studies* are descriptive and utilize one or two instances to illustrate a situation. This helps interpret other data, especially when there is reason to believe that readers know too little about a program (Davey, 1991).

An example of this type of case study would be to give a student information on the development of the IEP (Individualized Education Plan) and the purpose for using it in the public school system. The overview would provide the student and his or her parents with information written in common language that describes the IEP and provides a few examples of IEPs that have been developed in the past.

Illustrative case studies have some disadvantages. They require presentation of in-depth information on each illustration, and time on site for in-depth examination is not always available. The most serious problem concerns the selection of instances. The illustrative case must adequately represent the situation or program.

Exploratory case studies are condensed case studies undertaken before implementing a large scale investigation. Where considerable uncertainty exists about program operation, goals, and results, exploratory case studies help identify questions, select measurement constructs, and develop measures. The greatest danger in the exploratory study is that the findings may seem convincing enough to be released inappropriately as conclusions. Other dangers include the tendency to extend the exploratory phase and inadequate representation of diversity.

Critical instance case studies examine one or a few sites for one of two purposes. A very frequent application is the examination of a situation of unique interest, with little or no interest in generalizability. A second, rarer, application entails a highly generalized or universal assertion that is called into question and that one can test by examining one instance. This method is particularly suited for answering cause-and-effect questions about the instance or concern. The greatest hazard associated with use of this application is inadequate specification of the evaluation question.

Program implementation case studies help discern whether implementation complies with its intent. These case studies are also useful when there is concern about implementation problems. Extensive, longitudinal reports of what has happened over time can set a context for interpreting a finding of implementation variability. In either, generalization is desired, and the evaluation questions must be carefully negotiated with the customer. A requirement for an appropriately conducted program implementation study is investment of sufficient time to obtain longitudinal data and breadth of information. Multiple sites are typically required to answer program implementation questions. This imposes demands on training and supervision necessary for quality control.

Program effects case studies can determine the impact of programs and provide inference about reasons for success or failure. Like the program implementation case study, the evaluation questions usually require generalizability. For highly diverse programs, it may be difficult to answer the questions adequately to retain a manageable number of sites.

Cumulative case studies aggregate information from several sites collected at different times. The cumulative case study can be retrospective, collecting information across studies done in the past, or prospective, structuring a series of investigations for different times in the future. Retrospective cumulation allows generalization without the cost and time incurred conducting numerous new case studies; prospective cumulation also allows generalization without unmanageably large numbers of cases in process at one time.

Short-Term Analysis

Short-term analysis can be achieved by using the following methods. Formative evaluation, which is an internal function that feeds results back into the program to improve an existing educational unit, is one. This kind of evaluation is used frequently by teachers and school administrators to compare outcomes with goals. Another method is summative evaluation, which exists for the purpose of demonstration and documentation. Various ways of achieving similar goals can be compared. Summative evaluations assist school districts to analyze their unique characteristics and choose the program that will best achieve their pedagogical goals (Beswick, 1990).

Whether evaluations are long-term or short-term, the purpose of curriculum evaluation is to judge or determine the worth or quality of all of the courses collectively offered in school or college in a particular subject.

INSTRUCTIONAL EVALUATION

Instructional evaluation, or assessment, was once exclusively the teacher's domain. It consisted mainly of predetermined paper and pencil testing. Periodically, the students would read a book, write a report, and give an oral presentation, activities that would all have to live up to the expectations of the individual teacher. Assessment today is not necessarily based upon the sole, personal judgment of the teacher. Students are included. As the community demands more student accountability, students are becoming more involved in their own learning process.

Instructional evaluation is defined by Oliva (1997), in *Developing the Curriculum*, as the evaluation of instruction through the assessment of student achievement. Evaluation of the instruction is the evaluation of the effectiveness of the instructor. For example, does the teacher choose the right delivery system? Are the teacher's objectives clear? Do test items relate to objectives? Evaluation of instruction is also evaluation of the curriculum. It reveals the success of one dimension—how much the student achieves in areas that are assessed. It may also indicate whether the content has been adequately covered. Evaluation of instruction does not answer curricular concerns such as whether the subject matter was the right choice to begin with, whether its content is relevant, whether it meets student or societal needs, and whether the content has been selected wisely.

Methods of Instructional Evaluation

Measurement is the means of determining the degrees of achievement of a particular competency. Testing is the use of instruments for measuring achievement. The three phases of instructional evaluation are preassessment, formative evaluation, and summative evaluation. Evaluation that takes place before instruction is called preassessment. Evaluation that takes place during the instruction process is called formative evaluation. Assessment that takes place at the end of instruction is called summative evaluation.

The tool used in preassessment is the criterion referenced test or pretest. The criterion referenced test measures the entry skills that have been identified as critical to beginning instruction. According to Kibler, Degala, Miles, and Barker, there are four ways that criterion referenced tests can be used:

- for preassessment purposes,
- for formative testing,
- to determine whether components of the instructional model need modification, and
- to determine whether students have achieved the criterion levels of objectives.

The pretest is criterion referenced to the objectives the designer intends to teach. A pretest by itself is not sufficient to address all needs at the beginning of instruction. Students should perform poorly on a pretest but the instructor may not be able to gauge whether they did poorly for lack of general knowledge or specifically the knowledge required for entry level instruction.

A second type of test is designed to help students measure their skills against the skills of others. These types of tests are called norm-referenced tests. Norm-referenced measurement compares a student's performance on a test to the performance of other students who took the test. Norm-referenced testing is necessary when a limited number of spaces are to be filled from a pool of applicants. Norm-referenced measurement permits comparisons among people, with the primary purpose of making decisions about individuals.

Formative evaluation consists of formal and informal techniques of assessing the learning of students. Formative evaluation occurs during the process of instruction. It may include questions at different points during the instruction or checking students' responses to parts of the instruction. Instructors use formative evaluation to determine if the skills to be learned are being addressed. It allows instructors to determine if they need to provide remedial instruction to overcome difficulties.

Summative evaluation is the assessment that occurs at the end of a course or unit. The tools used are final exams, a post-test, or an actual demonstration of a skill or operation. It is used to determine if students have mastered the instruction.

Several new ways are available to assess student achievement. The new tools are called performance-based or authentic assessment. Authentic means "worthy of acceptance or belief, trustworthy" (Engel, 1994, p. 24). Assessments are authentic because they are valuable activities within themselves and involve the performance of tasks that are directly related to real world problems.

Educators, parents, and students have come to realize that standardized tests do not truly evaluate a student's growth in the content knowledge, skills, and instructional activities that occur in the classroom. Portfolios, authentic assessment measures, and alternative assessment activities are the latest buzzwords used to describe activities other than standardized tools for determining a student's achievement. Some of these buzzwords follow:

- Assessment—an exercise such as a written test, portfolio, or experiment that seeks to measure a student's knowledge in a subject area.

- Alternative assessment—any form of measuring what a student knows and is able to do other than through traditional standardized tests. Alternative forms of assessment include portfolios, performance-based assessments, and other means of testing students. These alternative assessments allow students, parents, and teachers to physically see actual growth of knowledge over a period of time, as opposed to standardized tests, which do not show the growth occurring.

- Authentic assessment—allowing the student to "become progressively self disciplined as a thinker . . . (and) to acquire the habit of inquiring and engaging in discourse with care and thoroughness" (Wiggins, 1993). Its purpose is to get students to take control of their own learning while maintaining relevance and a meaningful connection to what they are learning.

- Portfolio—a systematic and organized collection of a student's work throughout a course or school year that measures the student's knowledge and skills and often includes some form of self reflection by the student.

The portfolio is the most popular form of alternative assessment and is considered authentic assessment when done correctly. A portfolio is a collection of student writing samples assembled over a period of a course or longer. It is like a collection of snapshots of a student's writing. "Looking at them singly, each writing sample is simply an assignment or project whose relative success at meeting curricular objectives was determined long ago. Viewed collectively, however, these samples become a powerful, living demonstration of the student's growth as a writer over a period of time, as individualized as any assessment could possibly be" (Miller, 1997, p. 28).

A portfolio is called a performance-based assessment because the intent of the portfolio is for the student to assemble a collection of samples of his work, which in essence shows evidence of his accomplishments. Portfolios may contain creative writing, tests, artwork, exercises, reflective essays, notes on topics, and whatever other materials portray achievement. Standards and criteria for achievement in portfolios should be set. Some of the criteria may include completeness, effort, neatness, and creativity. Portfolios reveal students and allow teachers and students to work in the most productive ways possible. There are almost as many approaches to compiling and evaluating portfolios as there are proponents of this form of assessment. Portfolios can be used both formally and informally. Ideally, the portfolio captures the evolution of the student's ideas and can be used instructionally and as progress markers for the student, teacher, and program evaluator.

Portfolios are adaptable to a variety of educational settings. In Fort Worth, Texas, a fifth grade teacher used them in his math class. Educators in Kentucky and Vermont have made portfolios a part of their statewide assessment of students. Pittsburgh educators have used portfolios to assess learning in imaginative writing, music, and visual arts.

A portfolio has three major parts: biography, range of works, and reflections. The biography shows the developmental history of the child's progress and gives the reader an impression of how the student has progressed from the beginning to that point. The portfolio contains a variety of assignments. These could be the student's "best," "most important," "satisfactory," and "unsatisfactory" pieces of work as well as revisions. The student critiques her work by reflecting on how her performance has changed, what she has learned, and what she needs to do in order to improve.

Educators who use portfolios believe that these are practical and effective assessment tools for several reasons. Portfolios are easy to design, durable, and reusable. This form of assessment impacts the teacher's way of teaching and testing (i.e., by problem solving, communication, application, etc.) and promotes worthwhile learning while expanding the dimensions of education. It provides a developmental perspective that is easily observed by students, parents, and teachers. Finally, it can document a student's progress through school until graduation. Members of the NEA support the portfolio's use because it accurately reflects what the student has learned.

Not all educators support the portfolio. Some teachers use it to display students' best work. Used in this way, it will not accurately reflect performance and rate of progress and cannot be called an assessment measure. Rather than including a representative sampling of a student's work, teachers may guide students as to what to write and include. Storage is difficult because a portfolio, if used appropriately, can be big and bulky. Scoring is time consuming as well as inconsistent, and even if the scorers do agree, that does not guarantee that the portfolio measures what it was supposed to measure (Viadero, 1995). In Vermont, it took more than 160 scorers five days to assess 7,000 portfolios. These scorers were, understandably, influenced by their personal beliefs.

Unit Evaluation

Unit evaluation includes two major types of evaluation—diagnostic and summative. Diagnostic evaluation allows the teacher to learn what the students' learning potential is prior to the start of the instruction. Summative evaluation measures what the students have learned through implementation of the unit. The usual form of evaluation is a written test. The unit test can contain a mix of objective (answer with the facts) and subjective (essay) questions. These two types of evaluation assist with the planning of future methods of teaching a unit by providing, through student response to test items, information about how the instruction can be organized to become more effective.

Lesson Evaluation

Lesson evaluation occurs daily. Informal and formal evaluation occurs while the lesson is going on as well as upon its completion. Some informal methods of evaluation are observations of the students individually and as a group, assessment of students' contributions, review of homework, and overall impressions of the level of student understanding and success. Some formal methods of evaluation are quizzes, debates, and rating scales.

These evaluations are done constantly throughout the lesson to verify that students are comprehending the objectives. They allow for modifications to be made at any point in the lesson.

NATIONAL ASSESSMENT

"To compete and win in the twenty-first century, we must have a high standard of excellence that all states agree upon," President Clinton told Maryland legislators. "That is why I call for national standards of excellence in the basics, not federal government standards, but national standards representing what all our students must know to succeed in the new century."

That quote sounds wonderful, but is it entirely possible? One state's beliefs can be entirely different from another state's beliefs. Who's to say one is wrong and the other is right? According to the Constitution of the United States, education is under the authority of the individual state. As a result, the federal government cannot impose a national curriculum on the states without a constitutional amendment.

In 1944, Ralph W. Tyler and the Committee on Assessing the Progress of Education began to develop criterion referenced tests for nationwide assessment. Testing began in 1969 and encompassed ten areas: art, career and occupational development, citizenship, literature, mathematics, music, reading, science, social studies, and writing. Reassessments are performed biennially, and a report card showing patterns and trends is issued to the public after each assessment. From analysis of these national studies, curriculum workers can make comparisons of their local and state assessment data against national norms and can make inferences about areas in need or remediation. New national examinations that will reveal achievement of both students and schools are in the process of development. Dissatisfaction with the educational system runs so deep that educators, business people, parents, and others are voicing a desire for national assessment, an undertaking that will run counter to historic objections to a national curriculum and to revealing test scores of individuals and schools. The focus is now moving from the state level to the national level (Oliva, 1997).

When the National Assessment of Educational Progress (NAEP) was formed in 1969, it was federally funded by the National Institute of Education and became the only regularly conducted national survey of education at the elementary, middle, and high school levels. Supported by a grant from the National Center for Education Statistics of the Office of Educational Research and Improvement within the U.S. Department of Education, the NAEP measures the nation's educational system through a series of reading and mathematics tests that are given to students in grades 4, 8 and 12 in both public and private schools. The results are in three levels: basic, proficient, and advanced. Reading is basic to virtually all aspects of education. The reading test results for 1994 are shown in Table 10.1.

National standards will be necessary to ensure equal opportunity, as well as to provide a coordinating function. Standards tell all involved what is expected of them, and assessments tell them whether or not they are progressing (Ravitch, 1995). Republicans and Democrats seem to agree that a national assessment is needed to ensure learning in the core academic subjects. The current goal is to have these tests in the classroom by 1999. The tests will be based on NAEP's fourth grade reading and eighth grade math standards. National standards in other countries, such as Japan, Germany, and France, have proven to be successful.

TABLE 10.1
Results for 1994 of NAEP
Reading Tests

Grade	Basic	Proficient	Advanced
4	60%	30%	In all grades combined,
8	70%	30%	it was 3% to 7%.
12	75%	36%	

TABLE 10.2
Results of 1994 Phi Delta Kappan/Gallup Poll Inquiring Whether Certain Subjects Should Receive More or Less Attention

Subject	Higher	Less	Same	Don't know
Math	82%	1%	17%	*
English	79%	2%	19%	*
Science	75%	3%	22%	*
History, U.S.	62%	6%	31%	1%
Geography	61%	7%	31%	1%
Foreign Language	52%	16%	32%	*
Music	31%	22%	46%	1%
Art	29%	24%	46%	1%

* = less than ½ %

Interestingly, it appears that the demand for standards has come from the bottom, not from the top. "Quality assessment is reassuring to the tax payers. They can tell what they are getting for their investment in education" (Proffer, 1994). In the 1994 Phi Delta Kappan/Gallup Poll, responders were asked if more emphasis was needed on the subjects listed in Table 10.2, regardless of whether or not the subject should be required (Stanley & Gallup, 1996). These results are very interesting as an indication of what areas Americans thought were more important than others.

Students must be prepared to survive and be successful in the twenty-first century. Goals 2000 has drawn attention to the need for a national assessment. However, if left entirely up to the federal government to enact this assessment, it will be a long time coming. The Constitution gives that right to the states, and the right can be withdrawn only with a Constitutional amendment that is supported by a grass roots movement of voting citizens.

STATE ASSESSMENT

A Nation at Risk sparked several reform efforts at the state and national level by concluding that United States students were far behind other world leading nations. In response to this report, more than 36 states set minimum competencies for student achievement at various grade levels and for graduation from high school. For a period of fifteen to twenty years, during the height of the reform movement, states took their role as authority over public educational systems more seriously than ever. Assessment is but one phase in the exercise of that authority (Oliva, 1997). One example of the assessment reform movement of the 1980s is that of North Carolina's Charlotte Mecklenburg School System's institution of a graduation competency test. This test measures the minimum competencies that a student should master to be literate. Students are required to complete a senior essay or project that involves research and a presentation. The project or essay must be pre-approved and stages of development are monitored just as a dissertation would be monitored in the graduate school setting.

As another example of state assessment, in July 1996, the North Carolina Education Standards and Accountability Commission presented benchmark standards for students at grades 4, 8, 10, and 12, in addition to other recommendations. These benchmarks represented the first formal statewide attempt in North Carolina to hold students accountable for their performance. The Standards and Accountability Commission was created by the North Carolina General Assembly in 1993 to ensure that all graduates of public schools in that state mastered the skills needed to become productive workers and successful in life. The purpose of the commission was to develop high and clearly defined education standards, specify the skills and knowledge that high school graduates should possess to be competitive in the modern economy, and develop fair and valid assessments to assure that high school graduates met these standards. One example of the commission's recommendations is that high school students choose from college prep or college tech prep curricula with no option for a general curriculum (NCDPI, 1996).

In North Carolina in 1993, the first statewide grade level tests were administered. These tests are known as End of Grade (EOG) and End of Course (EOC). The EOG tests are taken by students in third through eighth grades and include assessment in reading and math (grades 3–8), social studies (grades 4–8), and writing (grades 4, 6, and 8). EOC tests are taken by high school students and include assessment of the core subjects of Algebra I, Biology, Economic/Legal/Political Systems, English I, Physical Science, and U.S. History, as well as some advanced classes, such as Geometry, Algebra II, Chemistry, and Physics.

Each year, a report titled, "Report Card, the State of School Systems in North Carolina," is published. The report focuses on the results of the annual EOG and EOC tests. Growth in each area is expected each year. In 1995, 40.8% of students in high school scored at or above the proficient level on the EOC tests combined. The elementary school fared a little better. On the writing test, 53.1% of fourth graders scored at or above the proficient level; 47.6% of sixth graders scored in or above the proficient range; and 62.5% of eighth graders scored at or above the proficient level. On the reading EOG test, a total of 66% of all tested grades scored at or above the proficient level; in math, 66.1%; and in social studies 61.1% of combined grades scored at or above grade level.

The EOG and EOC tests are a combination of standardized and factual tests. Every student in North Carolina takes the same test as all others in his grade level and subject area. Factual tests are subject-oriented. By definition, standardized testing administers the same test in the same manner to two or more students (Seldon, 1989).

Other factual and standardized tests are the SAT (Scholastic Assessment Test [formerly the Scholastic Aptitude Test]) and the ACT (American College Testing Program), taken for entrance into college. Test results are used to assist admissions officers in predicting how successful a student will be during his freshman year of college.

The SAT was originally created in 1925. In 1929, it was divided into math and verbal sections. More than 2 million high school students take the SAT each year. The ACT is taken each year by 1.3 million students who live predominantly in the Southeast, Midwest, and Rocky Mountain States (Toch, 1989).

The SAT and the ACT are different in format, content, and scoring. The ACT more closely matches a high school curriculum than the SAT. The ACT has four areas of assessment: English (written, grammar, usage), Science Reasoning (draw conclusions, research, similarities, develop hypotheses), Math (solving problems, application, reasoning, algebra, geometry) and Reading (reasoning, comprehension). The SAT has three areas of assessment: General Reading (author's meaning or suggestions, facts), Vocabulary (analogies and sentence completion), and Math (regular multiple choice, quantitative, comparisons, grid-in questions [new]). The Test of Standard Written English has been dropped. The SAT questions are presented in order of difficulty, while the ACT questions are not. The ACT does not penalize for guessing, while the SAT does—by taking off ¼ or ⅓ of a point for each incorrect answer. In 1990, the national SAT average was 900 (scale: 400–1600) and the ACT average was 20.6 (scale: 1–36). The 1995 SAT average for North Carolina was 838.

Most states use standardized tests to determine the success or failure of a student. Standardized tests are tests that are norm-referenced. Norm-referenced tests are used to compare the student's performance to that of those who have previously taken the test. Standardized tests present problems for certain populations. Norm-referenced standardized tests are poor indicators of quality and, at worst, they are misleading. They do not measure a student's progress against the curricula in a state but rather against a sample of students used to set the norm. They are designed to ensure that half of the students will score above average and half below. Barbara Sizemore's article in *Education Week* (1995, p. 1) states, "What African American students need most is a highly structured school with firm discipline that is focused on teaching them to take and pass standardized tests."

According to Theobald and Mills (1995), John Dewey promoted cooperative holistic curriculum and instruction and minimal individual evaluation. While Edward Thorndike promoted an individualized curriculum, breaking down the curriculum to its lowest skills or concepts, he did this through mass use of various sorts of individual tests. Of these two most significant influences on modern education, Thorndike seems to be winning.

EFFECTIVE SCHOOL SYSTEMS

One consequence of the evaluation process is that teachers and students are burdened with unnecessary testing that students resist or downplay because it is weakly aligned with the material they are currently studying. Furthermore, critics are so convinced that educators are unable to evaluate themselves or improve their schools effectively, that national objectives, standard curriculum, and narrowly gauged external evaluations are used and, in the opinion of some, overused (Ghory, 1996).

One aspect of state assessment is the standardized test. Controversy exists over the use of the standardized test today for many reasons: claims that it is out-of-date, unfair, equity issues, and costs. The design of a standardized test is basic and simple, fill-in-the-bubble multiple-choice test. However simple, the test was reliable and well-suited to the mass-manufacturing economy that existed in the United States in the early 1900s. But standardized tests do not work anymore (Viadero, 1994). Many are designed to ensure that students perform according to a normal curve, so that the tests must produce a group that performs below average to match the group that performs above average. Tests are sometimes rigged to produce these results to determine eligibility for compensatory or gifted programs. Greater opportunity to learn is continually and unfairly redistributed to those who have already learned well, not to those with greater needs for support in their learning. Rote drill and bubble-in testing do not prepare children for the workforce of tomorrow. To be competitive in the twenty-first century, individuals will have to think their way through their workdays by analyzing problems, proposing solutions, trouble-shooting and repairing equipment, communicating with others, and managing the resources of time and materials. Therefore, an assessment must be created that fosters thinking, problem-solving, and communicating skills. In the words of those educators who want state assessment change, "You get what you test" (Viadero, 1994, p. 3). In other words, by creating state assessments that elicit analytical problems and creative thinking questions, teachers will naturally teach these skills because all teachers teach to the test.

Two forms of questioning that teachers use that can be beneficial to the students when taking standardized tests are the factual information format and open-ended format. A fact is a "statement about concepts that is true or verified for a particular case on the basis of the best evidence available" (Martorella, 1996, p. 177). Of course, facts are a part of learning about history and the world, but these best serve to illustrate concepts and support generalizations. By teaching facts as the basis of identifying and organizing content, there is little transfer value from situation to situation. The open-ended, or constructed response, format allows the students freedom to initiate problem solving and think through ideas. The students are asked to respond in their own words—to "construct" their answers—to questions that may have multiple good answers. Students usually reason out their solutions as part of their answers.

Generally, students can answer these questions in just a few minutes. Open-ended questions assist students with the development of higher order thinking skills. In essence, students assume more responsibility for their own learning (Kindsvatter, Wilen, & Ishler, 1996). They propose solutions, gather data, and draw conclusions—all key responsibilities of the worker of the future. The essay in the SAT II written test and the SAT I grid-in questions in the mathematics section require that the students figure out the answer and express themselves on a subject. A possible weakness of these tests, and standardized tests in general, is that they "can make classifying a student a little too easy" (Lawton, 1996). Standardized tests use a specific number to tell what a student knows. Students are much more than the results of tests. Too much in life seems to be dependent upon standardized tests—promotion to next grade, graduation, college, and certification. But tests do not necessarily tell all the student knows or is capable of doing. Many students who do not perform well on standardized tests can successfully demonstrate the knowledge learned in another fashion.

Title III of GOALS 2000, "State and Local Education Systemic Improvement," provides support for the development and implementation of systemic education improvement plans at the state and local levels. *Status Report: State Systemic Education Improvement (*1995), by the Council of Chief State School Officers, provides a resource for state and federal policymakers. It is designed to help inform decisionmaking by identifying states' accomplishments and lessons learned in developing and implementing improvement activities. These include such items as Content Standards, Performance Standards, Opportunity-to-Learn Standards, and Governance and Management.

Local/School Testing Procedures

Local and school testing procedures differ from state to state. Mentioned previously, some states have defined procedures for different grades and different subjects within those particular grade levels. For example, in North Carolina, grade 9 has End-of-Course tests in English, Physical Science, Algebra, and History. Grades 1 and 2 have portfolio assessment. Grades 3–8 have tests in the core areas. Writing tests occur in grades 4, 6, 8, and 10. If a student does not pass the competency test in writing, reading, or math in the eighth grade, the particular test must be retaken until passed. If, upon graduation, the competency test has not been passed, the student will receive a certificate of attendance instead of a diploma. Currently, many high schools create a competency class for all three core areas for juniors who have not passed the eighth grade competency test. "So education became a world of tests and scales and graphs and correlations" (NCDPI, 1995).

In some school districts, students take a pre-test, measuring level of mastery of course objectives at the beginning of the year. Once that information is processed, the teachers give students an activity called "looping" at the beginning of each class to reinforce the information missed on the pre-test. This helps the students perform better on the test, and it assists the teachers by identifying what needs to be reinforced.

Some districts and individual schools use criterion referenced tests to gauge students' mastery of objectives at the beginning of the school year. The results of the testing are used to determine the baseline for beginning instruction. The aim of this form of preassessment is to determine the skills that the students have and how those will affect the delivery of instruction. For instance, if test results indicate that students do not have the capability to multiply 2-digit numbers by 2-digit numbers, the teacher can determine that 2 digit by 2 digit multiplication needs to be the beginning of instruction in math.

SUMMARY

Curriculum evaluation is defined as the evaluation of educational programs. The basic attributes of curriculum evaluation are utility, feasibility, propriety, and accuracy. Methods of curriculum evaluation are long-term and short-term analysis. Short-term analysis should be used on short projects or in order to decide if long-term analysis is needed. Whether evaluations are long-term or short-term, the purpose of curriculum evaluation is to judge or determine the worth or quality of all of the courses collectively offered in school or college in a particular subject.

Instructional evaluation is the evaluation of the instructor. Evaluation of instruction does not answer curricular concerns such as whether the subject matter was the right choice to begin with, whether its content is relevant, whether it meets students' or societal needs, and whether the content has been selected wisely (Oliva, 1997). Tools that are used in instructional evaluation are formative and summative tests, criterion-referenced and norm-referenced tests.

Evaluation, if used correctly, can promote student learning. This is the real reason for all educational reform and the goal that all educators must strive to attain. Better schools begin with a curriculum that is designed to meet the needs of each student, challenge students through promotion of higher level thinking skills, and prepare students for the challenges that will face them in the future—the twenty-first century workplace.

Some educators believe new forms of assessment, such as portfolios and authentic assessment, are the answer. These two forms of assessment contain documents that the student has prepared based on an idea or concept instead of a multiple choice test that only judges factual information or short-term memory ideas. The nation's leaders, presidents, and state boards of education continuously attempt to create curriculums and tests that will promote student learning. However, the attempts are always criticized and the public still argues for more change. Teachers, on the other hand, are tired of constant change; they want constant results. Various standardized tests have been under the educational microscope due to the politically correct nature of America's democratic society and the limited opportunities available to many students. Even though America has been in constant turmoil over education and the growth of its students in comparison with other nations, the unprecedented need to rise above and meet the global challenges is the catalyst that motivates America's education and its facilitators. " . . . (U)nless somebody really has meaningful standards and a system of measuring whether you meet those standards, you won't achieve your goals. . . . we can get there together. We have to start now with what you're trying to do. We have to have high standards and high accountability. If you can achieve that, you have given a great gift to the future of our country" (President Clinton, 1996).

Evaluation of curriculum, instruction, and student performance does need to change. American schools have been stagnant for the last 100 years. There has been very limited change in education since the Committee of Ten, the Committee of Fifteen, the Committee of Nine and in methods of evaluation since the late 1800s and early 1900s. Authentic assessment and portfolios are good ideas, but still have some "bugs" to work out, especially through training teachers how to use these assessment measures successfully. School systems and teachers tend to get locked into the traditional ways of teaching and evaluating students. They need help, and must come to the realization that they need to change. School systems must practice what they preach. Curriculum and instructional evaluation procedures need to be understood by teachers. The results of this kind of testing should be used to determine the skill levels of students and should be the baseline for beginning instruction. Teachers should be cautioned not to look only at test scores when assessing student success.

Teachers should familiarize themselves with the new performance assessment procedures and operations such as portfolio, open-ended, and authentic assessment. Teachers are going to be increasingly called upon to assess students in a more in-depth way. The new tools will allow students to be part of the evaluation process and understand it better.

Many challenges await the teacher of the twenty-first century. The diversity of America, the global communications of the present and future, and the nature of skills needed, especially high-order thinking skills, create many challenges that educators in the past did not have to contend with in creating their lessons or curricula. Society has changed. Curricula must change along with it to help students meet the future challenges in their workplaces. Education is supposed to prepare students to become effective citizens and skilled workers. The teacher is the best and really only guide who can reach each and every student. Therefore, curricula must meet the needs of the students by creating subject matter that is valuable and relevant to the future that awaits them and their mentors—the classroom teachers.

❖ ❖ ❖   DISCUSSION QUESTIONS

1. How can national standards and assessment affect education today?
2. Compare and contrast evaluation methods in education today with education 20 years ago. Has it changed? How? If not, why not?

❖ ❖ ❖   CLASS ACTIVITIES

1. Develop a chart that shows how alternative assessment, authentic assessment, and portfolios can be used in conjunction with your current teaching methods. How can use of these assessments improve or not improve instruction?

❖ ❖ ❖   REFERENCES

A system of high standards: What we mean and why we need it. (Spring, 1996). *American Educator, 20.*

AFT criteria for high-quality standards. (Spring, 1996). *American Educator, 20,* 28-35.

Beswick, E. (1990). Evaluating educational programs. *ERIC Digest,* Series 54.

Bradley, (1995). Even as popularity soars, portfolios encounter roadblocks. *Education Week on the Web, 14.*

Charlotte Mecklenburg Schools. (1994). Criterion referenced tests: What's really happening. Division of Accountability Services.

Charlotte Mecklenburg Schools. (1997). Charlotte Mecklenburg schools end-of-grade science best packet. Division of Accountability Services.

Clinton, W. (1996, Spring). President urges standards that count: excerpts from President Clinton's address to the national education summit. *American Educator, 20,* 8-12.

Davey, L. (1991). Application of case study evaluations. *ERIC Clearing House on Test, Measurement, and Evaluation.*

Engel, B. (1994). Portfolio assessment and the new paradigm: New instruments and new places. *The Education Forum, 59,* 22–27.

Ghory, W. J. (1996, April). Reclaiming evaluation: The Cinderella of school reform. *Equity & Excellence in Education, 29,* 91–96.

Gillespie, C. S., Gillespie, R. D., Ford, K. L., & Leavell, A. G. (1996, March). Portfolio assessment: Some questions, some answers, some recommendations. *Journal of Adolescent & Adult Literacy, 39,* 480–91.

Kindsvatter, R., Wilen, W., & Ishler, M. (1996). *Dynamics of effective teaching* (3rd ed.). White Plains, NY: Longman Publishing.

Lawton, M. (1996, May 22). Board endorses draft plan for NAEP overhaul. *Education Week on the Web*, 1–2.

Martorella, P. (1997). *Teaching social studies in middle and secondary schools* (2nd ed.). Upper Saddle River, NJ: Merrill/Prentice Hall.

Measuring up: Questions and answers about state roles in educational accountability. (1988, November). (OERI Study Group: Superintendent of Documents: stock number 065-000-00352-0) (ED395383). Washington, DC: U.S. Government Printing Office.

National Assessment of Educational Progress (NAEP). (1995). *1994 reading: A first look.* Washington, DC: National Center for Education Statistics.

North Carolina State Board of Education. (1995). *Report card 1995: The state of school systems in North Carolina.* Raleigh, NC: North Carolina Dept. of Public Instruction.

Oliva, P. (1997). *Developing the curriculum.* United States: R. R. Donnelley.

Payne, D. A. (1992). *Measuring & evaluating educational outcomes.* New York: Macmillan.

Proffer, L. (1994). *A vision of competence.* Washington, DC: National Conference of State Legislators.

Ravitch, D. (1995*). National standards in American education: A citizen's guide.* Washington, DC: The Brookings Group.

Robinson, J. (1995). *A guide to the ABCs for teachers.* Wilmington, NC: State Board of Education, North Carolina Department of Public Instruction.

Rowan-Salisbury Schools Board of Education (1989). *Rowan-Salisbury schools board of education policy handbook.* Salisbury, NC: Author.

Schafer, W. (1996). Using performance assessments: Possibilities and pitfalls. *Reading Today*, (13).

Seldon, R. (1989). Report from Washington: Standardized testing: Helpful? *PTA Today, 14*(5), 28–30.

Shafritz, J. M., Koeppe, R. P., & Soper, E. (1988). *The facts on file dictionary of education.* New York: Facts on File.

Stanley, E. M., & Gallup, A. M. (1996). 28th annual Gallup poll: The public's attitude toward the public schools. *Phi Delta Kappan, 78.*

Status report: State systemic education improvements. (1995, August). Washington, DC: Council of Chief State School Officers: ED387891.

Theobald, P., & Mills, E. (1995). Accountability and the struggle over what counts. *Phi Delta Kappan, 76,* 462–466.

Toch, T. (1989, December 11). Putting a new SAT to the test. *US News and World Report,* p. 60.

Viadero, D. (July, 1994). Teaching to the test. *Education Week on the Web* (http://www.edweek.org/), pp. 1–12.

Wiggins, G. (1989). Teaching to the (authenticity) test. *Educational Leadership, 46*(7), 41–48.

Wiggins, G. (1993). Assessment: Authenticity, context and validity. *Phi Delta Kappan, 75*(3), 200–214.

William, P. (1989, December). Using customized standardized tests. *ERIC Digest,* 141–144.

❖ ❖ ❖ SUGGESTED READINGS

Gay, L. R. (1996). *Educational research.* Upper Saddle River, NJ: Prentice Hall.

Glazer, S. M. (1994). Authentic assessment, evaluation, portfolios: What do these terms really mean, anyway? *Reading Today,* p. 12.

Greene, R. (1997, February 11). Students say school's not tough enough. *The Charlotte Observer,* p. 7A.

Haladyna, T. M. (1997). *Writing test items to evaluate higher order thinking.* Needham Heights, MA: Allyn & Bacon.

Hass, G. (1980). *Curriculum planning: A new approach.* Boston, MA: Allyn & Bacon.

Miller, H. M. (1997). No more one legged chairs: Sharing the responsibility for portfolio assessment with students, their peers and their parents. *Middle School Journal,* 28.

Robinson, G. E., & Craver, J. M. (1989). *ERS report: Assessing and grading student achievement.* Arlington, VA: Educational Research Service.

❖ ❖ ❖

Name Index

SUBJECT INDEX